MESSIAH

Volume 1

ALSO BY MATT DORFF AND MARK AREY

The Book of Revelation

MESSIAH:

ORIGIN

Messiah: Origin
Published by Zondervan
Grand Rapids, MI 49530, USA

Requests for information should be addressed to:
Zondervan
5300 Patterson Ave SE
Grand Rapids, MI 49530

Printed in the USA

13 14 15 16 17 18 /DCI/ 10 9 8 7 6 5 4 3 2 1

PREFACE

Messiah: Origin is unlike any Bible you have ever read. Yes,
every word is Scripture, taken from the four Gospels and freshly
translated from the original Greek. Those who profess a belief
in Christ read in these four accounts a single truth. And even
though the four Evangelists each wrote their own divinely-
inspired account of the life, death and resurrection of Jesus, the
four Gospels comprise a single story.

    We are inviting all readers to experience the story of Jesus
anew in this visualized narrative harmony of Matthew, Mark,
Luke and John. We understand that we are trending with the
modern consumer. *Star Wars* is a series of movies and more; *The
Lord of the Rings* and *Harry Potter* are book and movie series
and more. Even the Bible has become a cable miniseries. But the
film/video medium would be hard-pressed to tell the story using

solely the words of the Bible. Only the text of Scripture can do that.

The Bible may still be the bestselling book in the world, but Biblical literacy has been declining for decades. This narrative harmony is designed to bring you back to the story of Jesus through the format of today's serials. The text is composed exclusively of sacred Scripture with the verses arranged in a linear narrative. We hope to make it feel new again, and that you will read these familiar passages with fresh eyes.

This is not a new idea. Long before the New Testament was compiled there were different ways Christians read and listened to Scripture. The epistles of the apostle Paul were letters to communities and individuals, which over time were shared among the local churches. The Gospels were read aloud during worship services in arrangements that developed into lectionary versions. And there were ancient attempts at creating what we call today a "narrative harmony" that contains the whole story of the Lord Jesus Christ in a single, continuous account. One such ancient harmony had a unique influence on the establishment of the canon of the New Testament. Less than 100 years after the death of the last apostle, a man named Tatian compiled the "Diatessaron" (from the Greek meaning "through the Four"). The "Four" are Matthew, Mark, Luke and John, and Tatian's compilation helped to establish their authority and authenticity.

During my 30 years as a Greek Orthodox clergyman, my rich prayer life in the language of the New Testament, and particularly hearing the original read aloud, has profoundly impacted me. I was struck by how the lectionary Gospels used for worship present the story of Jesus in purposeful narrative combinations. When the opportunity came to arrange a narrative harmony of my own, I went to the original Greek to pull together a single narrative that reflects the unity of the Good News of Jesus Christ. It has been a challenging process that has required rigorous selection and conscientious choices.

For example, the genealogies of Matthew and Luke are included in Volume 1, but placed at the end as an appendix. And where certain events are repeated, I give only one example, leaving the reader to take the rewarding journey of exploring the Gospels individually. The harmony never tries to replace the four Gospels, rather, it becomes a gateway back to them. Experiencing the richness of the life of Jesus in one narrative will open a door to the originals in all their unique and distinctive glory.

In *Messiah: Origin* what links and drives the verse arrangement (listed at the start of each chapter and in the index) is Kai Carpenter's enchanting artwork, expertly guided by the visual storytelling alchemy of Matt Dorff. Together they have created illustrations into which the text has been placed to generate a narrative flow, a forward story motion. Think of it as a reverse illuminated manuscript. Ancient illuminated manuscripts employed artists to illustrate around the text; ours places the text into the illustration. We have searched the venerable and ancient Christian traditions of illustrated texts, lectionaries and Gospel harmonies to bring out of those storehouses, as Jesus said, "new treasures as well as old" (Matthew 13:52).

The Bible is unlike any book you have ever read. We turn and return to its narratives, parables, poetry and teachings again and again—to be inspired, comforted and instructed. The Bible is much more than the sum of its words and stories. The Bible is life. We hope this presentation will bring life to you and to those you love.

Mark Arey
New York City
June 2013

INTRODUCTION

Images...

An evening star...a newborn...a virgin...shepherds... wise men...angels...

Poetry...

Silent night...first noel...o little town...Immanuel...joy to the world...

A story oft told...

Just look at any calendar...the four-numbered year... that is the quantity of time since this story entered our universe. Do we grant any other narrative such respect? Is not the copyright of every other story linked to the initial publication of this one?

It is only a First Chapter and yet it has been called "the greatest story ever told." It is at least one of the most moving. I dare say more art and poetry has been inspired by this story than any other in human history – save, of course, for the Final Chapter, the conclusion to the tale this *Messiah: Origin* inaugurates.

A story telling...

Yes, it's well known and we have heard most of it before...but have you ever noticed how full a tale it becomes... how much of the telling is actually poetry...how much is imagery...how much actually is art begging for incarnation?

Dreams are important to this story...and songs...the prayer of a man so old he wants only to die...and of a girl so buoyant she sings of the poor being vindicated, tyrants overthrown...but what has happened to history? Jews flee to Egypt to escape the baby-killing pharaoh...sorcerers stream from Persia to worship the Messiah...this seems all backwards or inside out.

Tables are being turned, that's for sure...in the world of this narrative, babies count the most; young girls and old women come in second; men, maybe third; but kings are as (frighteningly) anachronistic as they are (ultimately) irrelevant.

A story yet told...

It is the First Chapter of the tale of an unimaginable life. Note the diversity – and unity – of response. Angels and humans – women and men – rich and poor – Jews and Gentiles – all end up on their knees, in reverence before the inauguration of what they could not have imagined.

And yet...there is an antithesis. Hatred and fear so

powerful...so vile it would distort prophecies of hope into sleuthing tools for determining who should die...so cowardly it would pit armed men against infants and toddlers.

Between those two extremes, any number of reactions might be noted...from "Go Tell It On the Mountain" to "cherish and seal it in one's heart." Where will you be on the spectrum of response?

It has been called "the greatest story ever told." It is at least one of the most moving. So now...look...and see...and be moved.

Mark Allan Powell
Editor, *HarperCollins Bible Dictionary*
Author, *Introducing the New Testament: A Historical, Literary, and Theological Survey*

"We have found the Messiah!"

– Gospel of John 1:41

PROLOGUE

JOHN 1:1–18

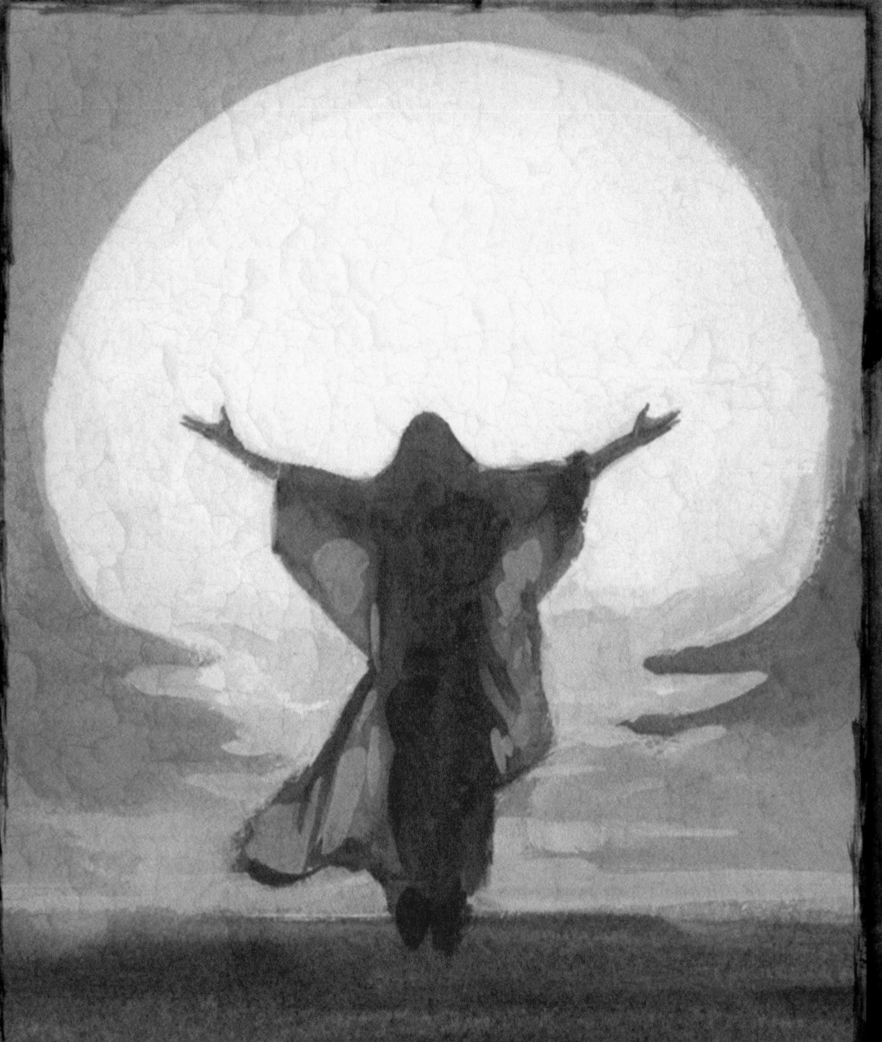

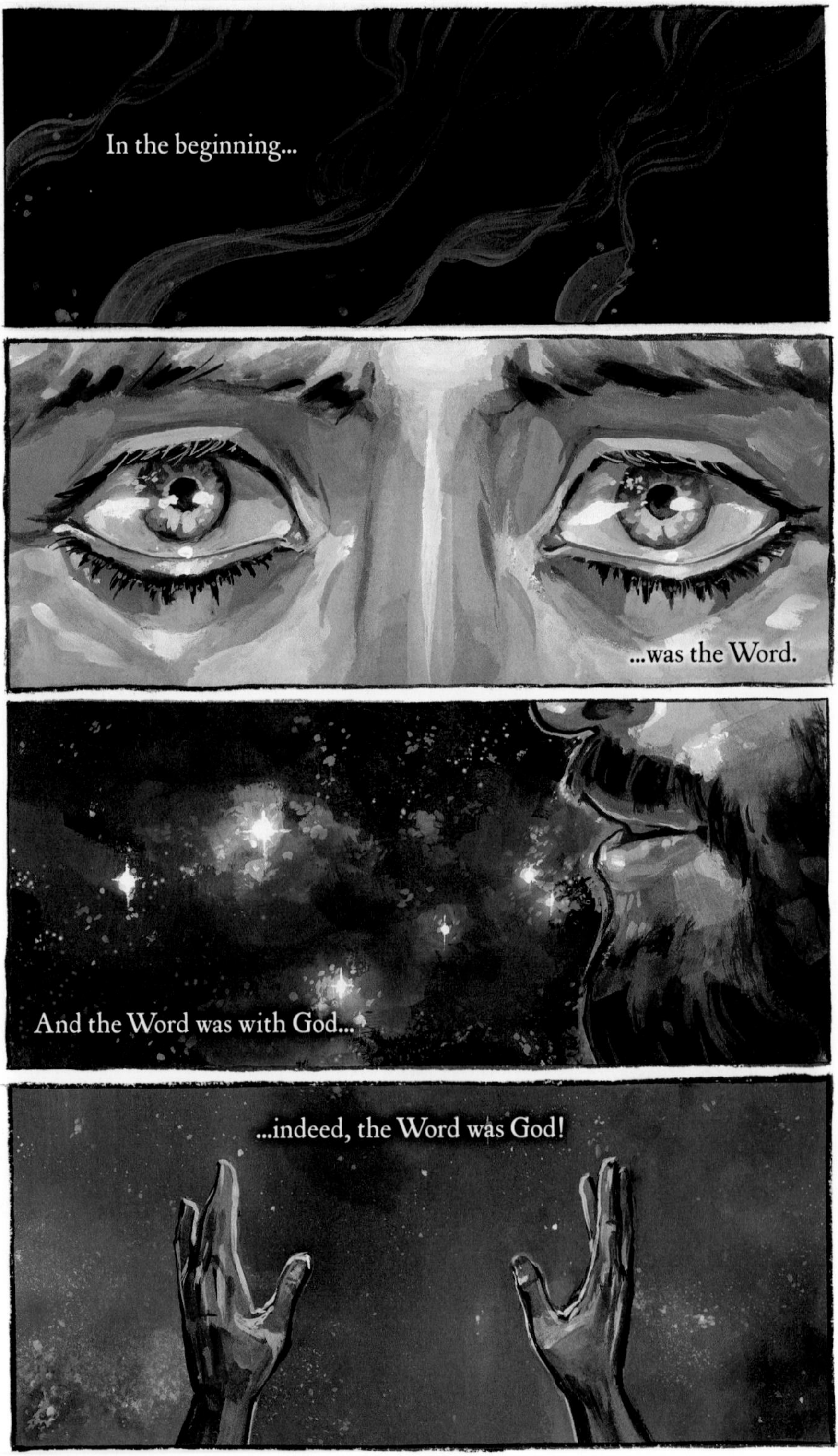
In the beginning...
...was the Word.
And the Word was with God...
...indeed, the Word was God!

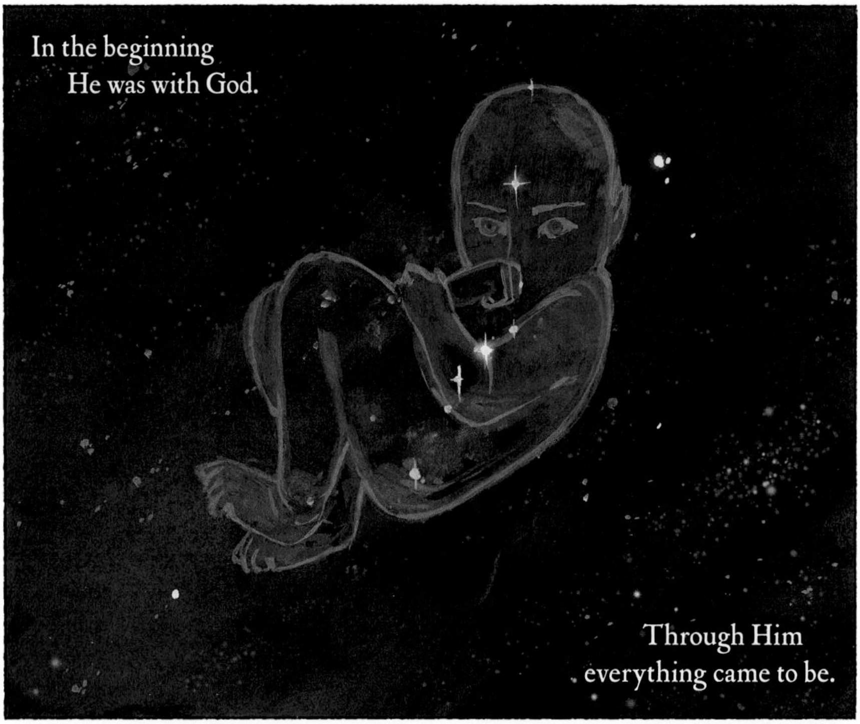
In the beginning
He was with God.
Through Him
everything came to be.

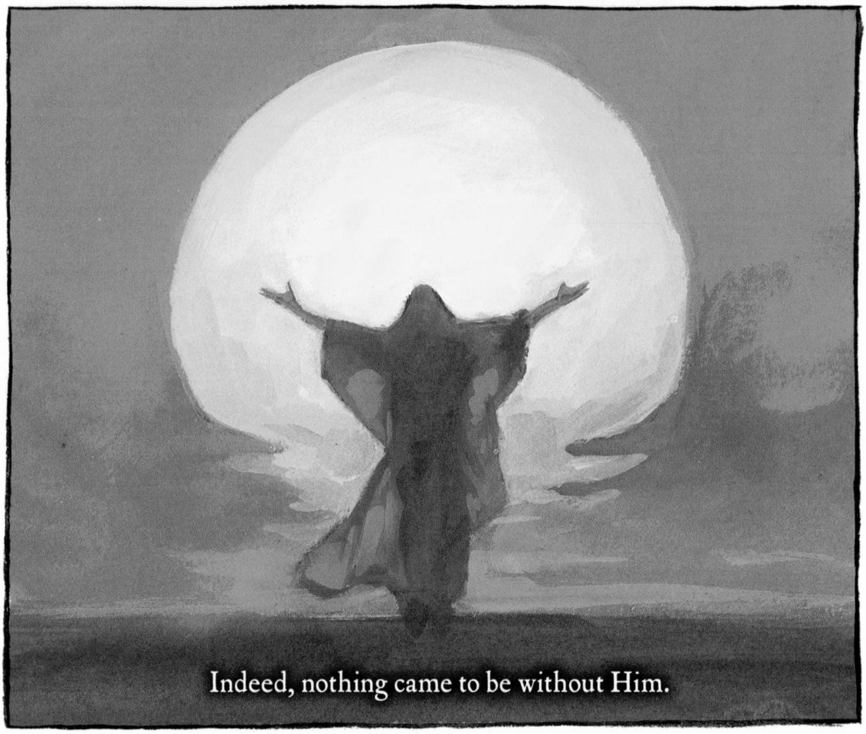
Indeed, nothing came to be without Him.

In Him was Life,
and His Life was
the Light of humanity.

And the Light shines on
in the darkness, never overcome
by the darkness!

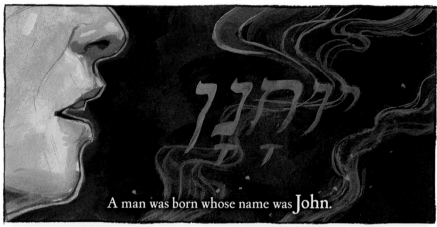

A man was born whose name was John.

He was sent by God.

He came to bear witness to the Light...

...so that all might believe through him.

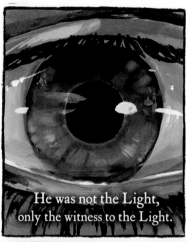

He was not the Light, only the witness to the Light.

The true Light, the Light Who enlightens every person coming into the world, was the Word.

In the world He was...

...and the world came to be through Him.

Yet the world did not know Him.

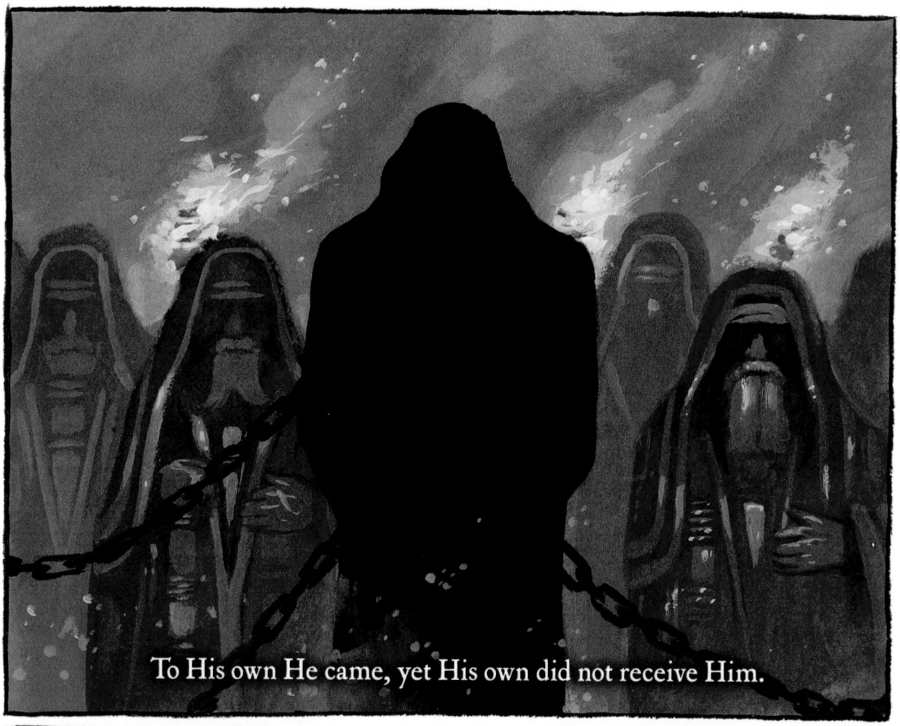
To His own He came, yet His own did not receive Him.

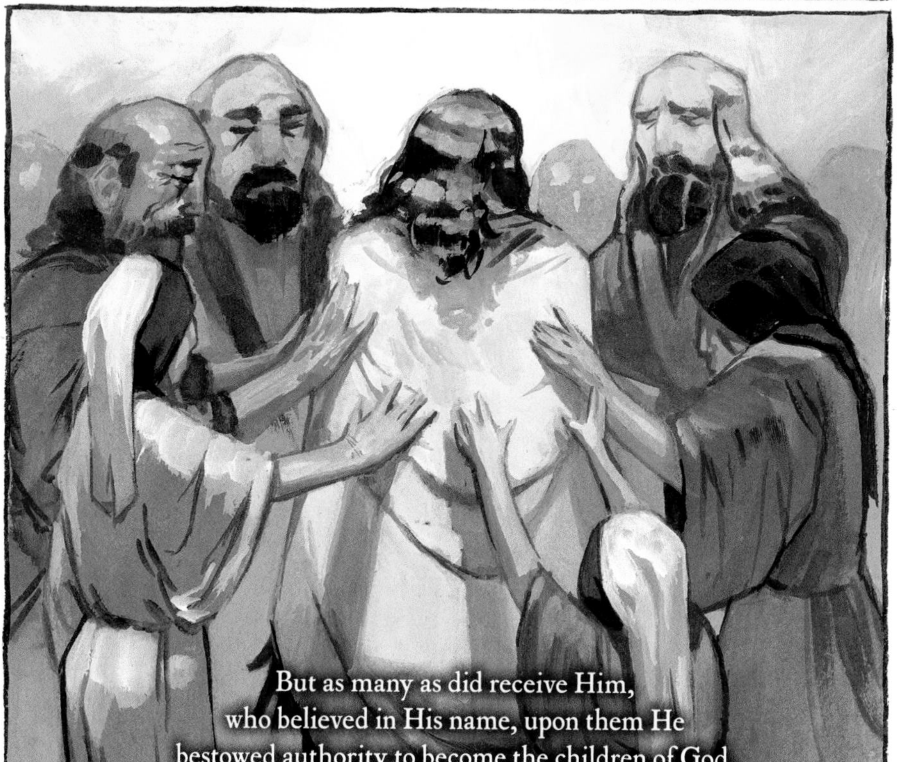
But as many as did receive Him,
who believed in His name, upon them He
bestowed authority to become the children of God.

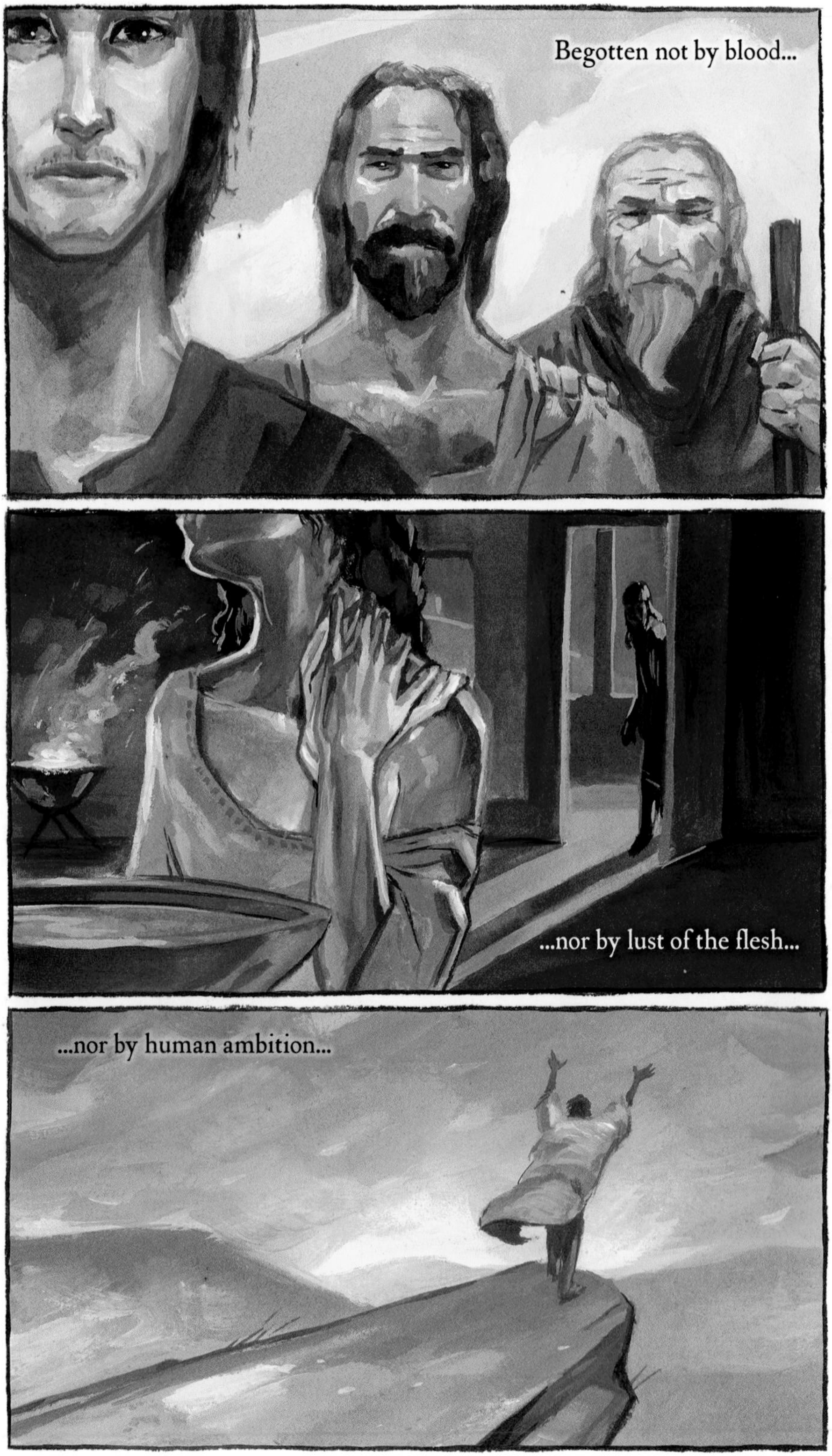
Begotten not by blood...
...nor by lust of the flesh...
...nor by human ambition...

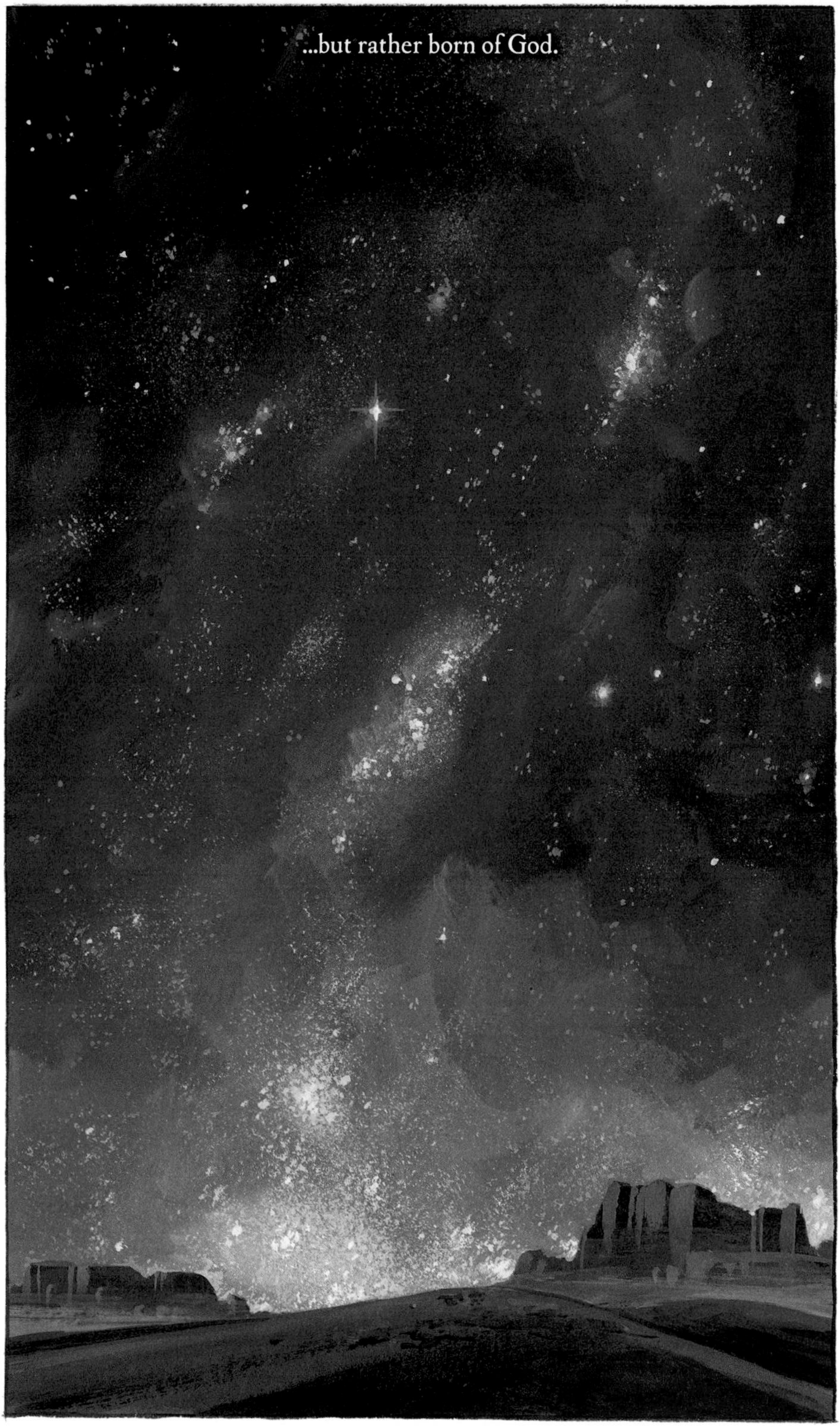
...but rather born of God.

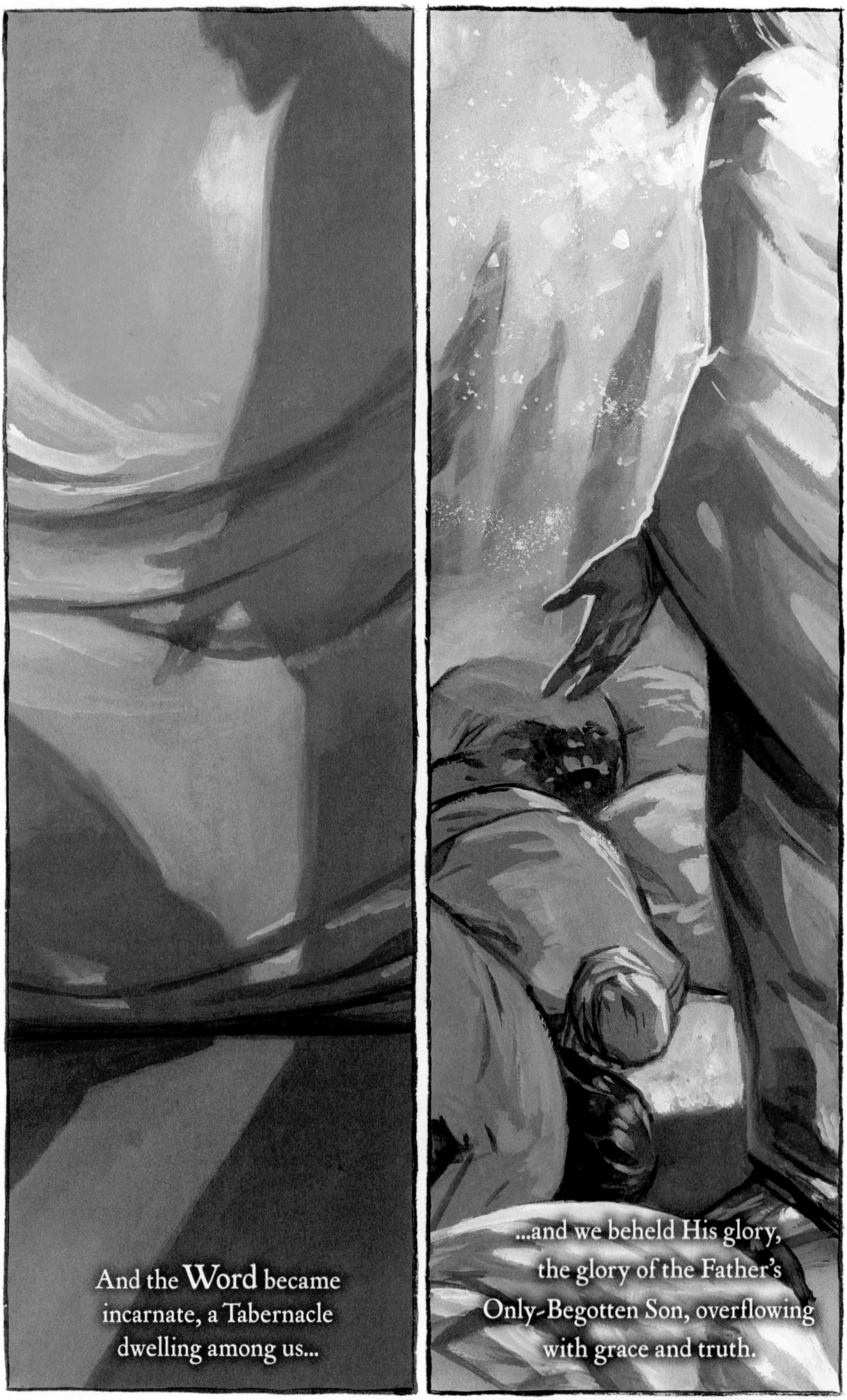
And the Word became incarnate, a Tabernacle dwelling among us...
...and we beheld His glory, the glory of the Father's Only-Begotten Son, overflowing with grace and truth.

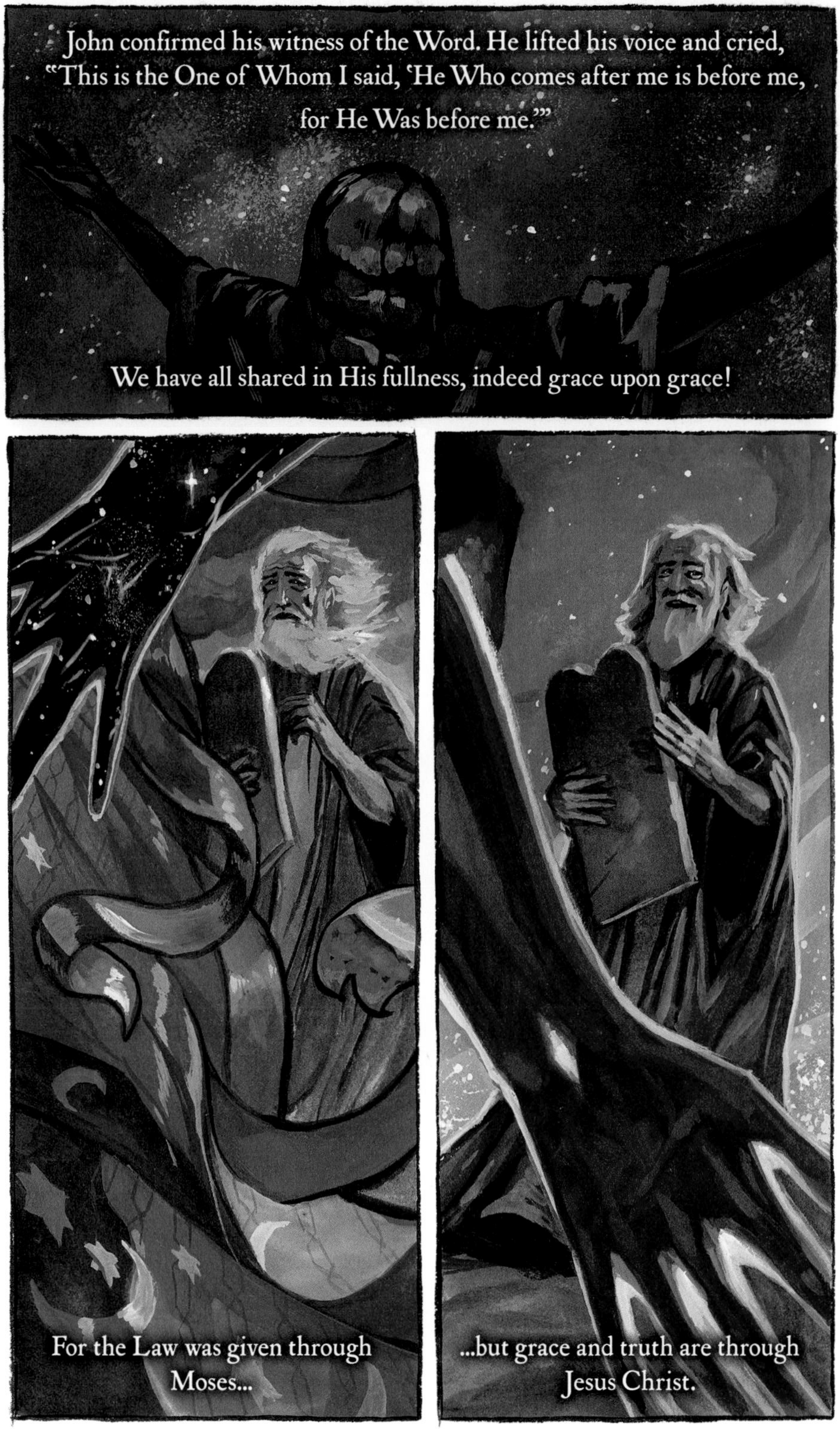
John confirmed his witness of the Word. He lifted his voice and cried, "This is the One of Whom I said, 'He Who comes after me is before me, for He Was before me.'"
We have all shared in His fullness, indeed grace upon grace!
For the Law was given through Moses...
...but grace and truth are through Jesus Christ.

No one has ever seen God.

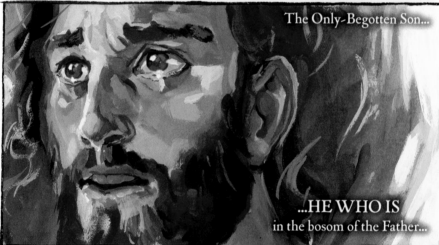

The Only-Begotten Son...

...HE WHO IS
in the bosom of the Father...

...He has revealed God

ANNUNCIATION
OF THE NATIVITY OF JOHN THE BAPTIST

LUKE 1:5–25

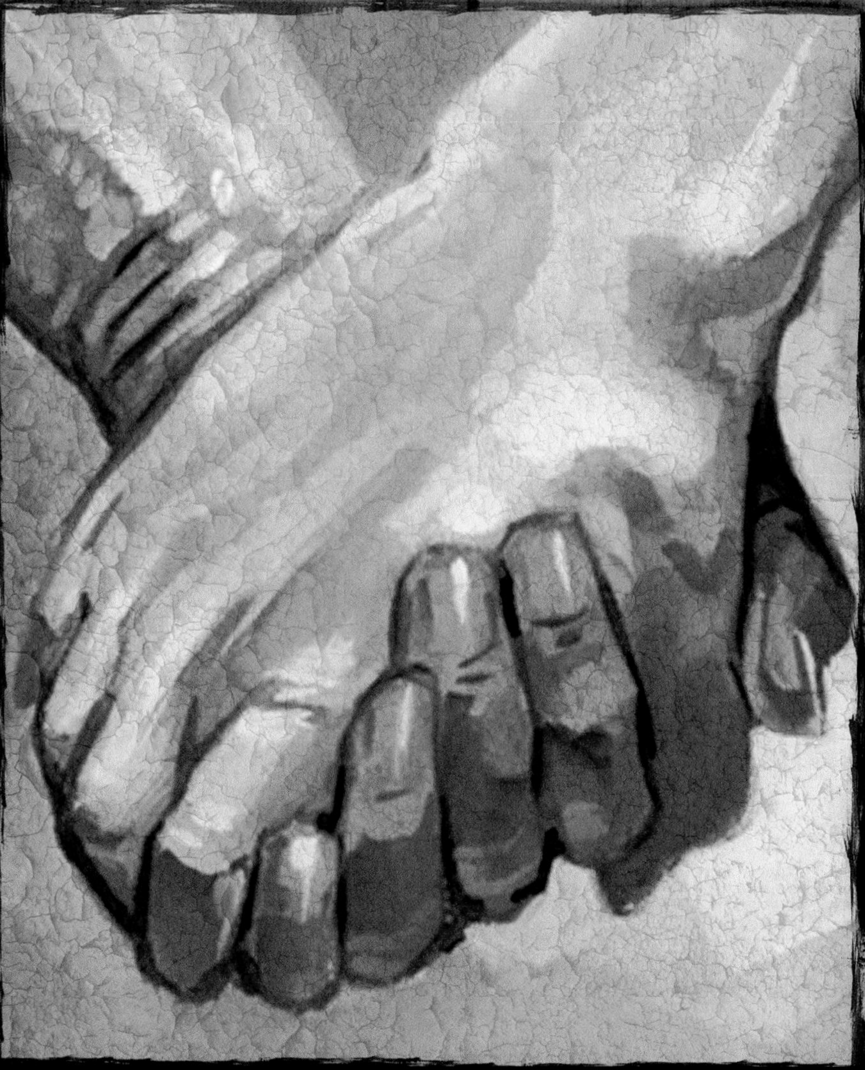

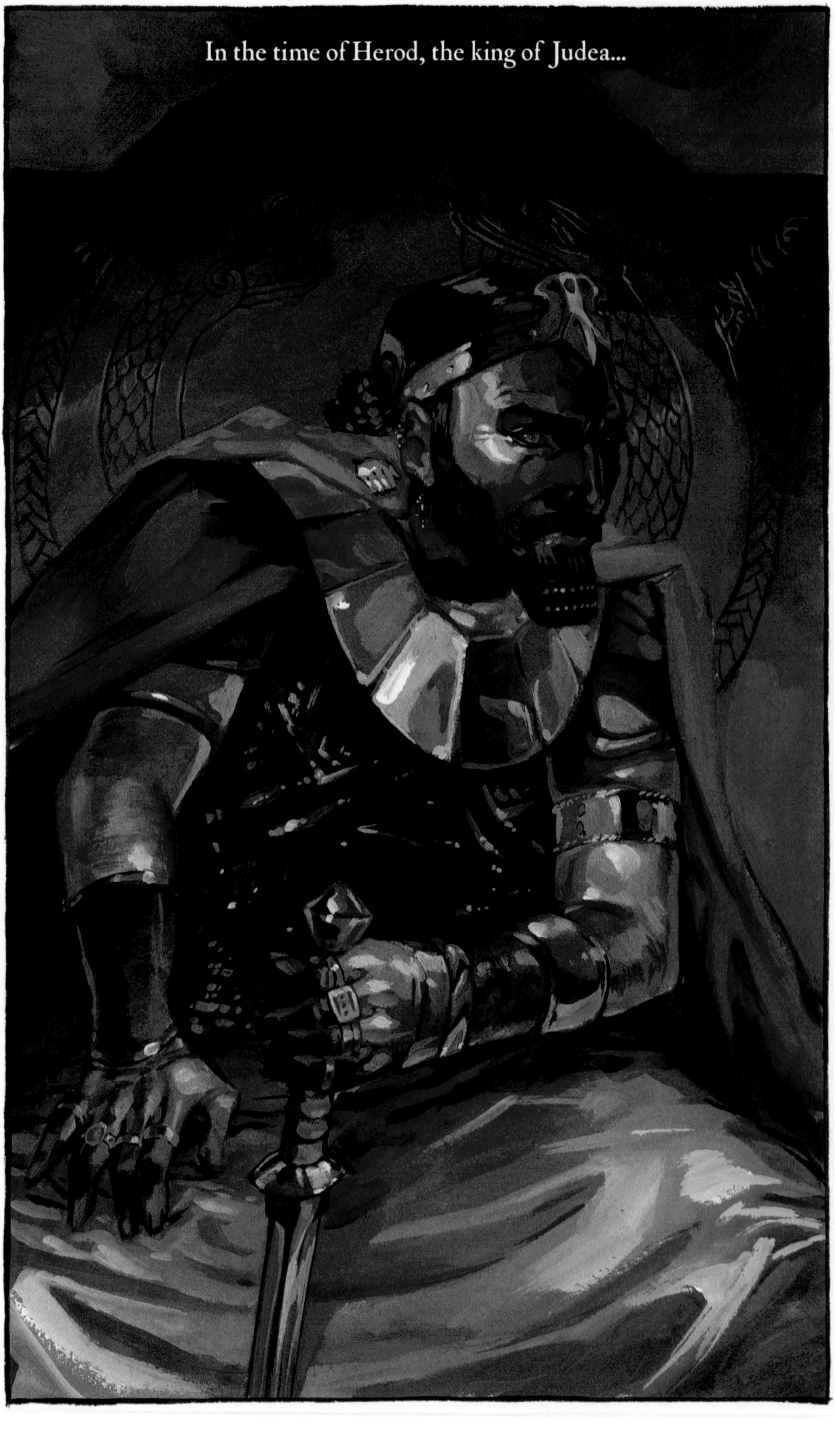
In the time of Herod, the king of Judea...

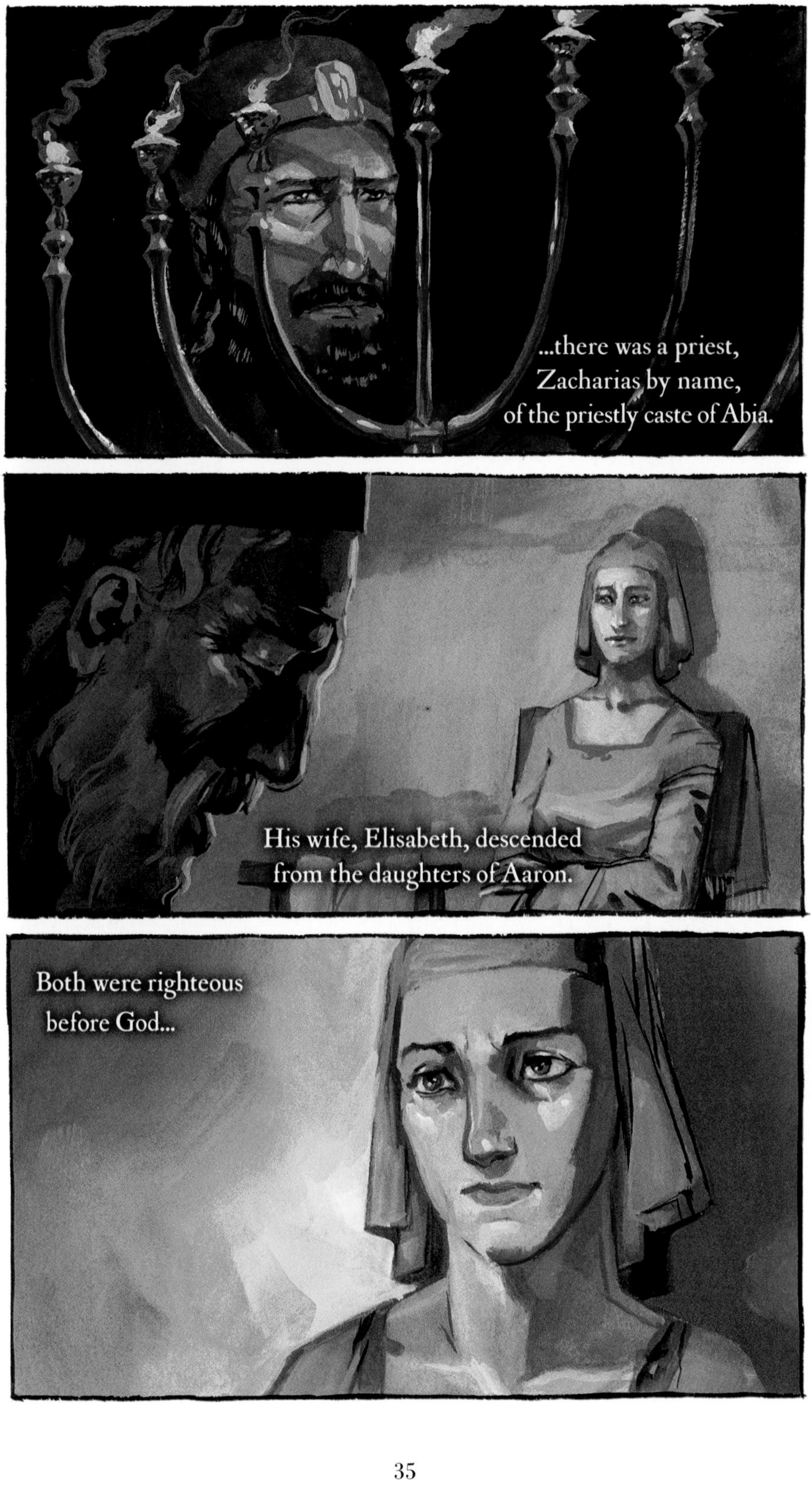
...there was a priest, Zacharias by name, of the priestly caste of Abia.
His wife, Elisabeth, descended from the daughters of Aaron.
Both were righteous before God...

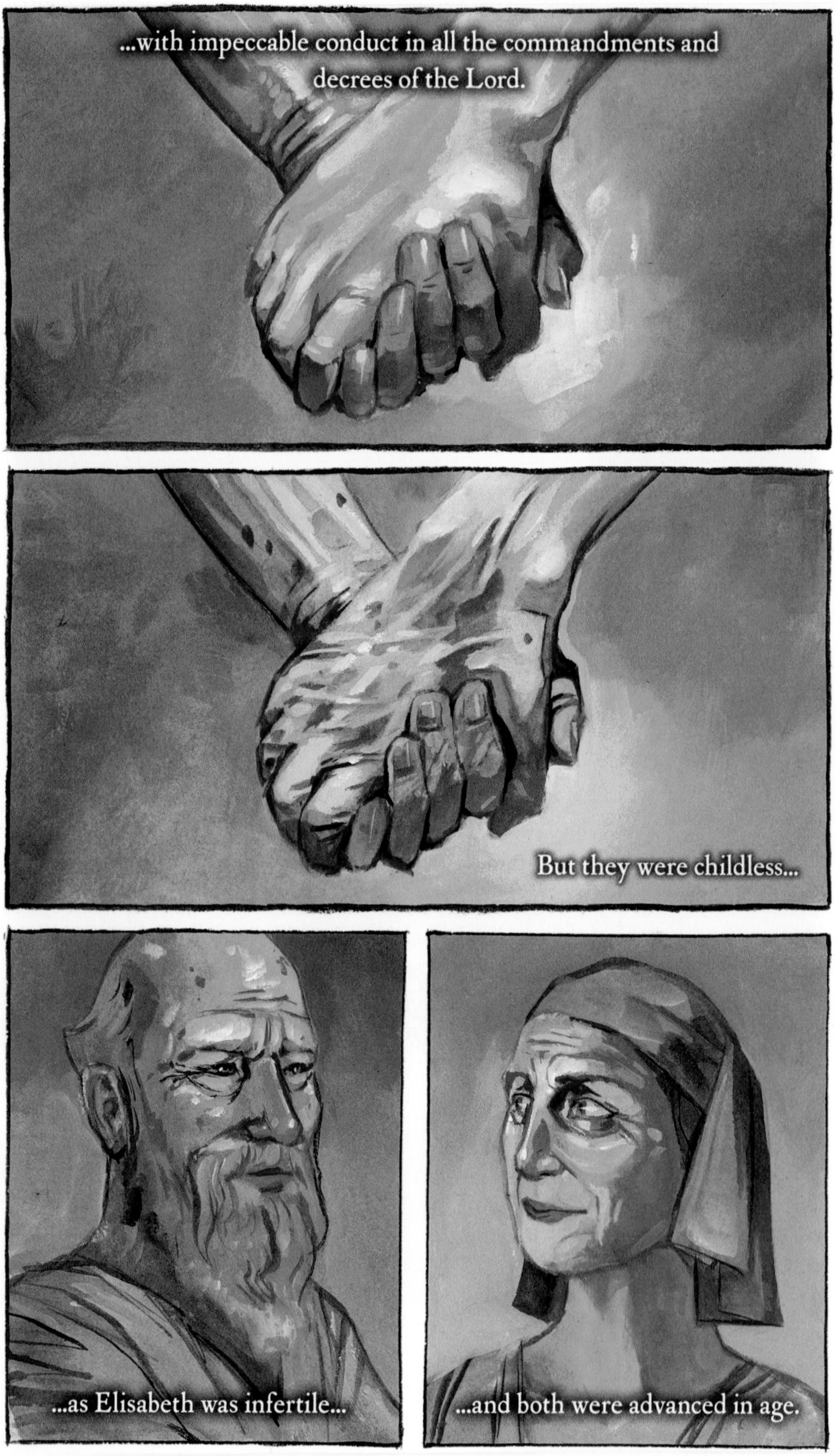
...with impeccable conduct in all the commandments and decrees of the Lord.
But they were childless...
...as Elisabeth was infertile...
...and both were advanced in age.

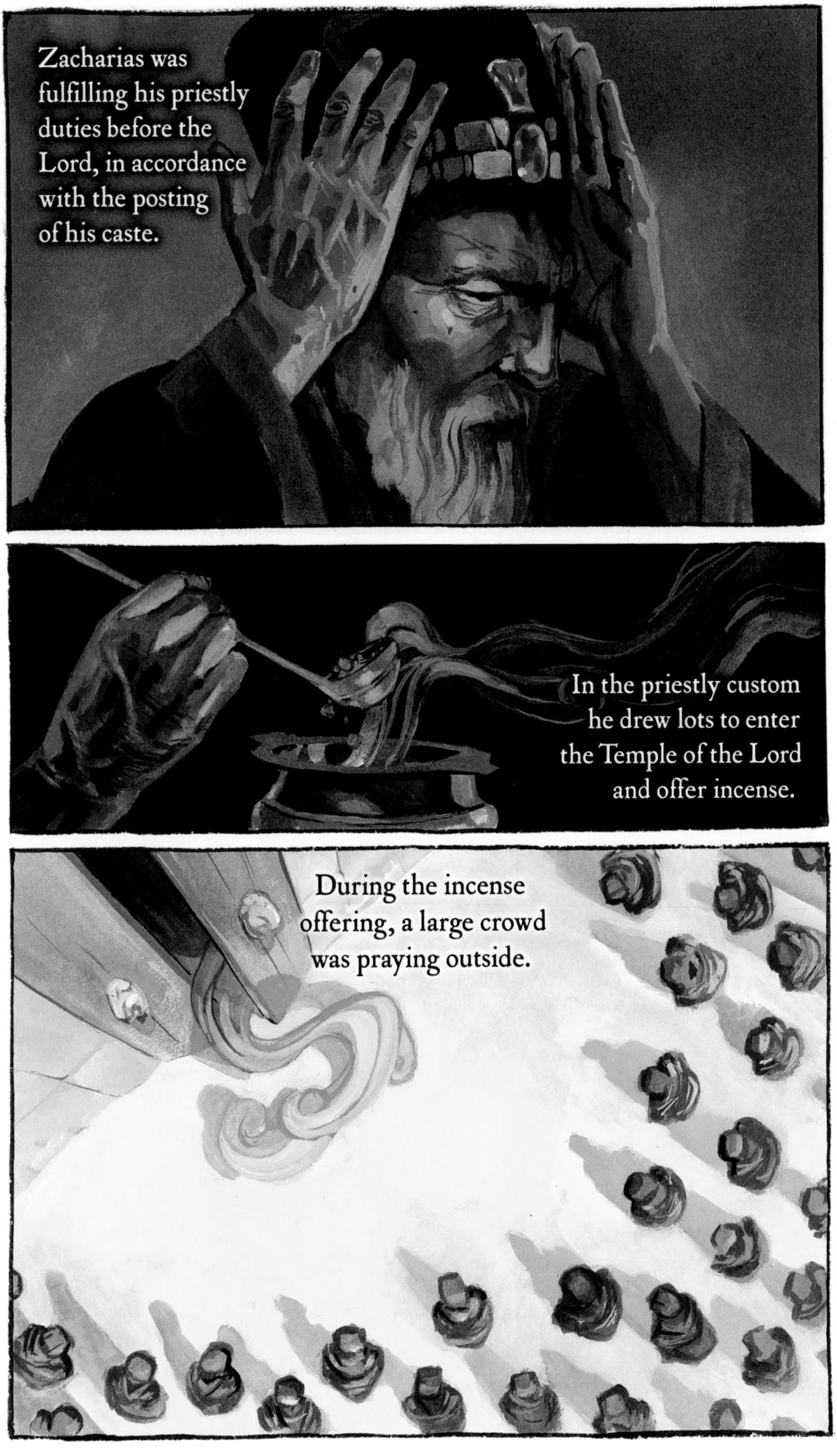
Zacharias was fulfilling his priestly duties before the Lord, in accordance with the posting of his caste.
In the priestly custom he drew lots to enter the Temple of the Lord and offer incense.
During the incense offering, a large crowd was praying outside.

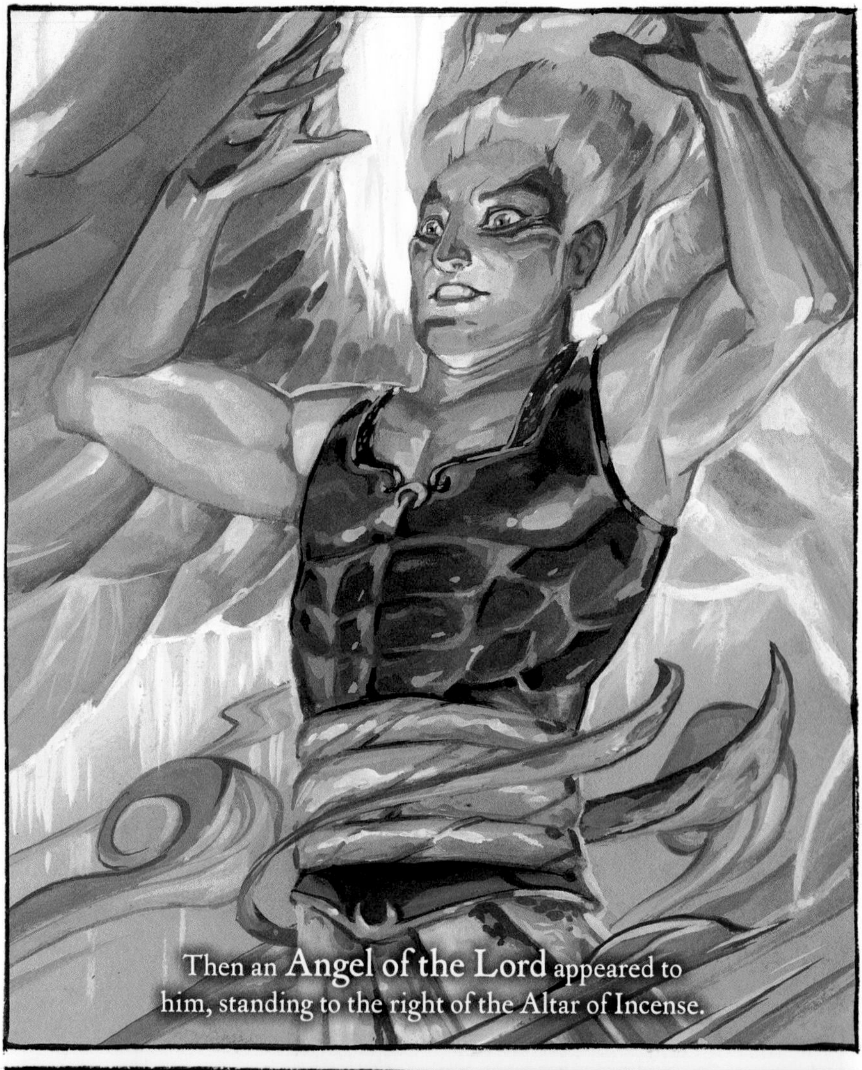
Then an Angel of the Lord appeared to him, standing to the right of the Altar of Incense.

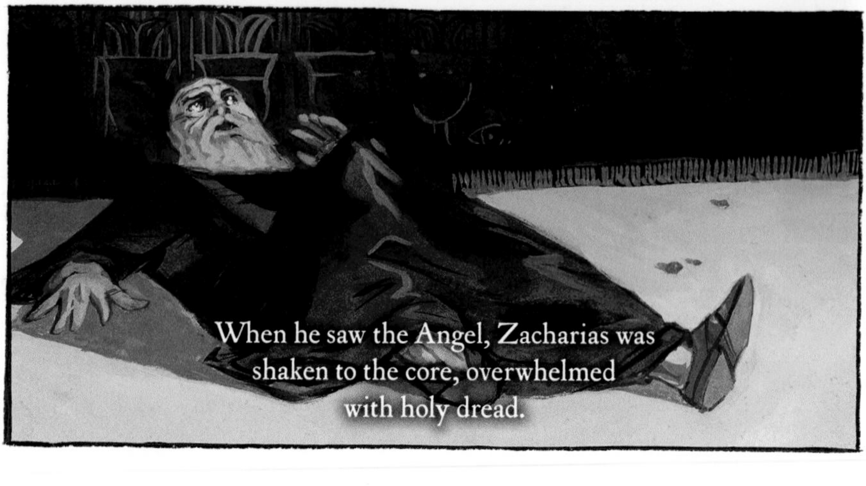
When he saw the Angel, Zacharias was shaken to the core, overwhelmed with holy dread.

The Angel addressed him:
"Zacharias, do not be afraid.
Your prayer has been heard."

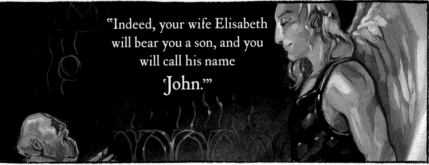

"Indeed, your wife Elisabeth
will bear you a son, and you
will call his name
'John.'"

"He will bring you joy and gladness, and
many will rejoice at his birth."

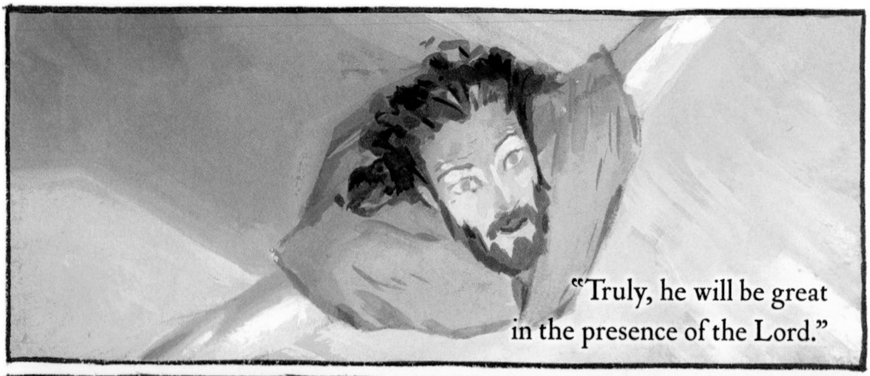
"Truly, he will be great in the presence of the Lord."

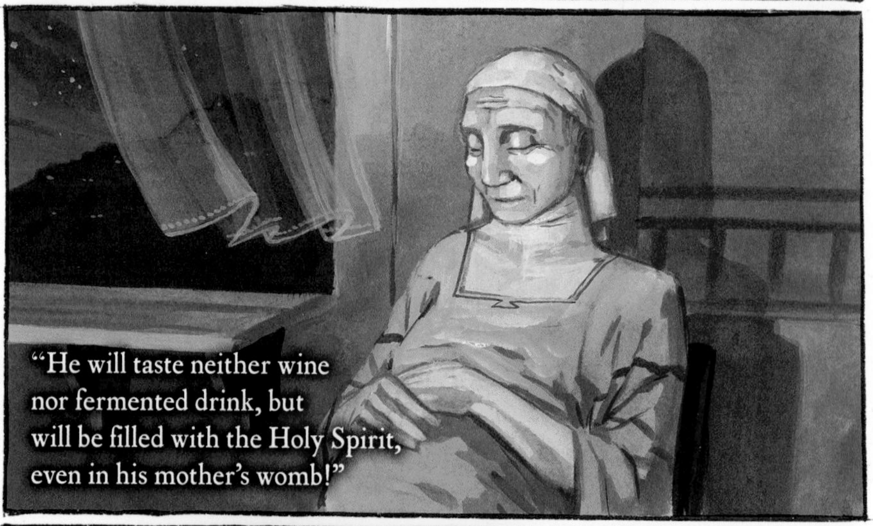
"He will taste neither wine nor fermented drink, but will be filled with the Holy Spirit, even in his mother's womb!"

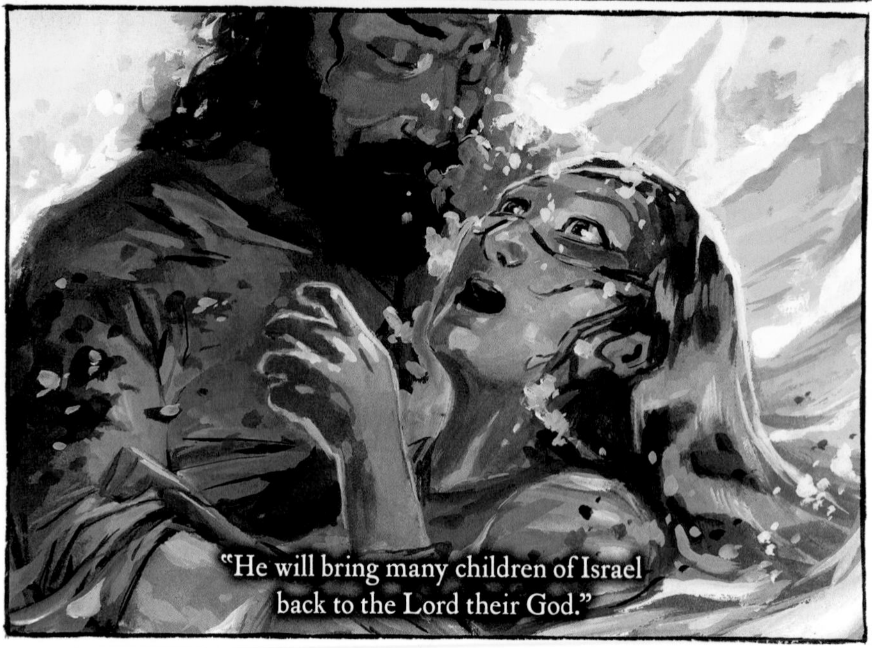
"He will bring many children of Israel back to the Lord their God."

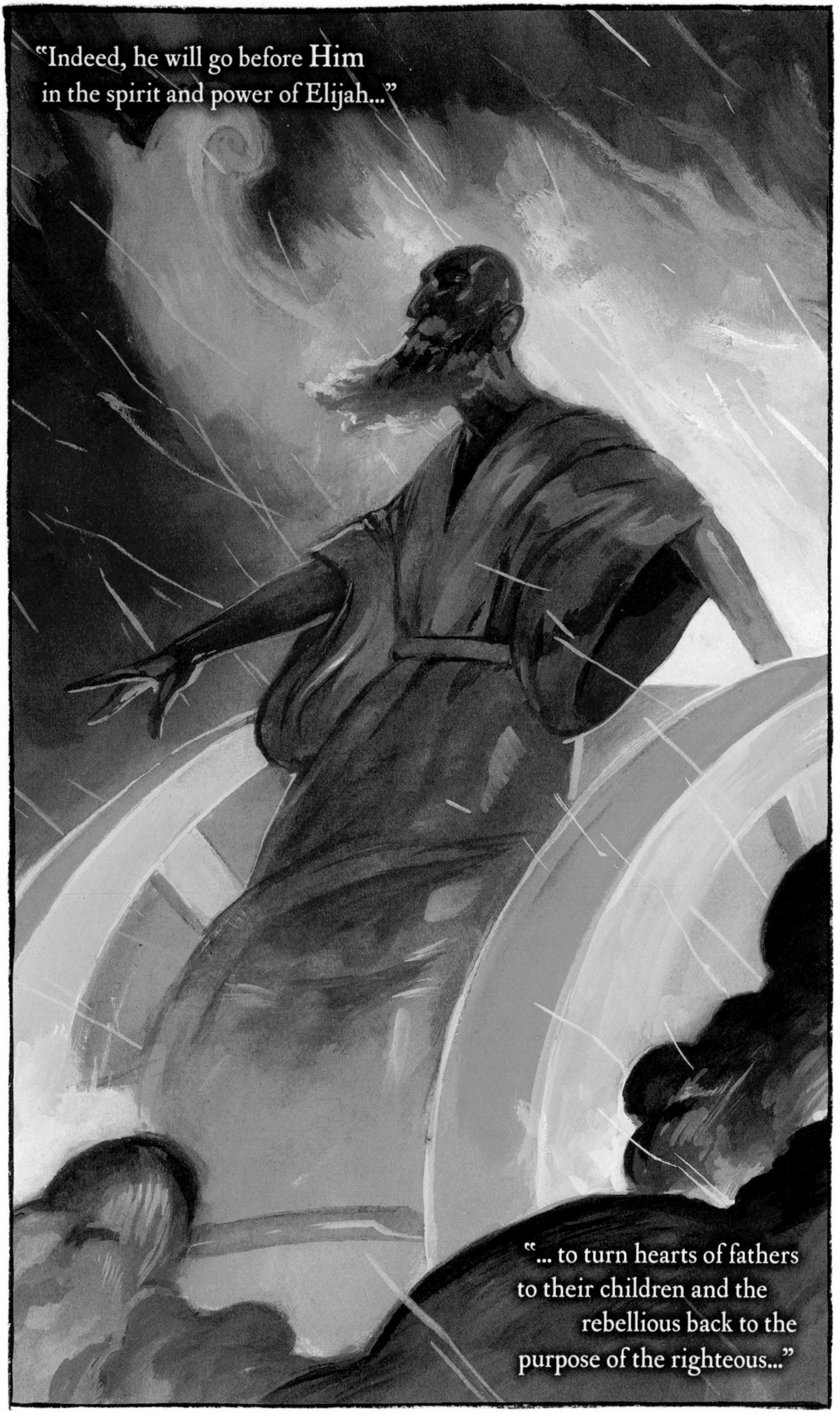
"Indeed, he will go before Him in the spirit and power of Elijah..."
"... to turn hearts of fathers to their children and the rebellious back to the purpose of the righteous..."

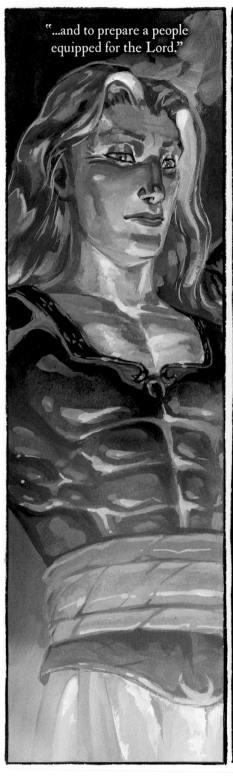

"...and to prepare a people equipped for the Lord."

Zacharias replied, "How can I know this? I am an old man, and my wife is well beyond her days."

The Angel answered, "I am Gabriel who stands before God! I am sent to speak these things to you and proclaim the Good News!"

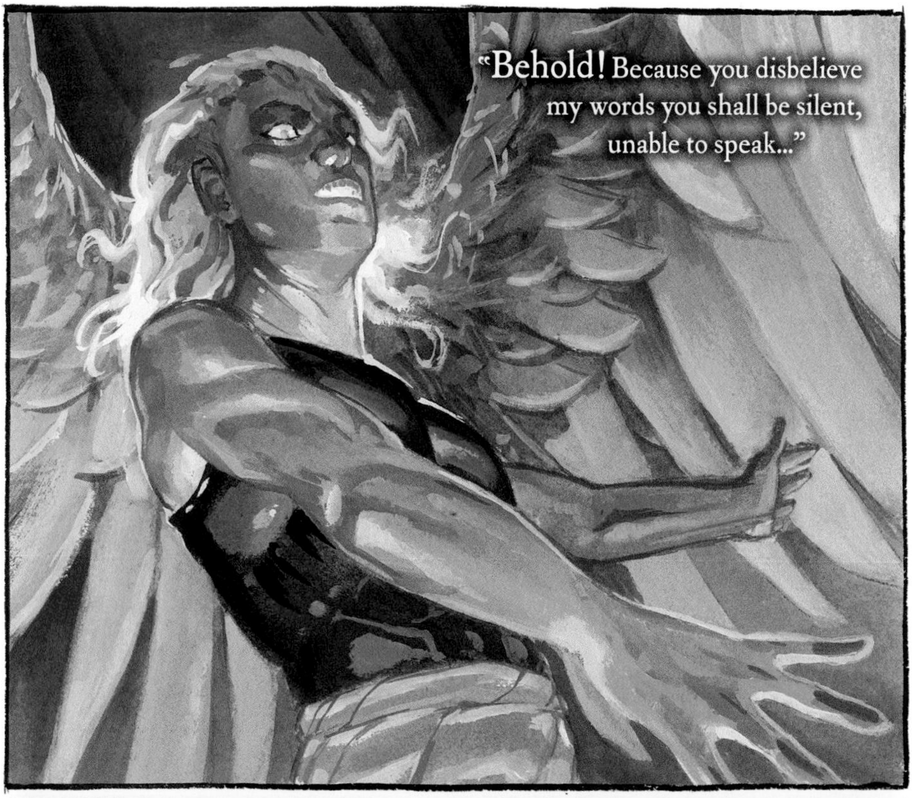
"Behold! Because you disbelieve my words you shall be silent, unable to speak..."

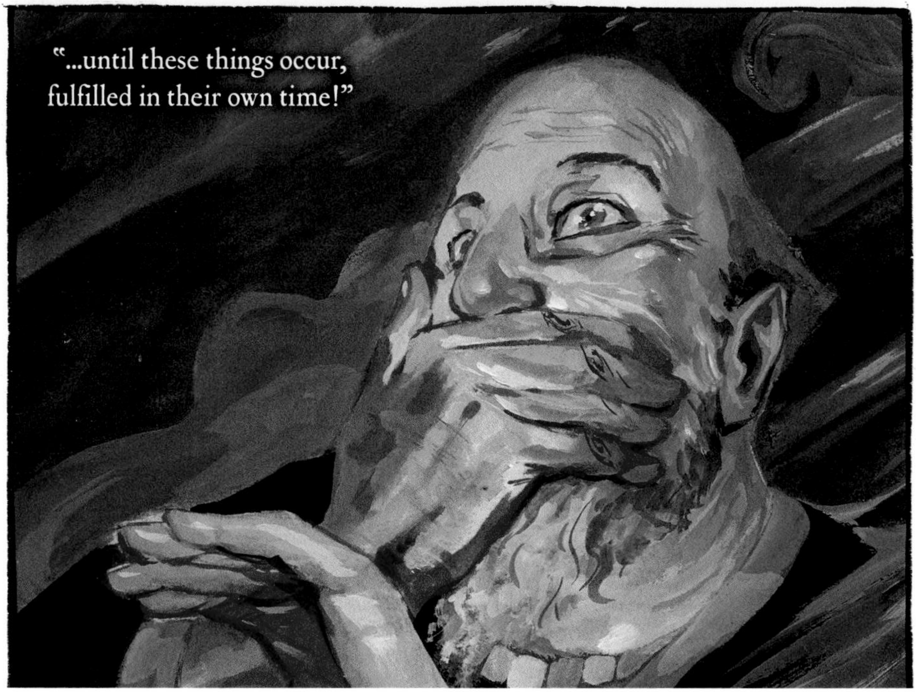
"...until these things occur, fulfilled in their own time!"

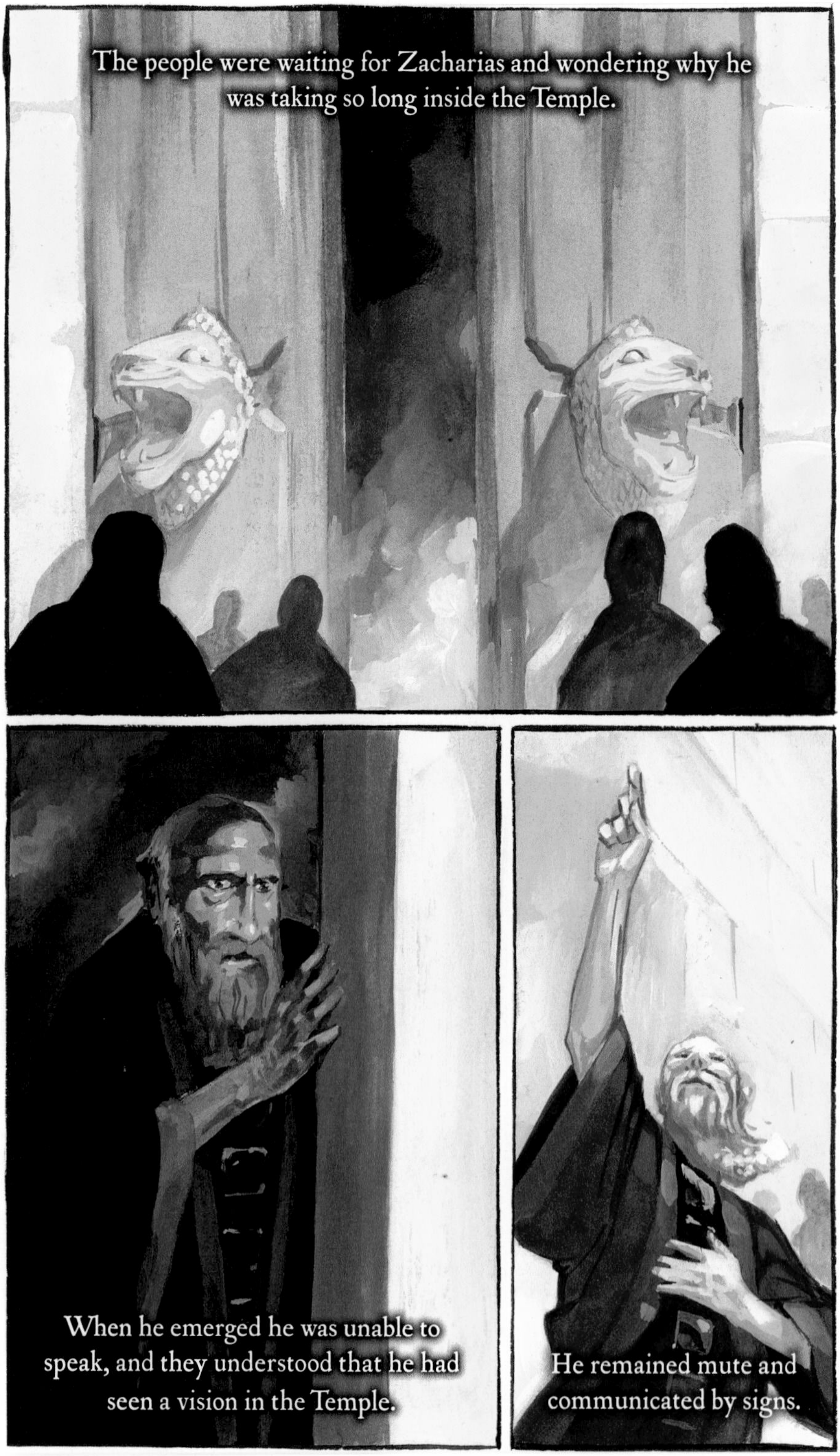
The people were waiting for Zacharias and wondering why he was taking so long inside the Temple.
When he emerged he was unable to speak, and they understood that he had seen a vision in the Temple.
He remained mute and communicated by signs.

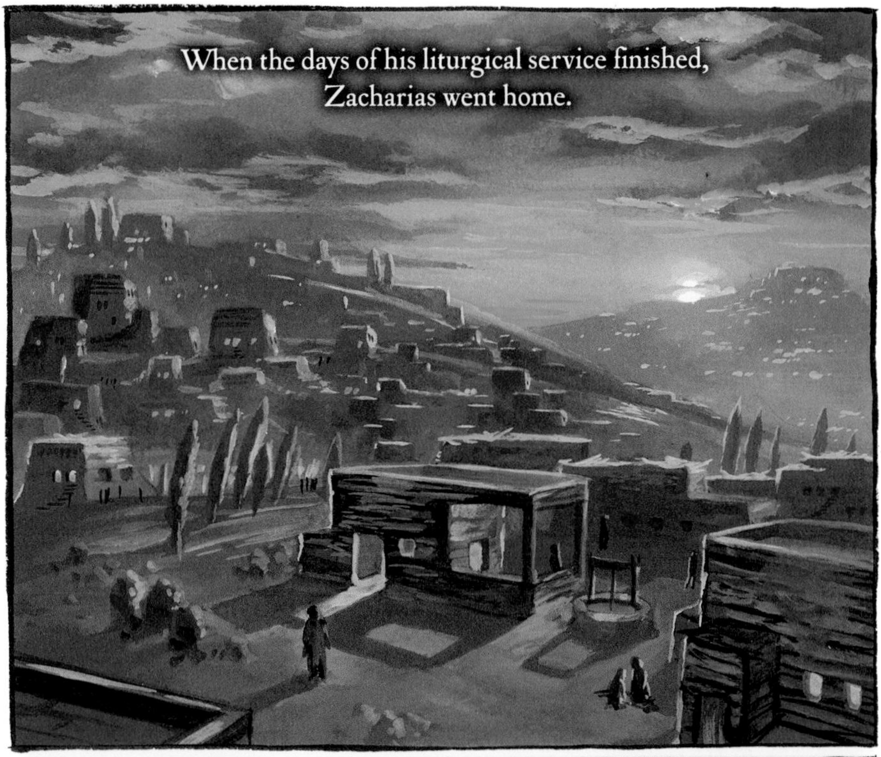
When the days of his liturgical service finished,
Zacharias went home.

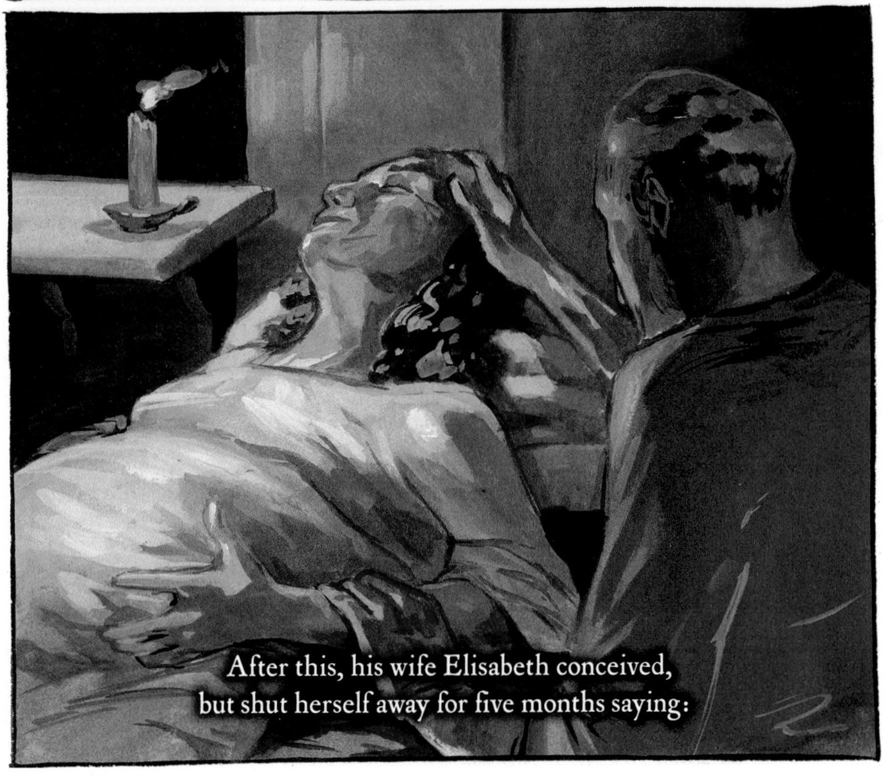
After this, his wife Elisabeth conceived,
but shut herself away for five months saying:

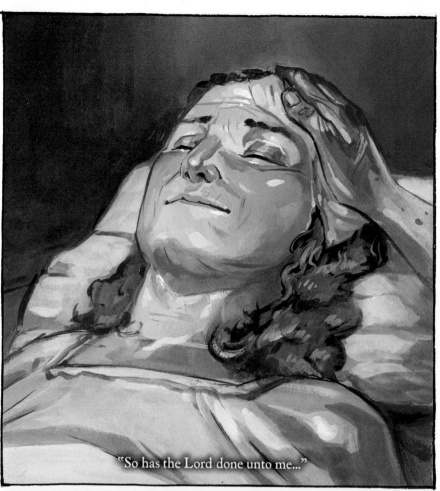

"So has the Lord done unto me..."

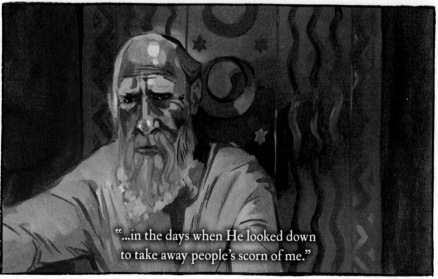

"...in the days when He looked down
to take away people's scorn of me."

ANNUNCIATION
OF THE NATIVITY OF THE MESSIAH

LUKE 1:26–38

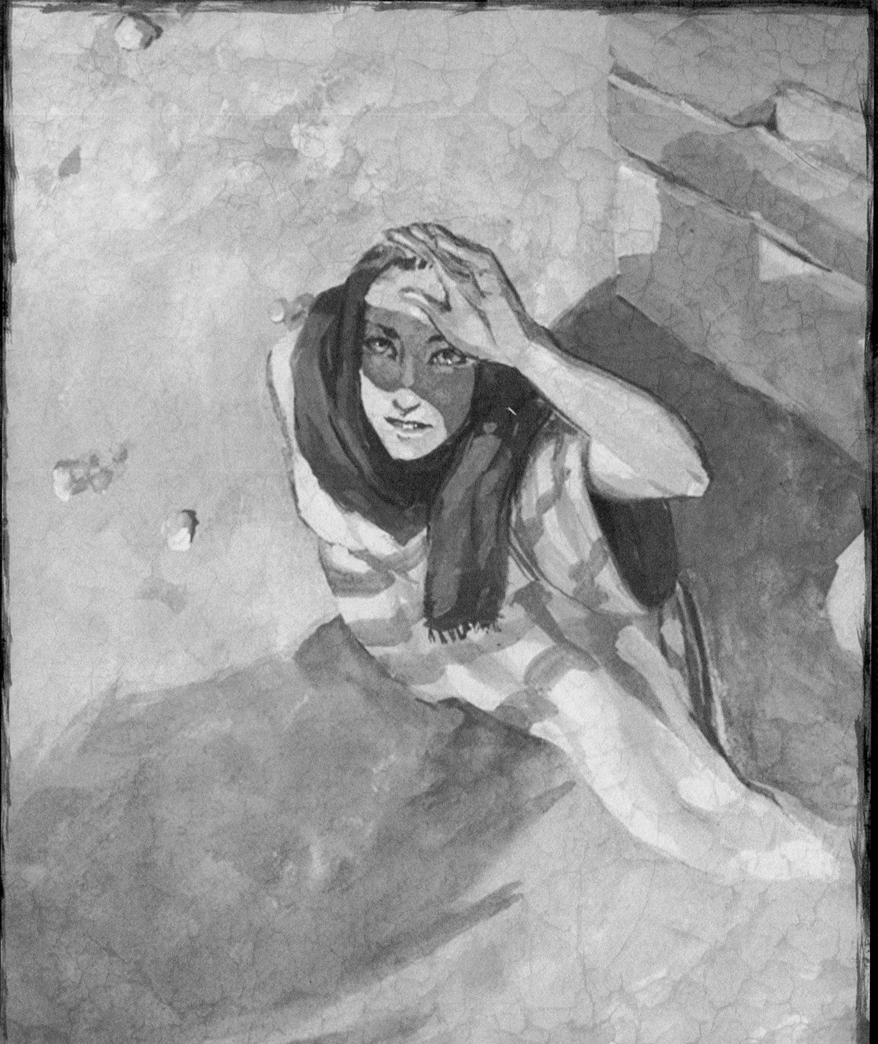

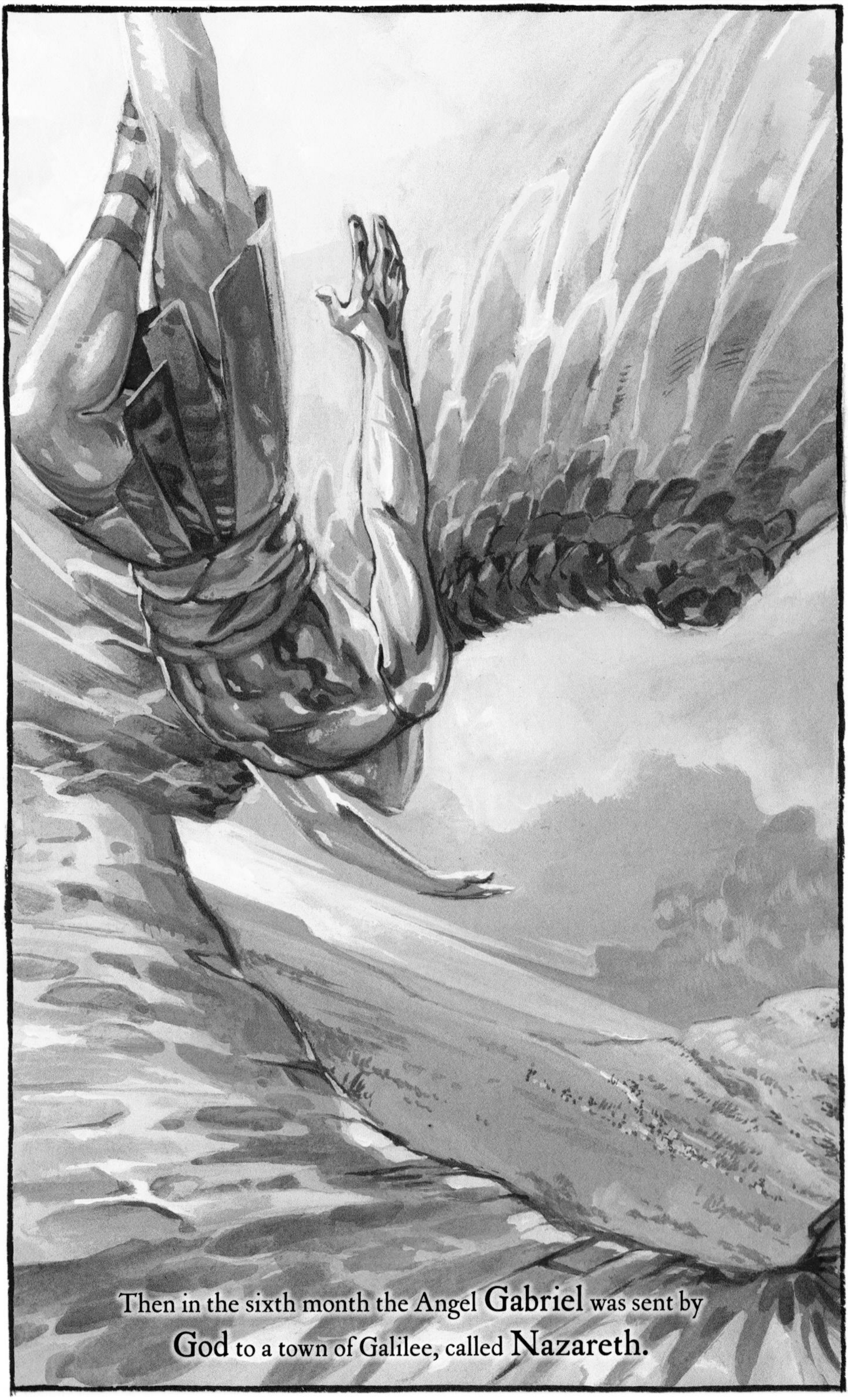
Then in the sixth month the Angel Gabriel was sent by
God to a town of Galilee, called Nazareth.

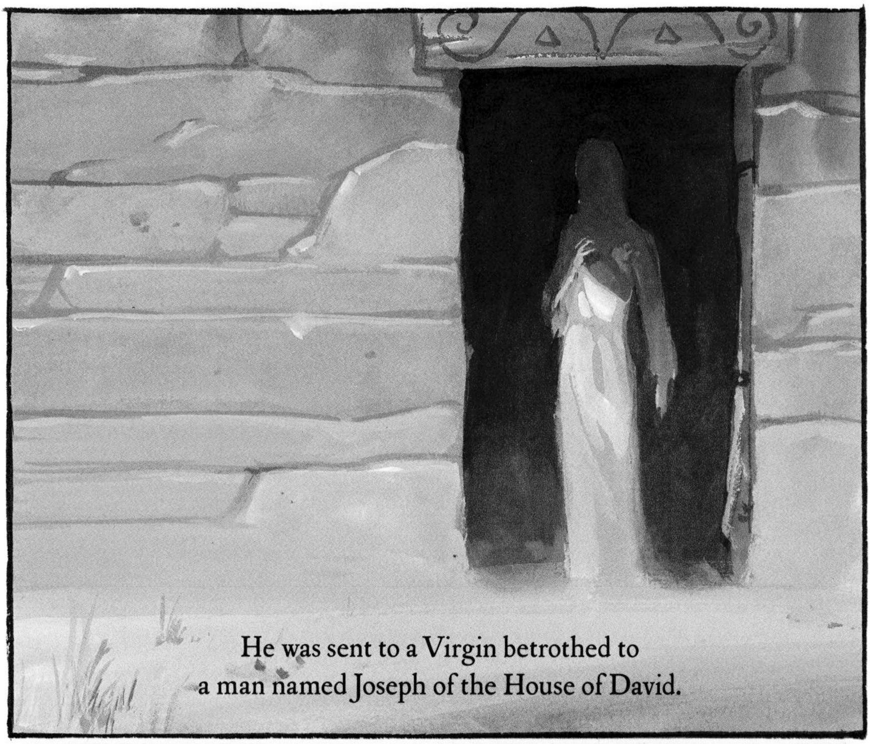
He was sent to a Virgin betrothed to
a man named Joseph of the House of David.

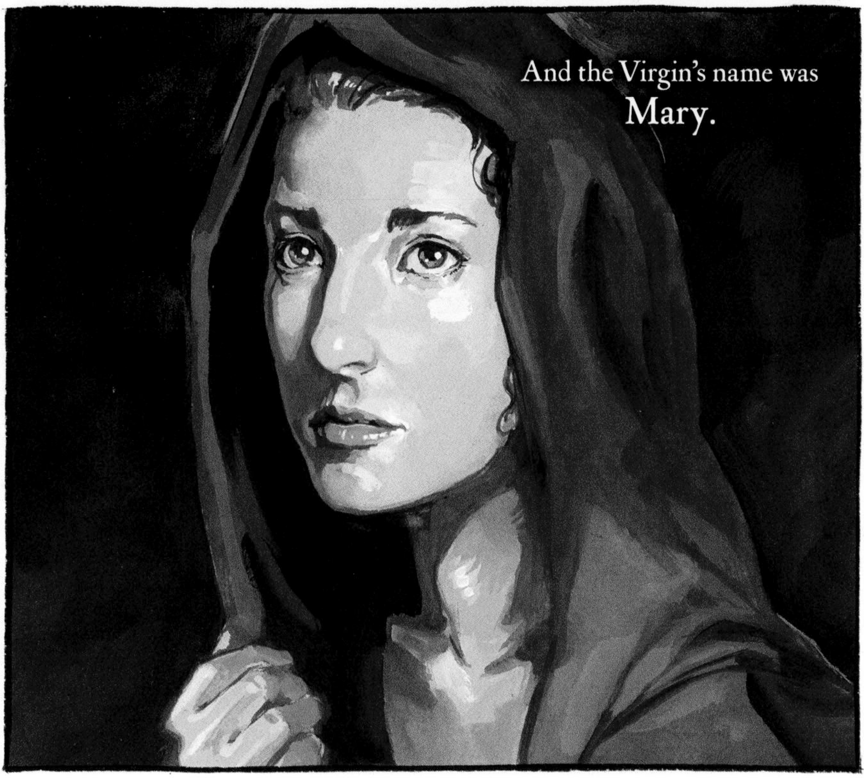
And the Virgin's name was
Mary.

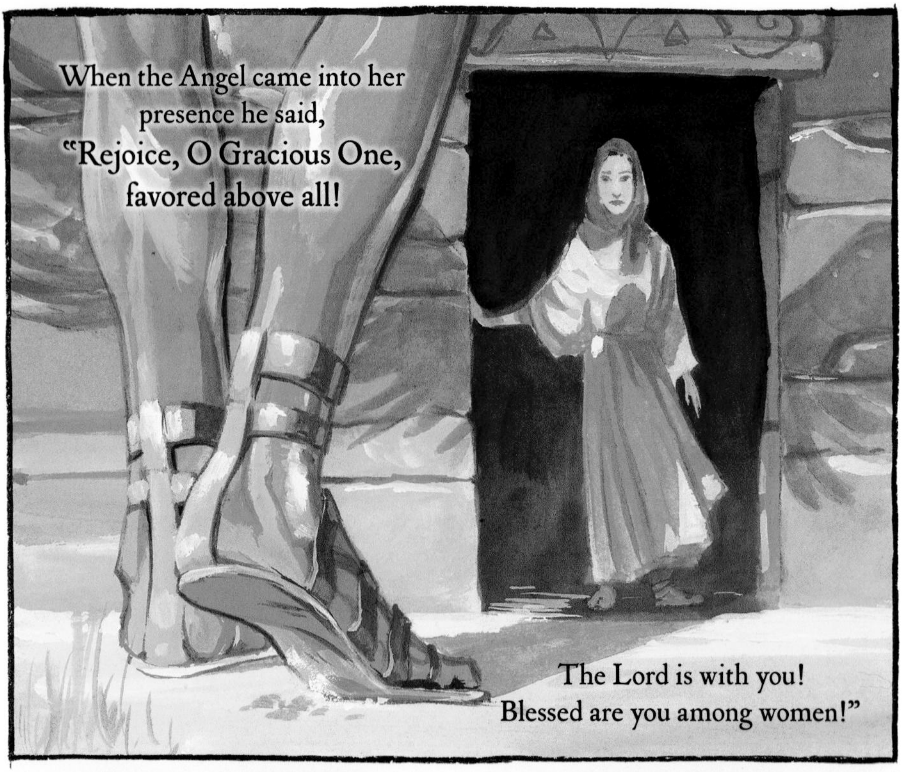
When the Angel came into her presence he said, "Rejoice, O Gracious One, favored above all!
The Lord is with you! Blessed are you among women!"

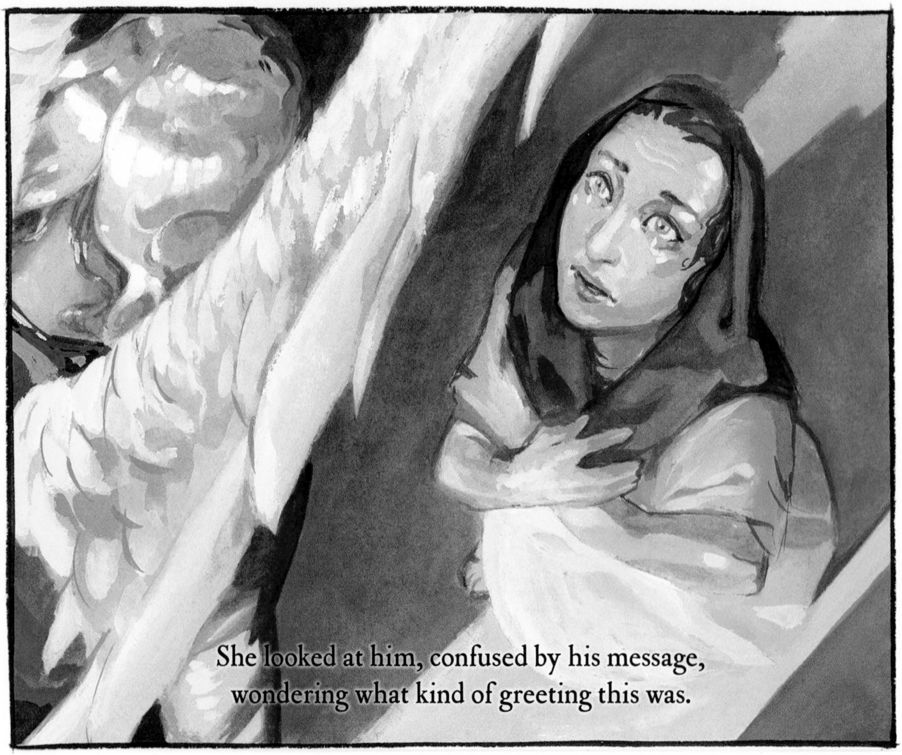
She looked at him, confused by his message, wondering what kind of greeting this was.

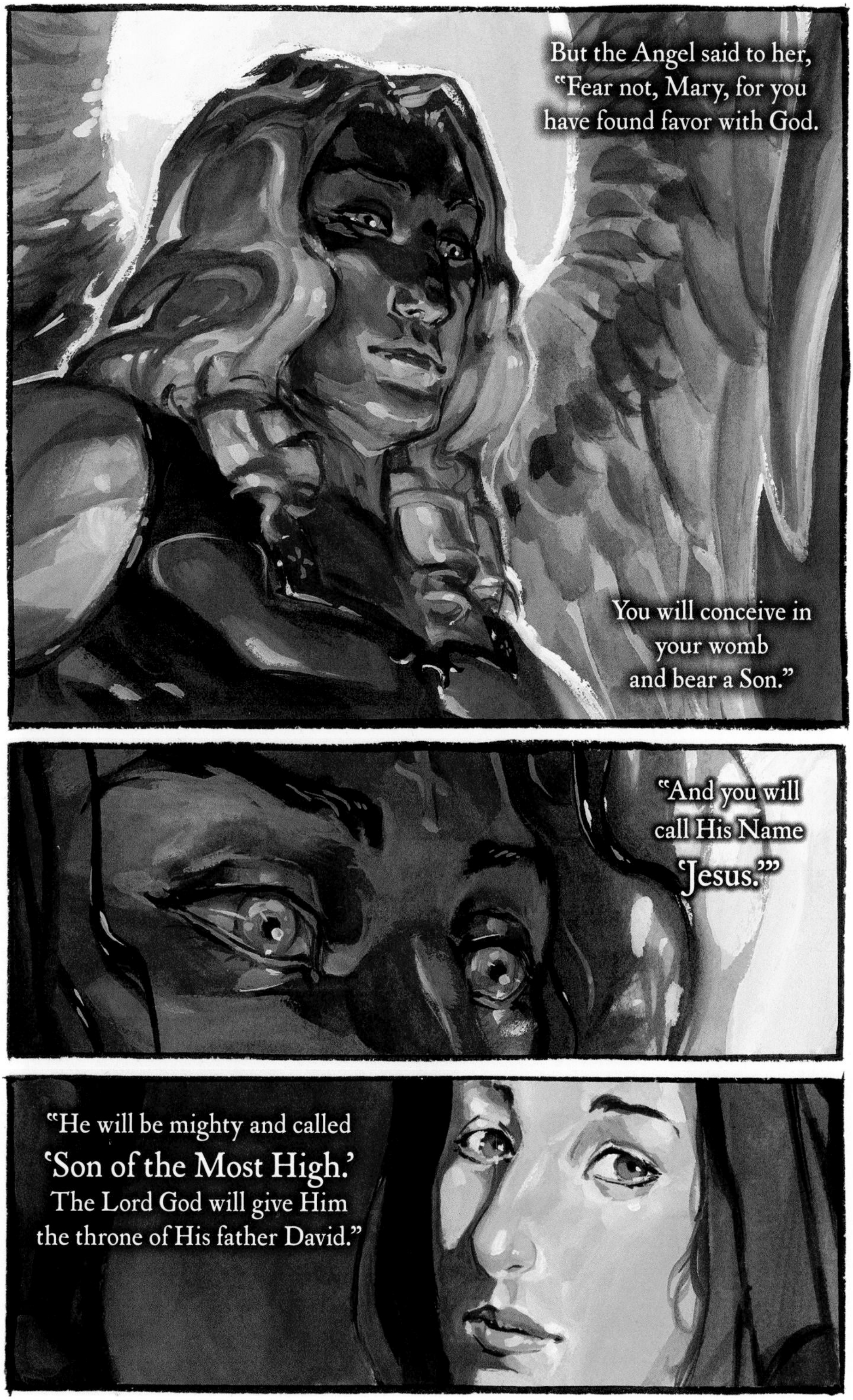
But the Angel said to her, "Fear not, Mary, for you have found favor with God.
You will conceive in your womb and bear a Son."
"And you will call His Name 'Jesus.'"
"He will be mighty and called 'Son of the Most High.' The Lord God will give Him the throne of His father David."

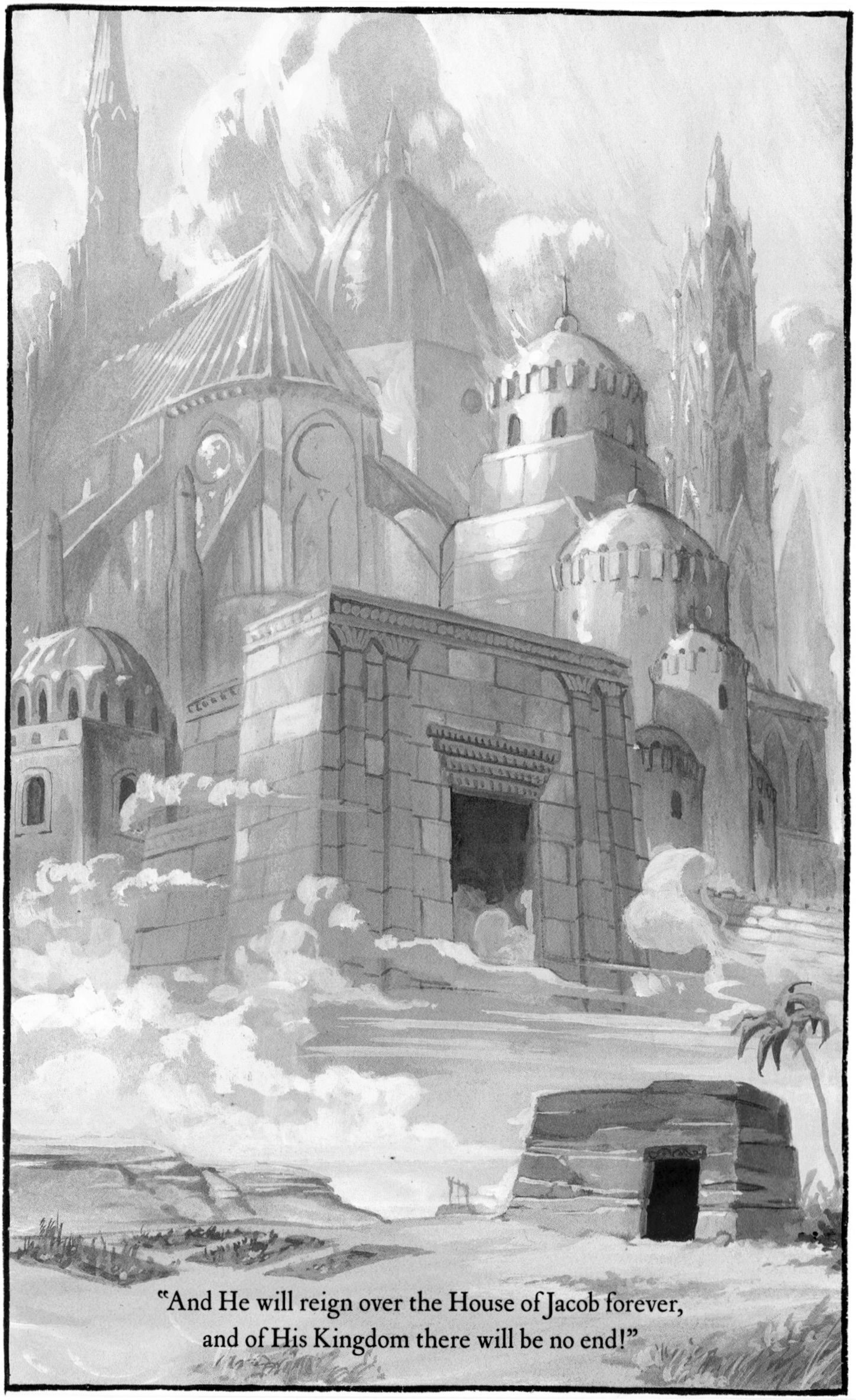

"And He will reign over the House of Jacob forever,
and of His Kingdom there will be no end!"

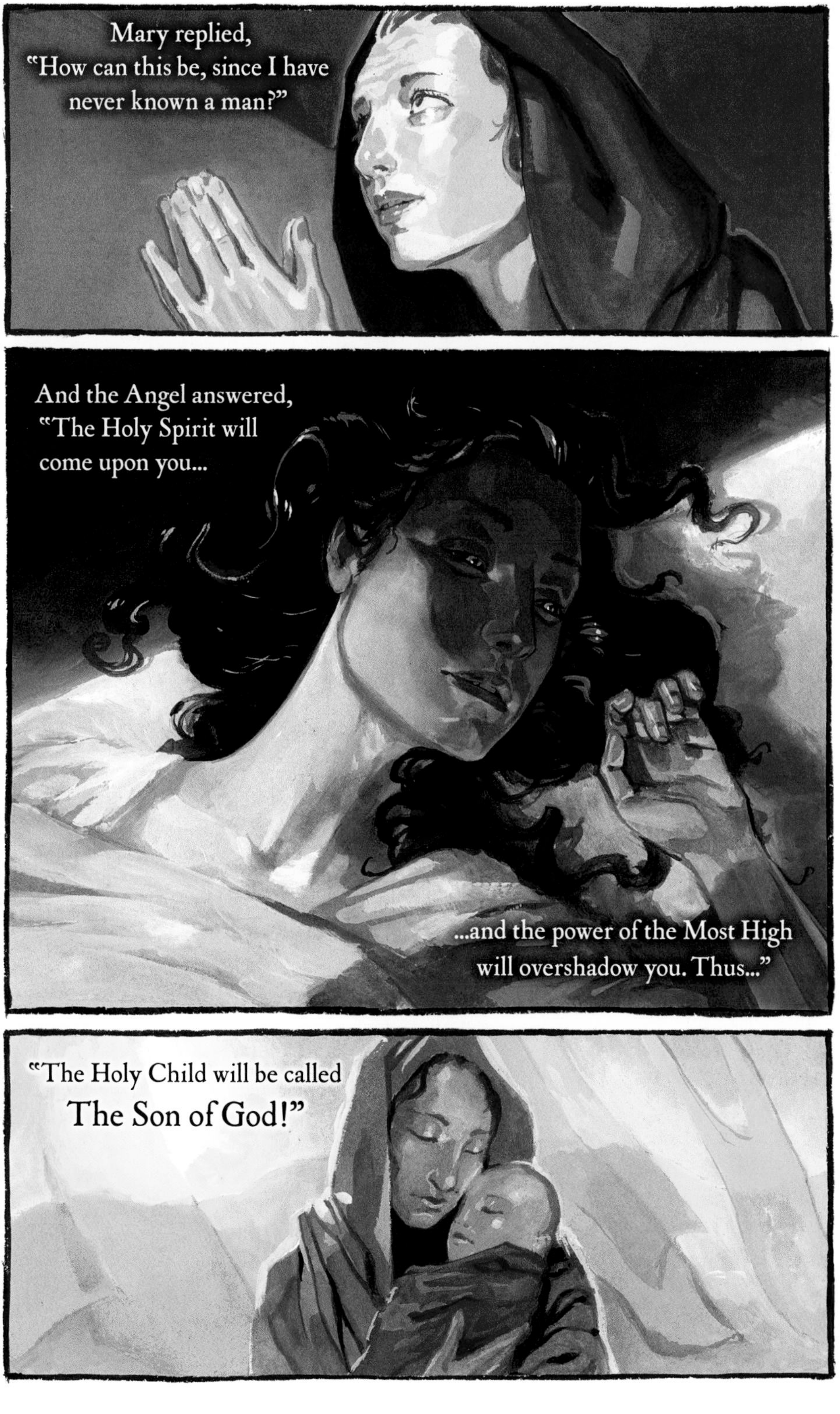
Mary replied,
"How can this be, since I have never known a man?"
And the Angel answered,
"The Holy Spirit will come upon you...
...and the power of the Most High will overshadow you. Thus..."
"The Holy Child will be called
The Son of God!"

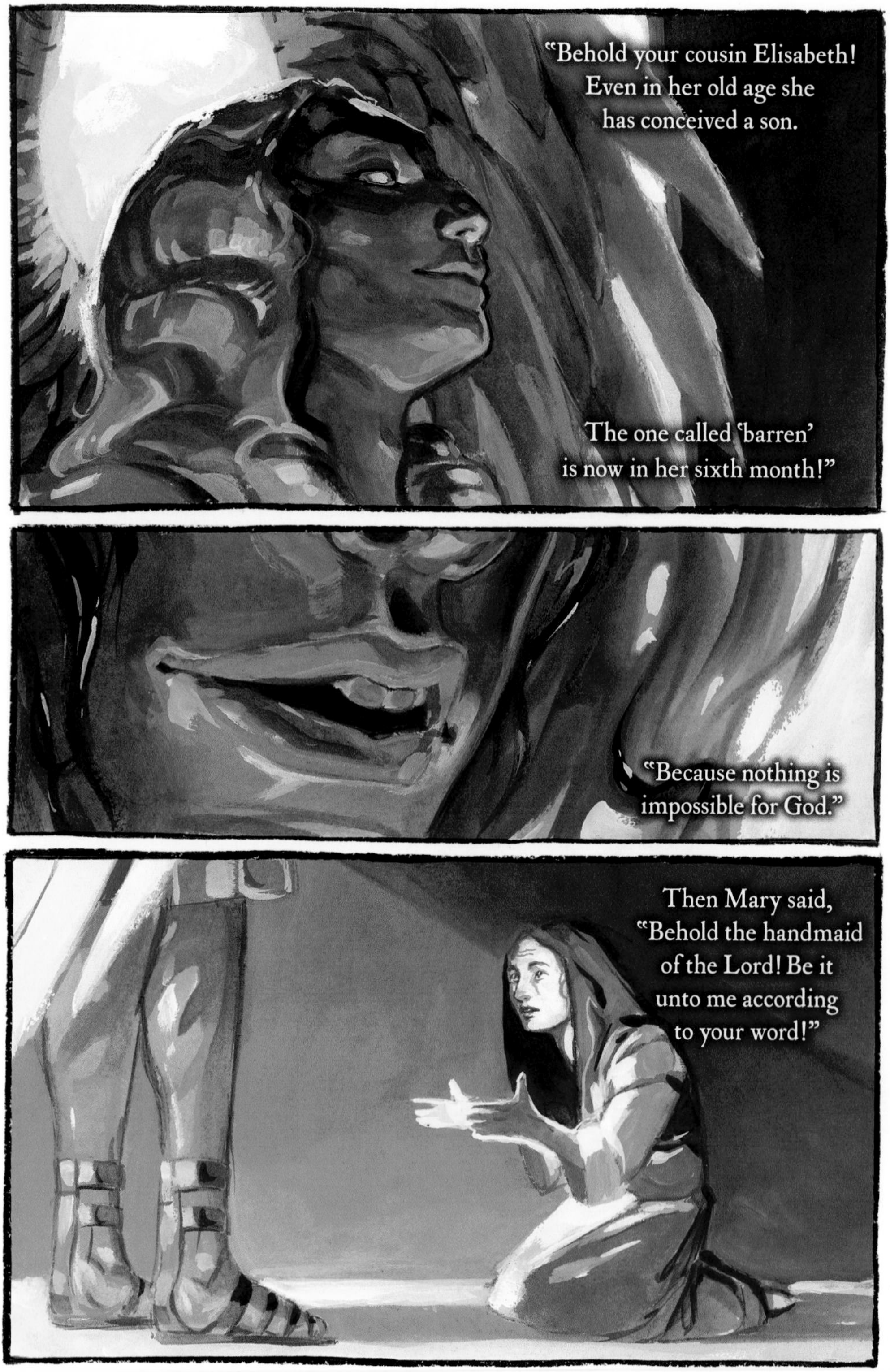
"Behold your cousin Elisabeth! Even in her old age she has conceived a son.
The one called 'barren' is now in her sixth month!"
"Because nothing is impossible for God."
Then Mary said, "Behold the handmaid of the Lord! Be it unto me according to your word!"

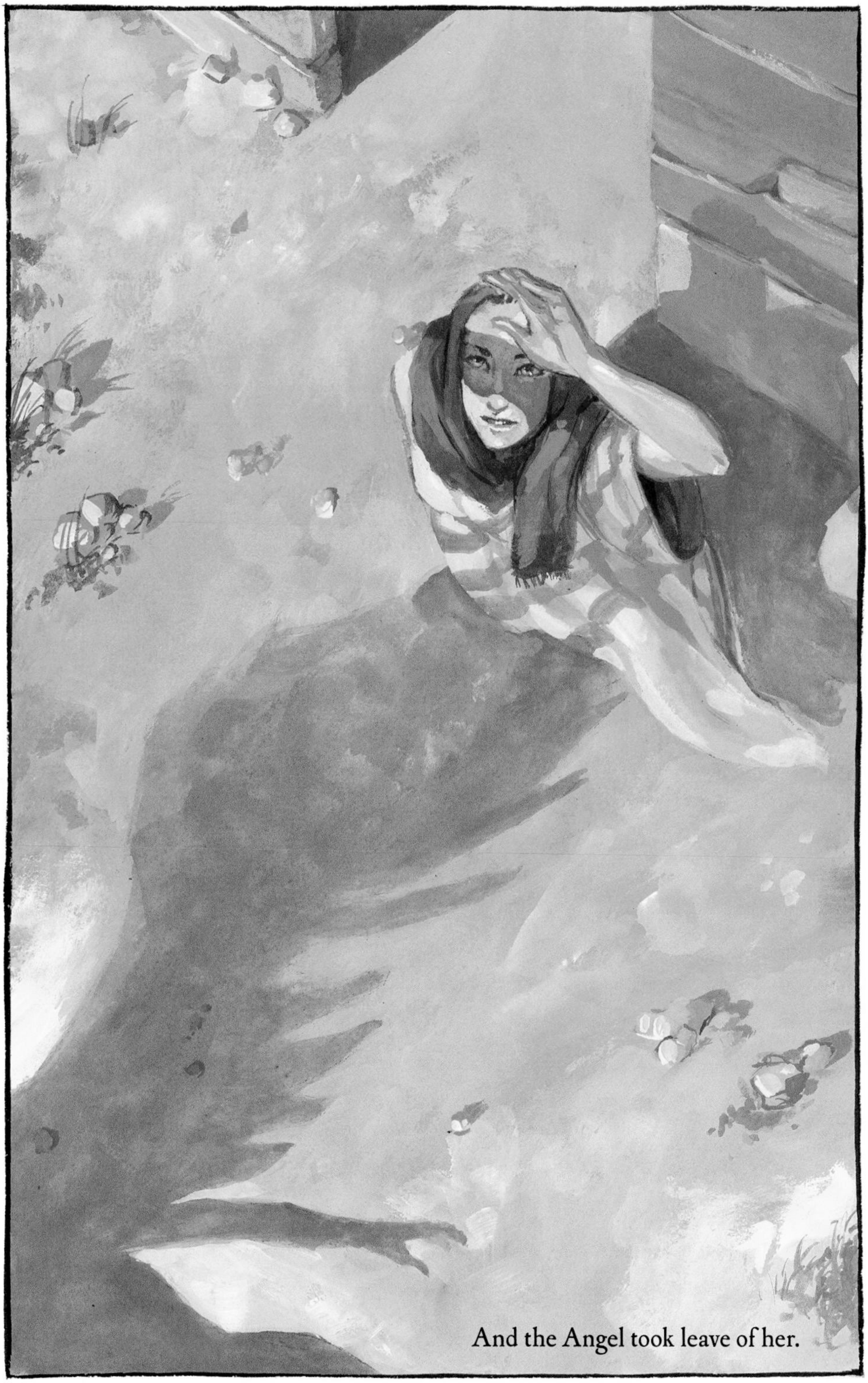
And the Angel took leave of her.

MARY AND ELISABETH

LUKE 1:39–56

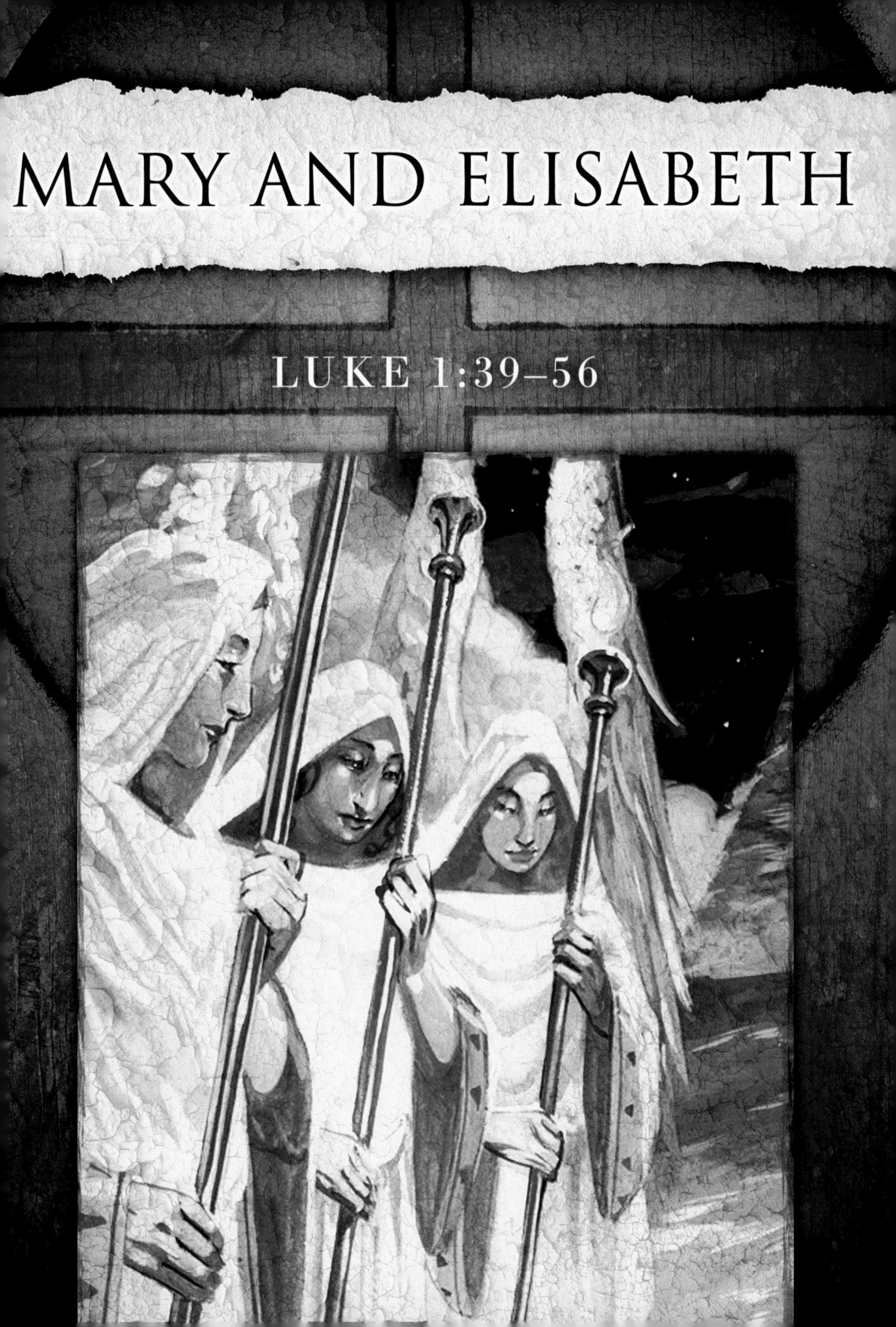

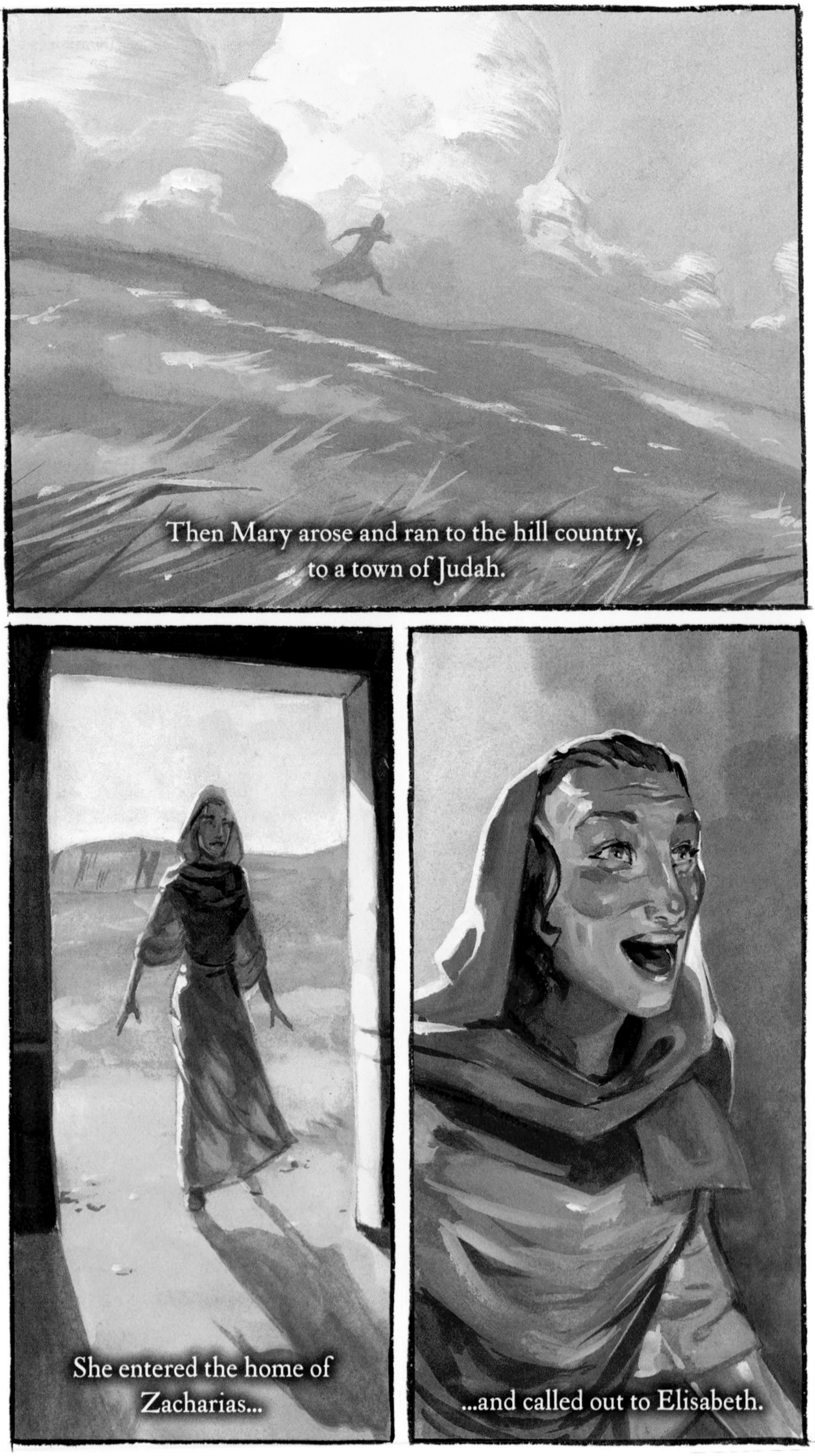
Then Mary arose and ran to the hill country,
to a town of Judah.
She entered the home of
Zacharias...
...and called out to Elisabeth.

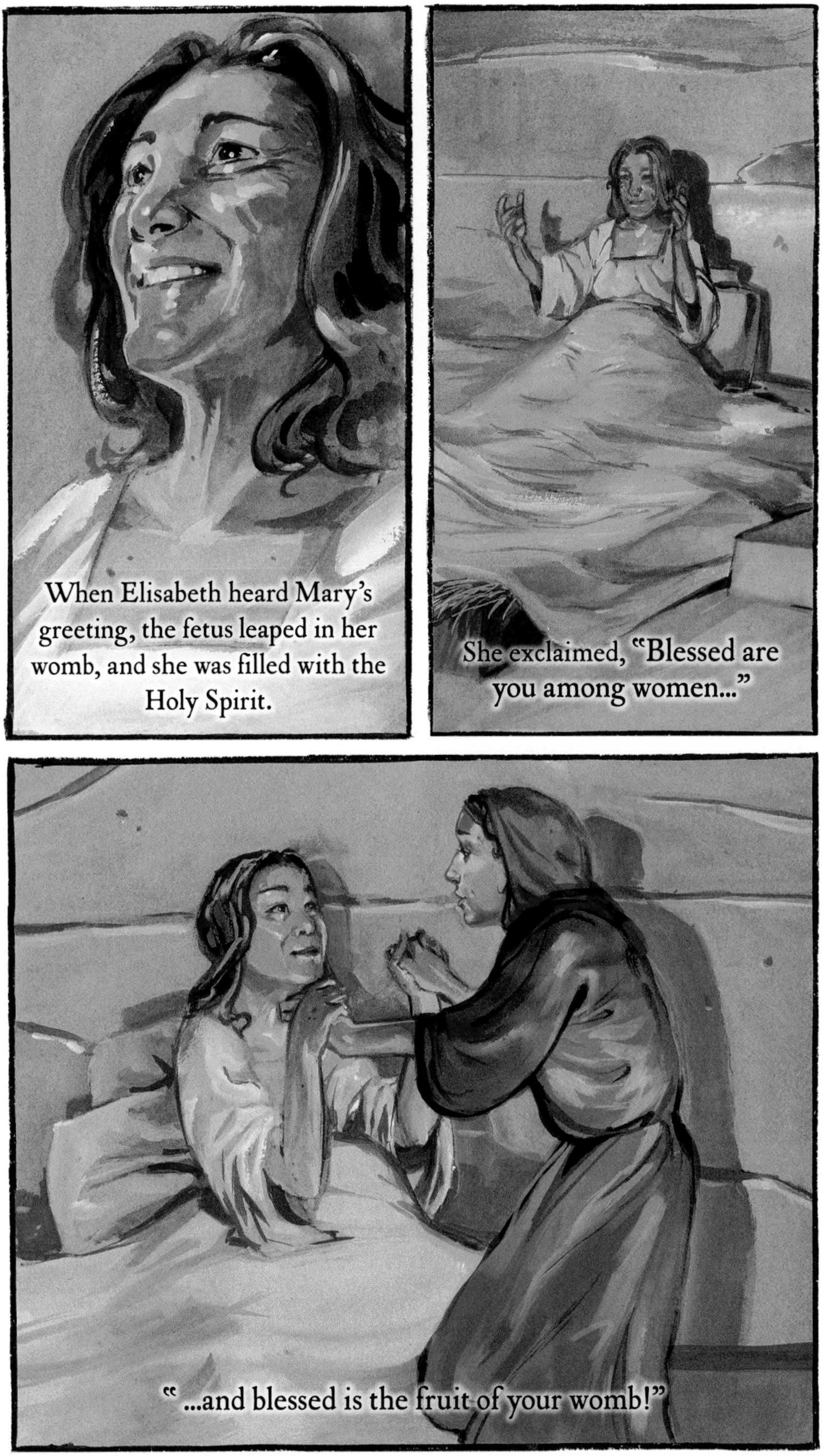
When Elisabeth heard Mary's greeting, the fetus leaped in her womb, and she was filled with the Holy Spirit.
She exclaimed, "Blessed are you among women..."
"...and blessed is the fruit of your womb!"

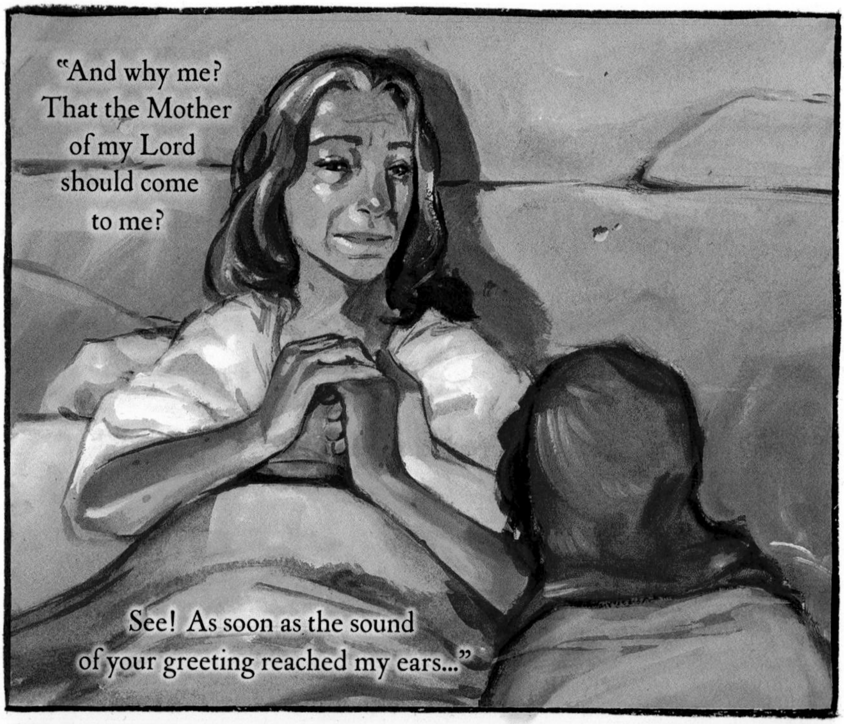
"And why me? That the Mother of my Lord should come to me?
See! As soon as the sound of your greeting reached my ears..."

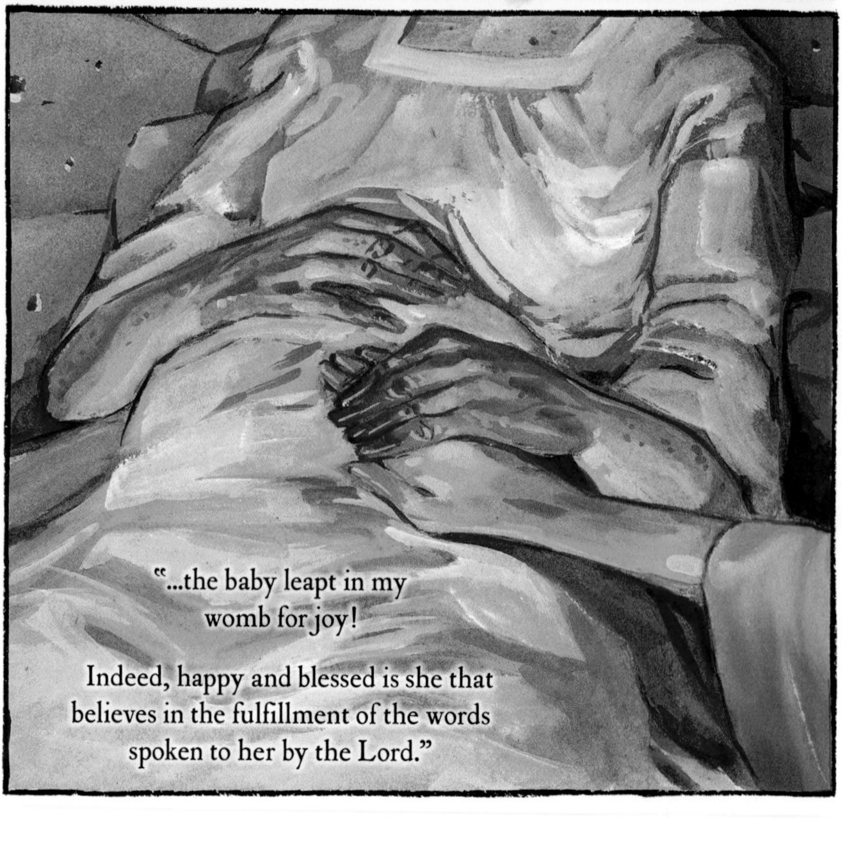
"...the baby leapt in my womb for joy!
Indeed, happy and blessed is she that believes in the fulfillment of the words spoken to her by the Lord."

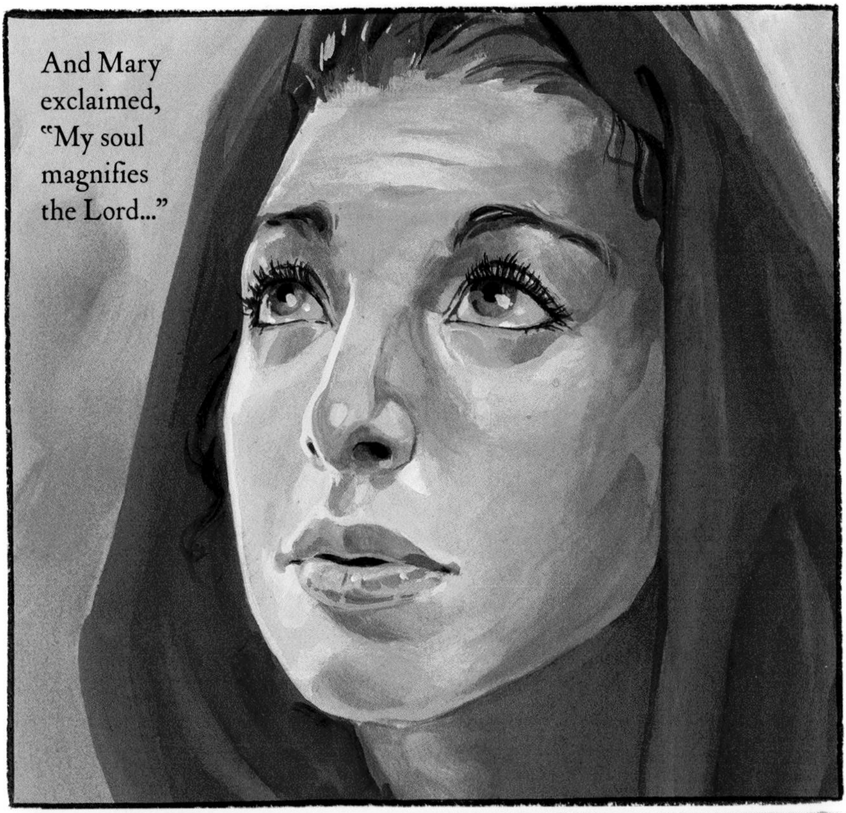
And Mary exclaimed, "My soul magnifies the Lord..."

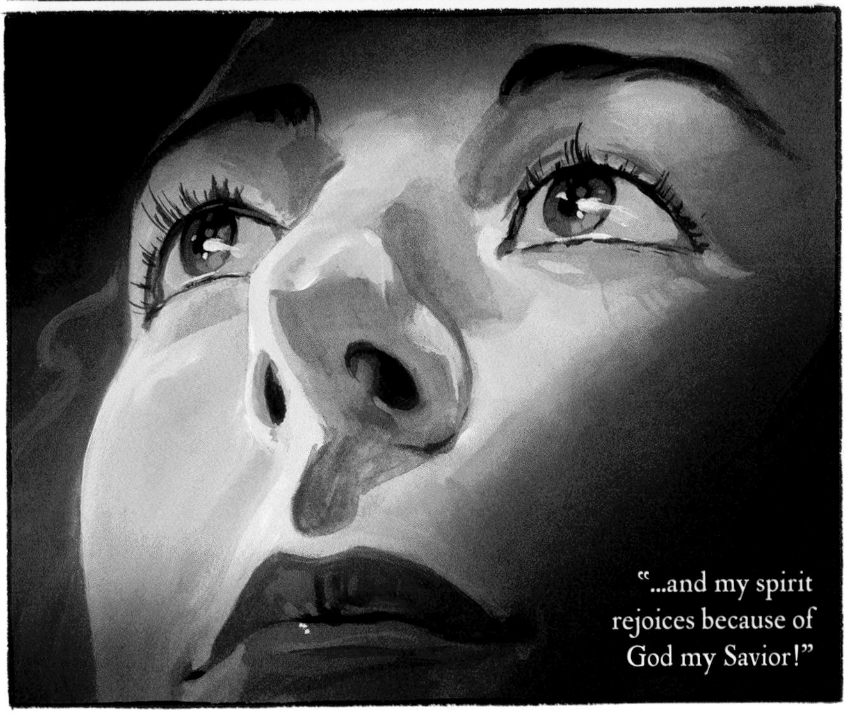
"...and my spirit rejoices because of God my Savior!"

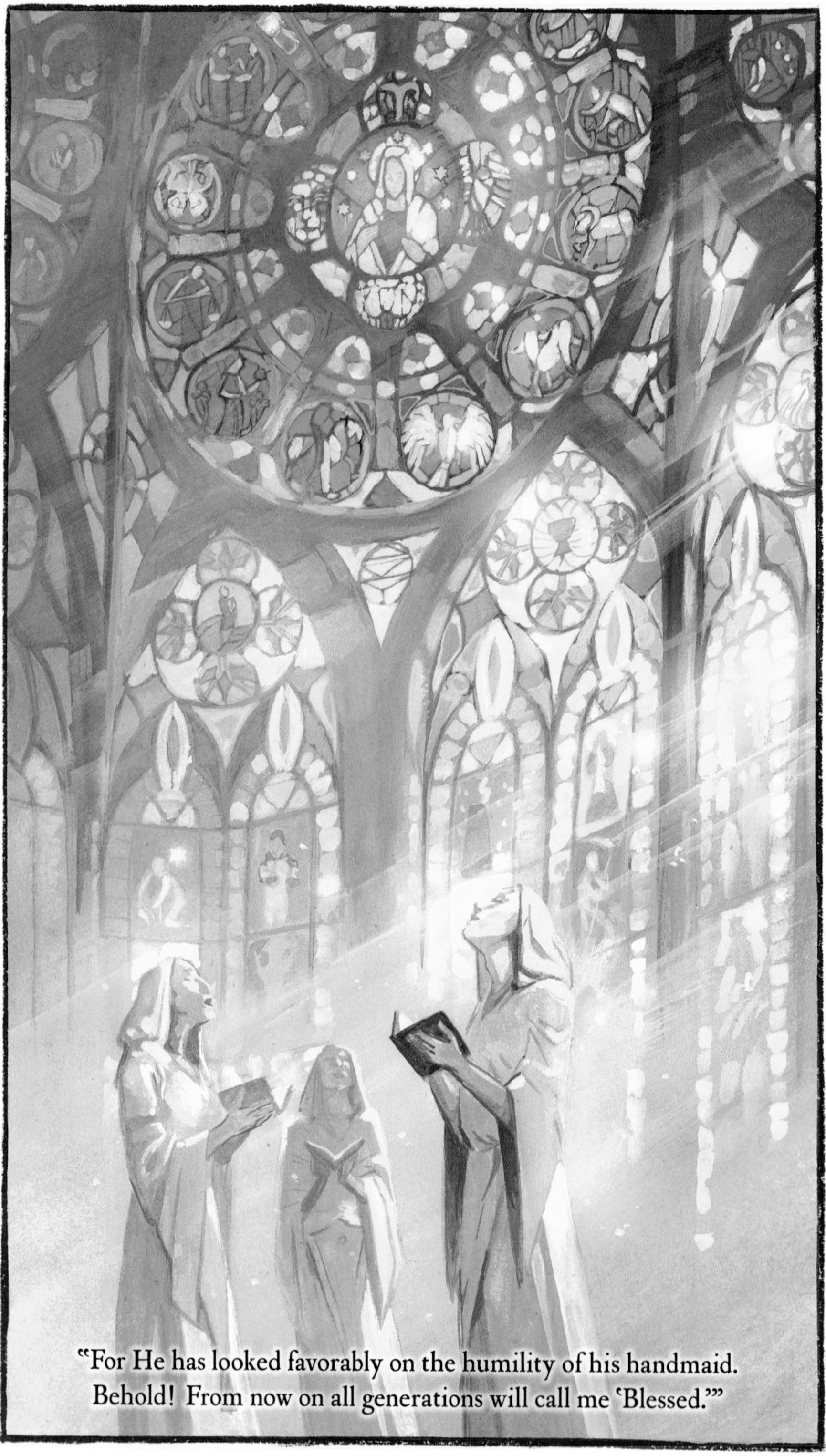

"For He has looked favorably on the humility of his handmaid.
Behold! From now on all generations will call me 'Blessed.'"

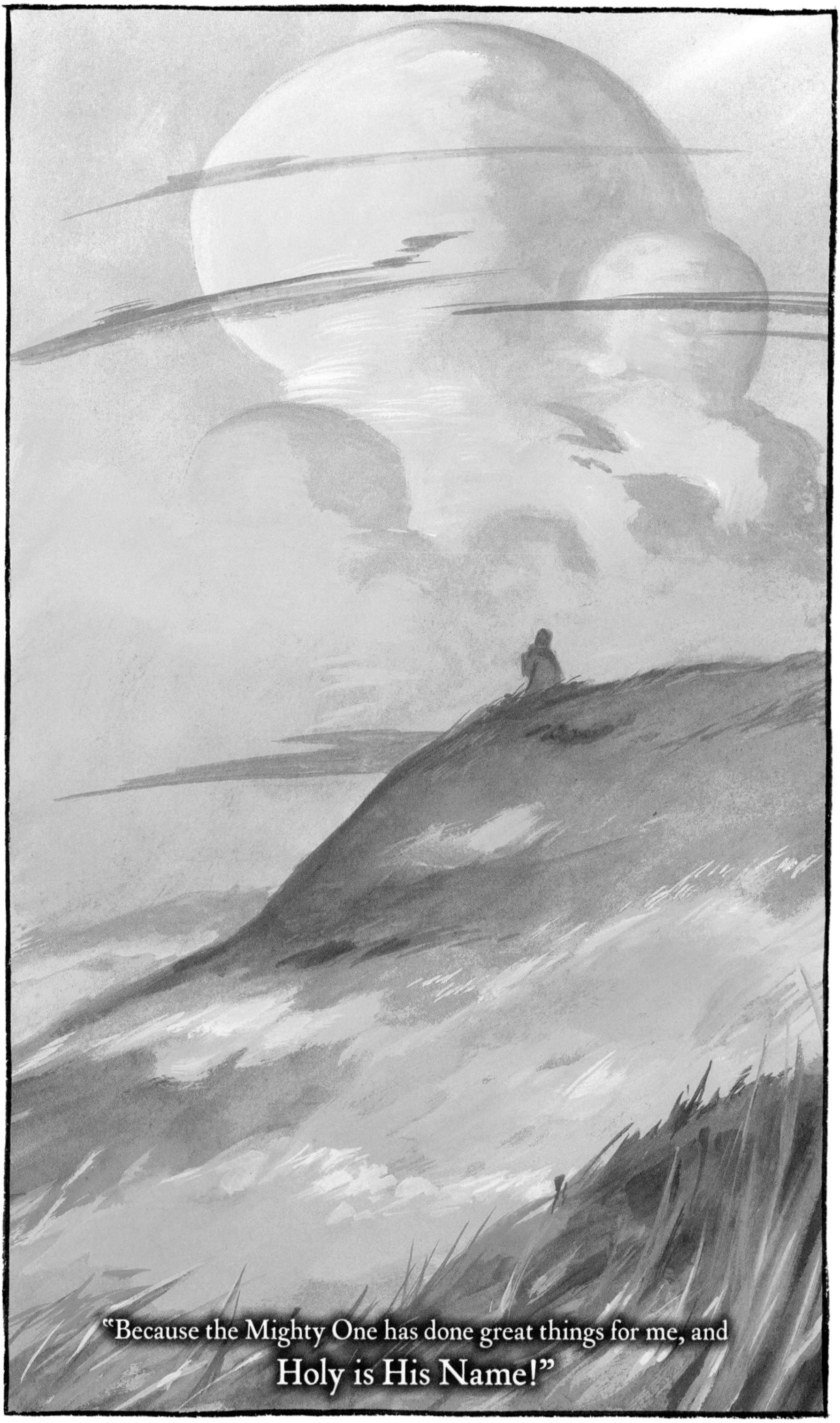
"Because the Mighty One has done great things for me, and
Holy is His Name!"

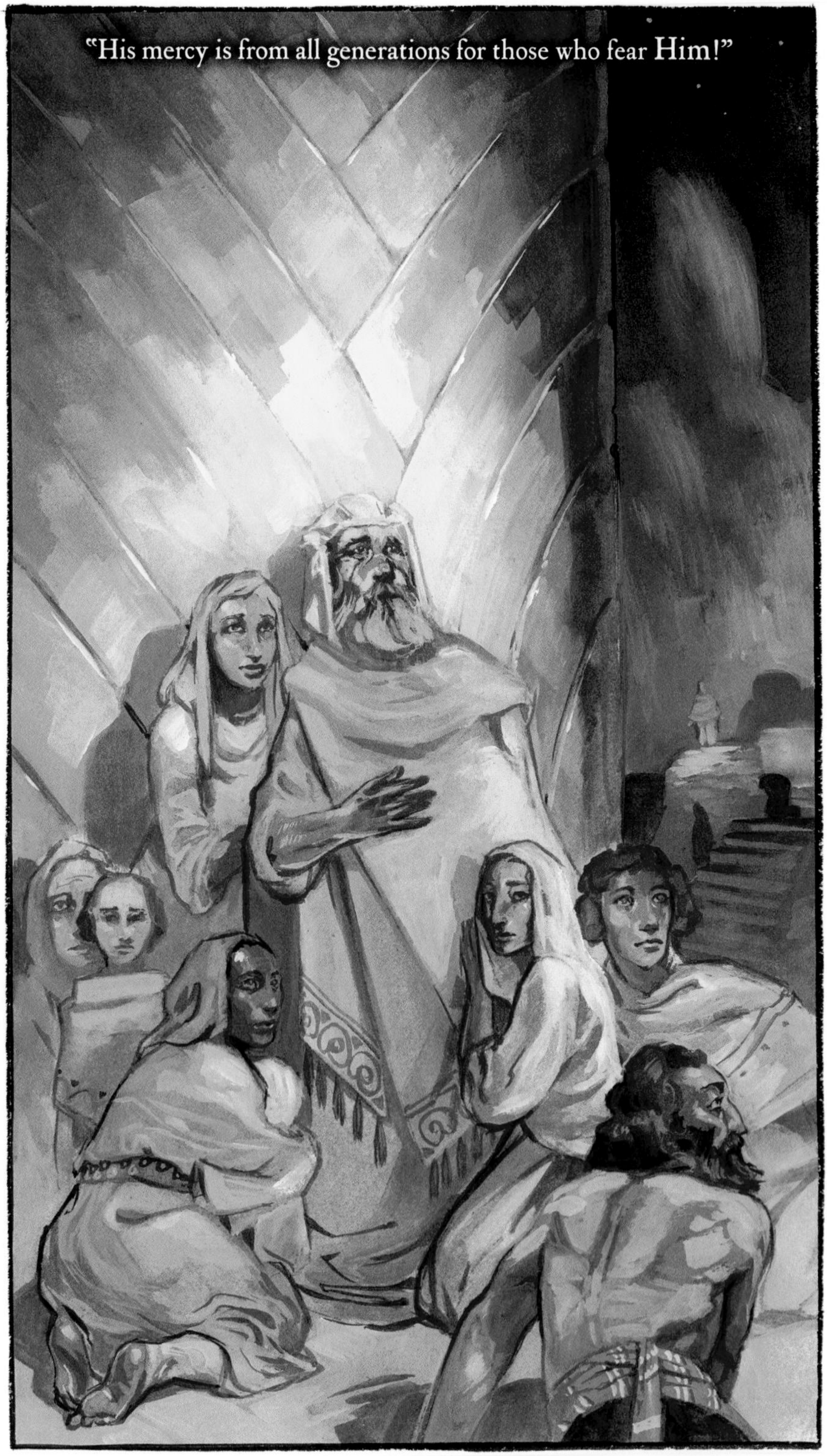
"His mercy is from all generations for those who fear Him!"

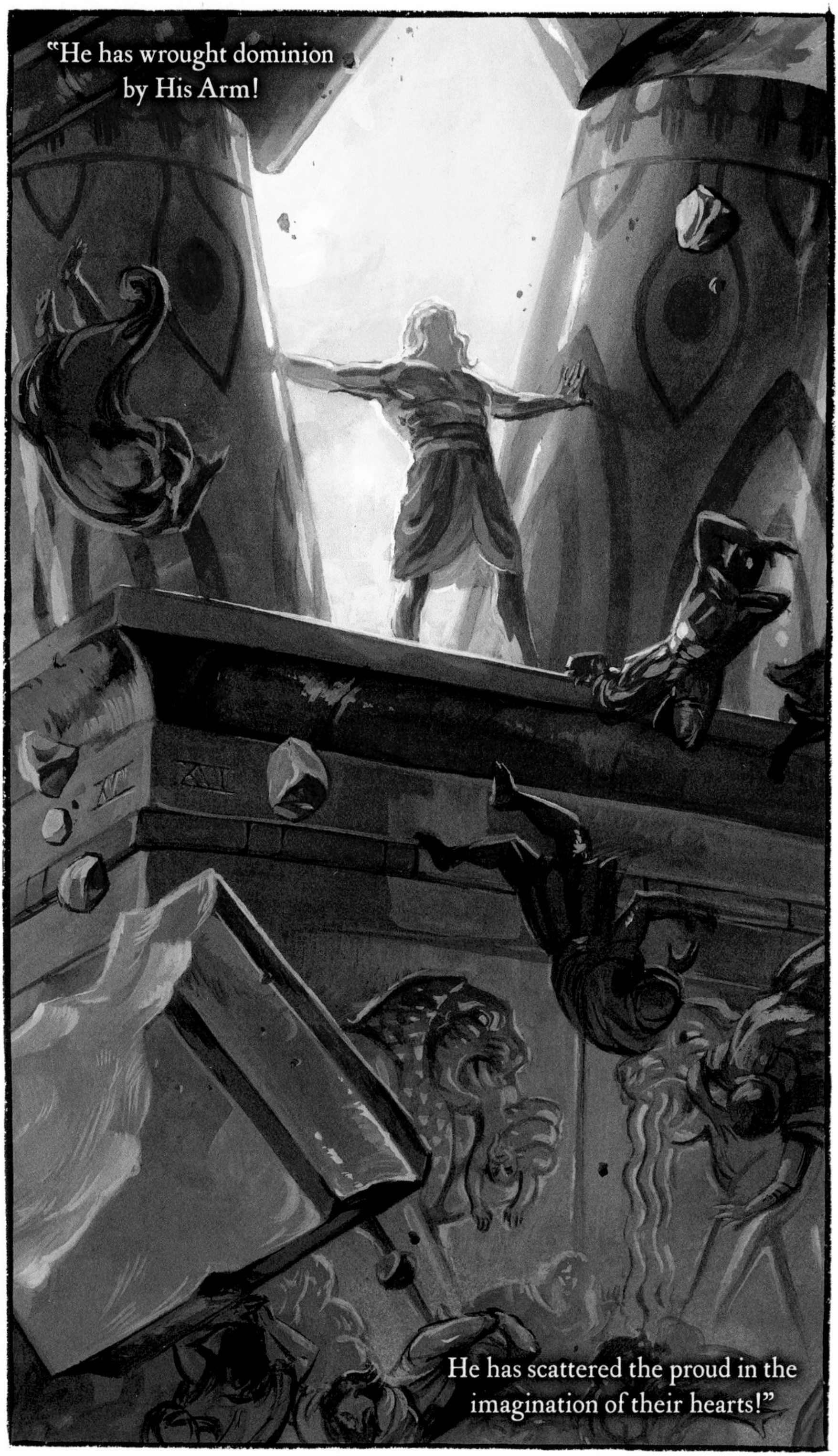
"He has wrought dominion
by His Arm!
He has scattered the proud in the
imagination of their hearts!"

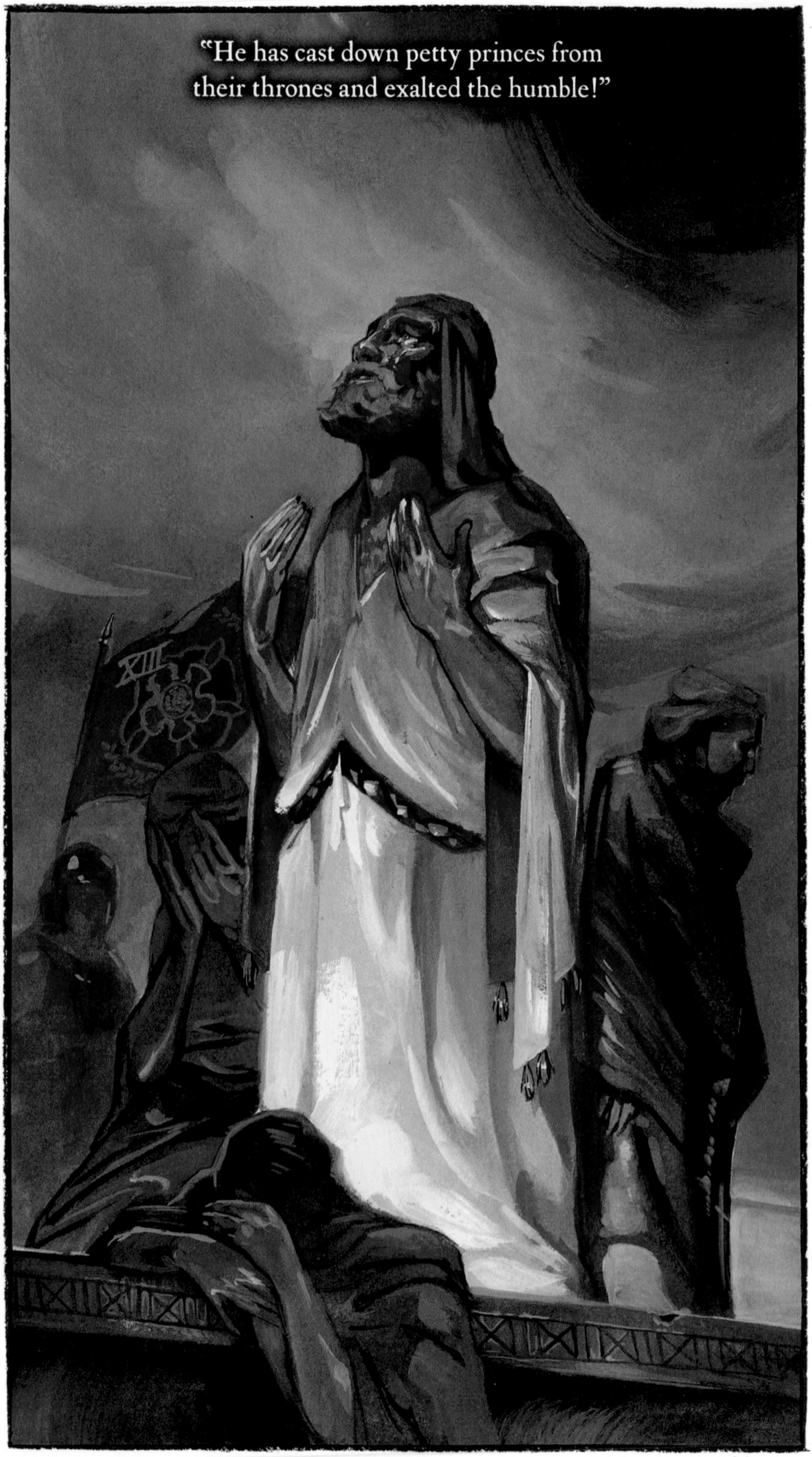
"He has cast down petty princes from their thrones and exalted the humble!"

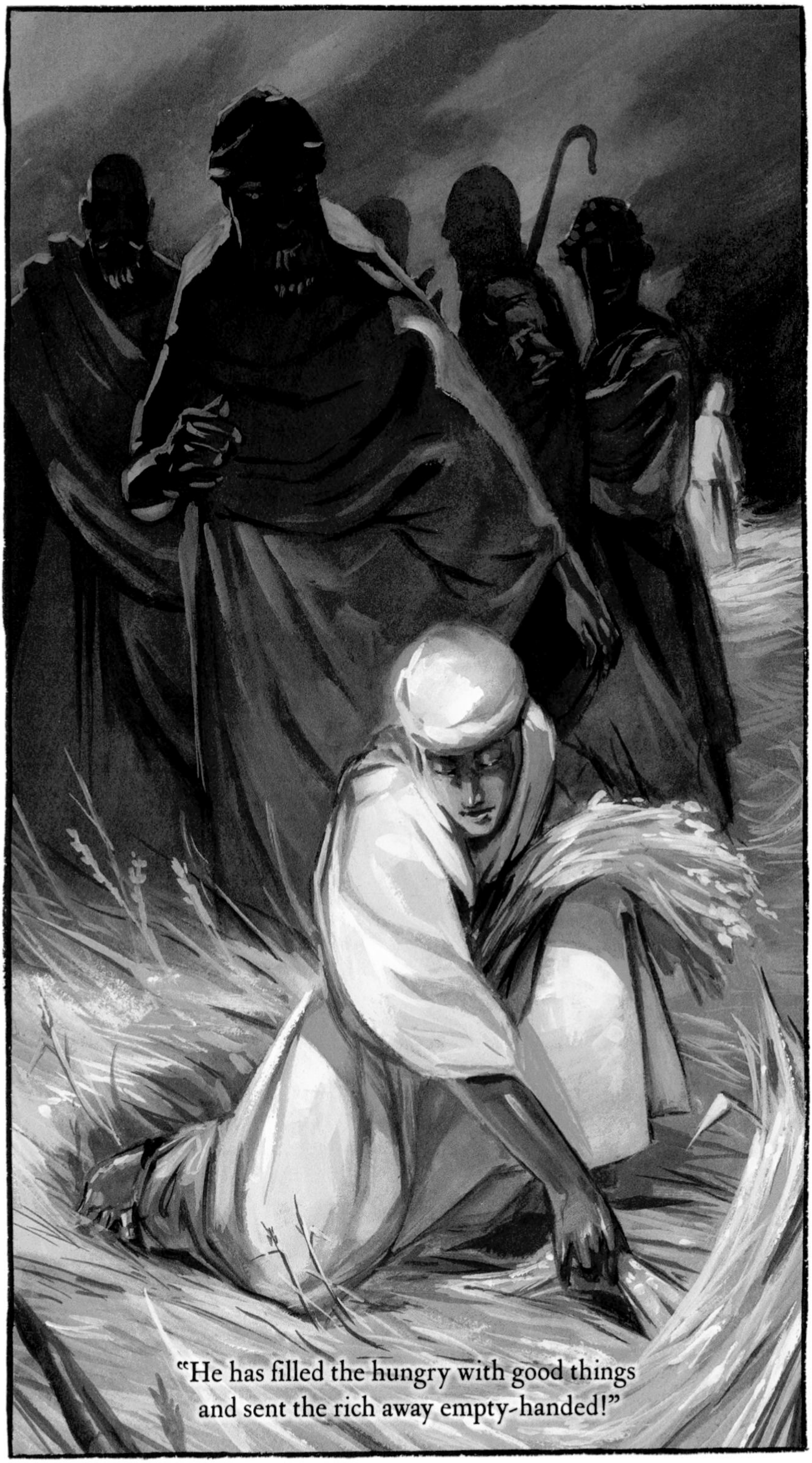
"He has filled the hungry with good things
and sent the rich away empty-handed!"

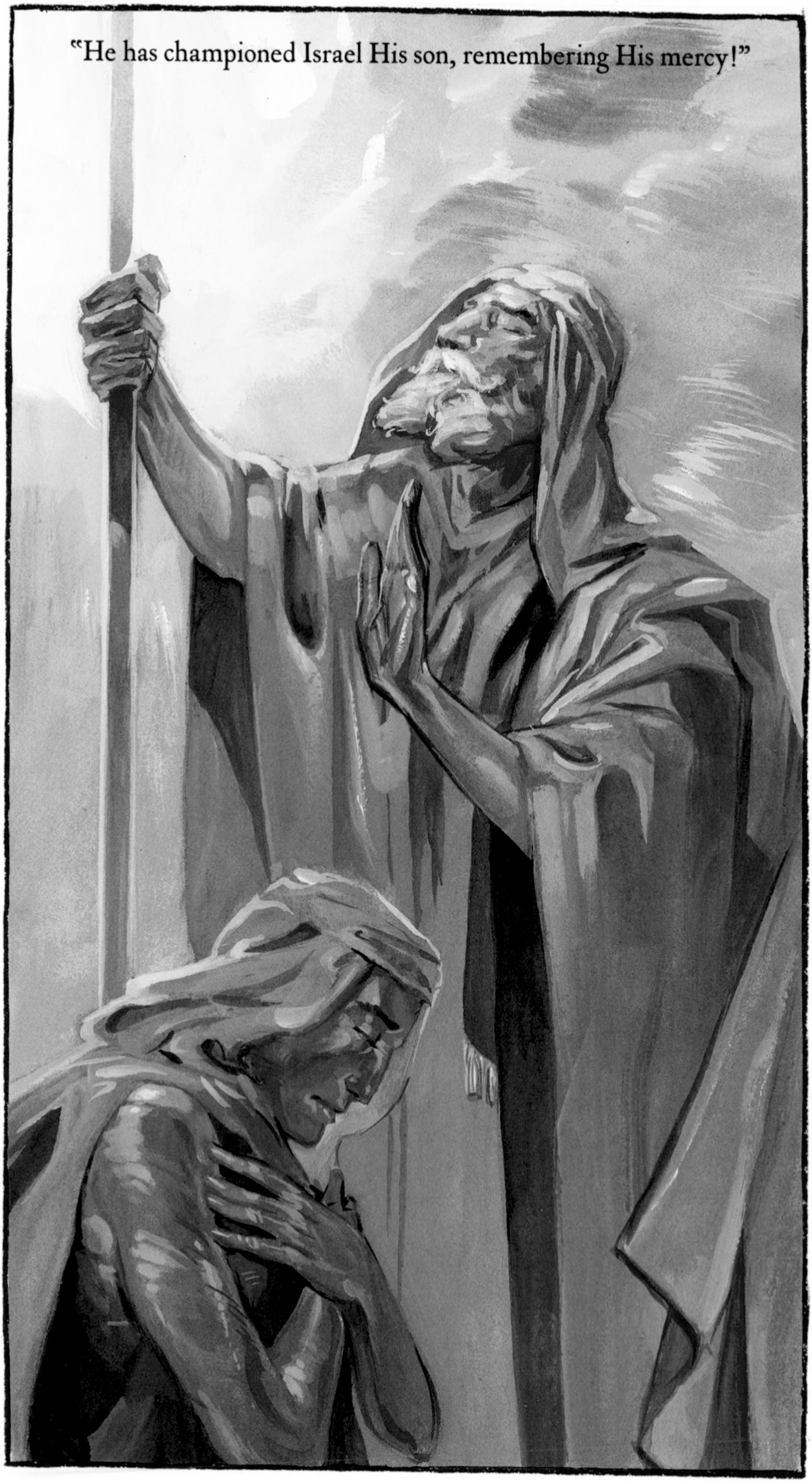
"He has championed Israel His son, remembering His mercy!"

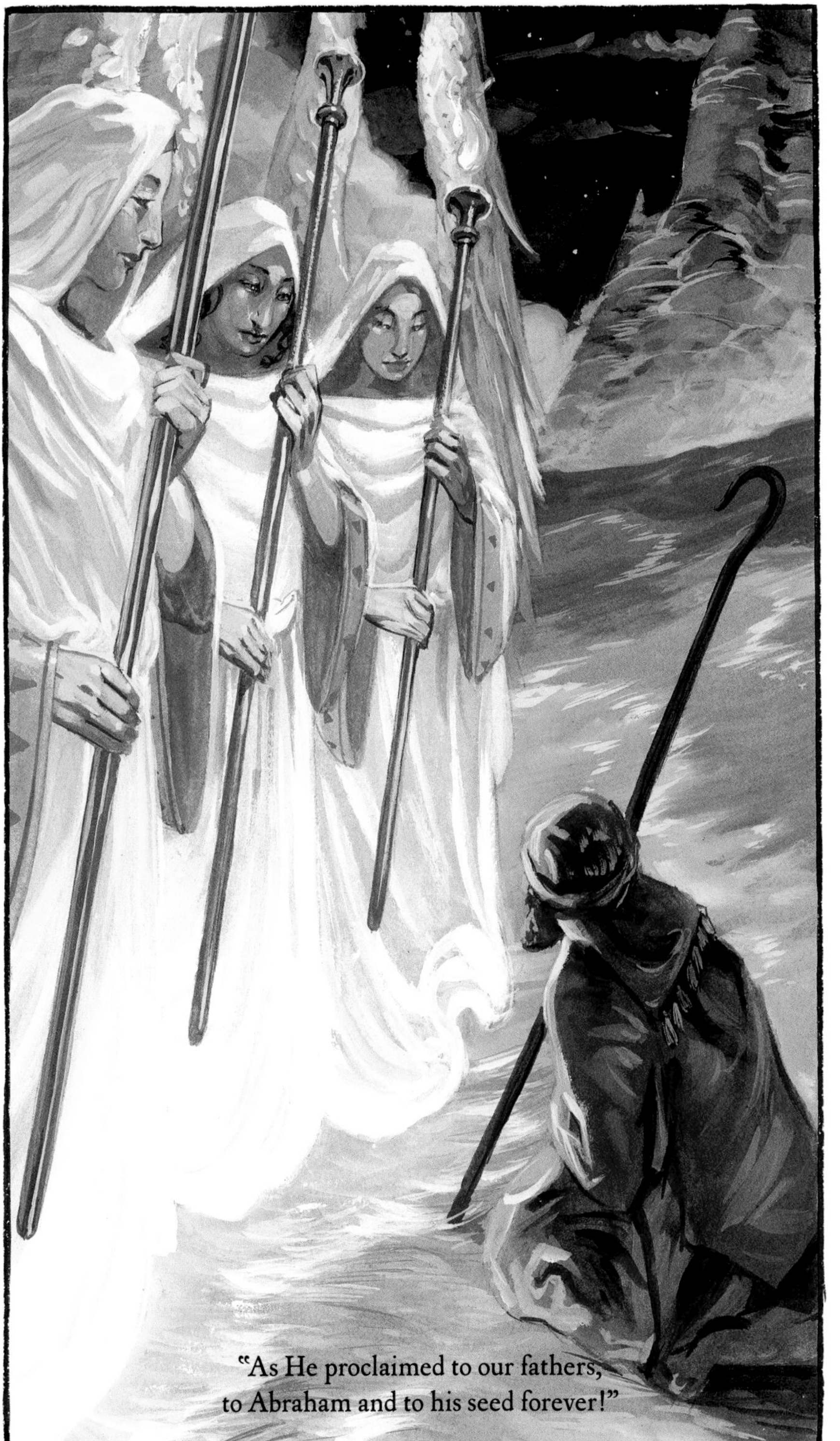
"As He proclaimed to our fathers,
to Abraham and to his seed forever!"

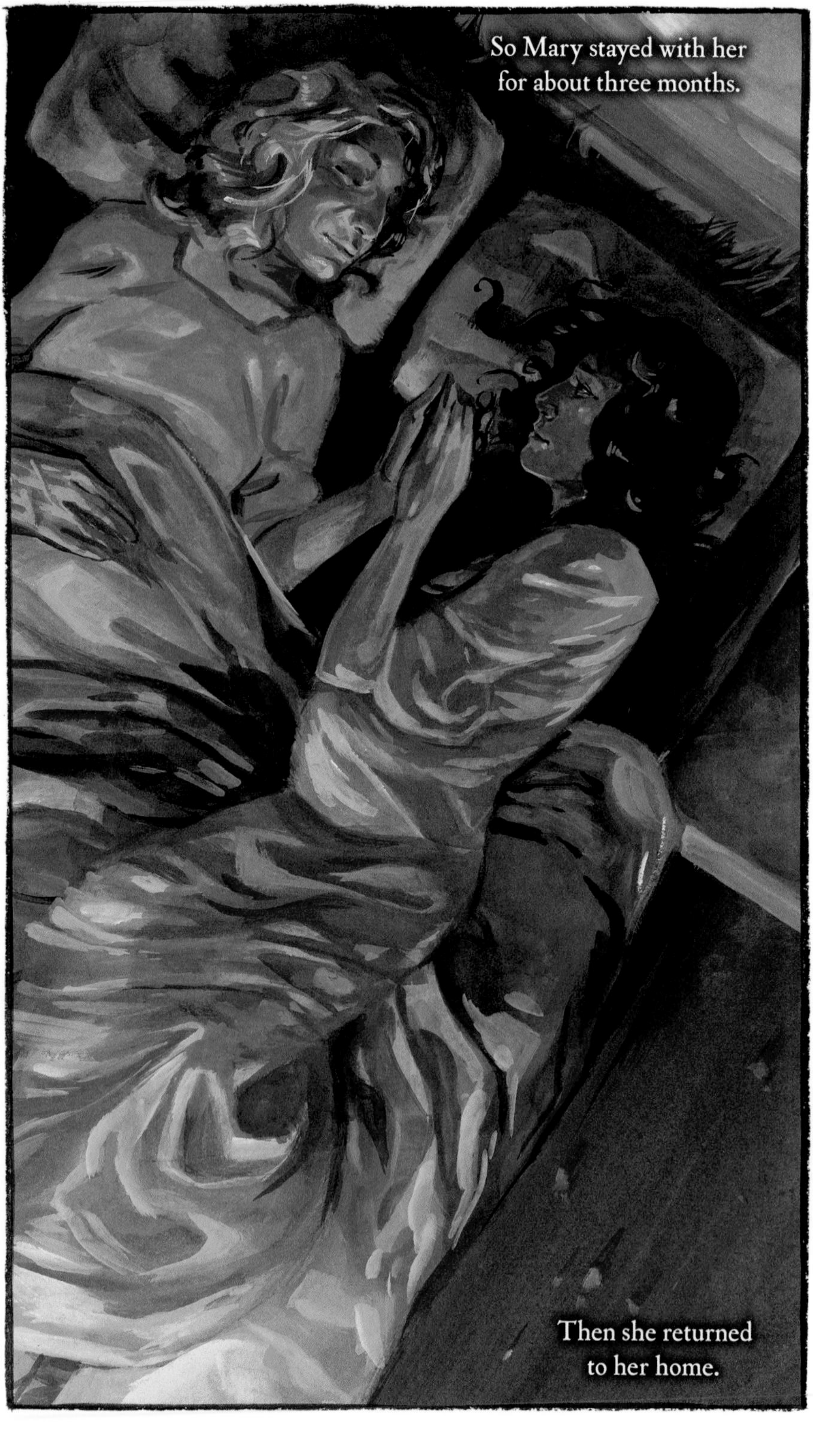
So Mary stayed with her for about three months.
Then she returned to her home.

BIRTH OF JOHN

LUKE 1:57–80

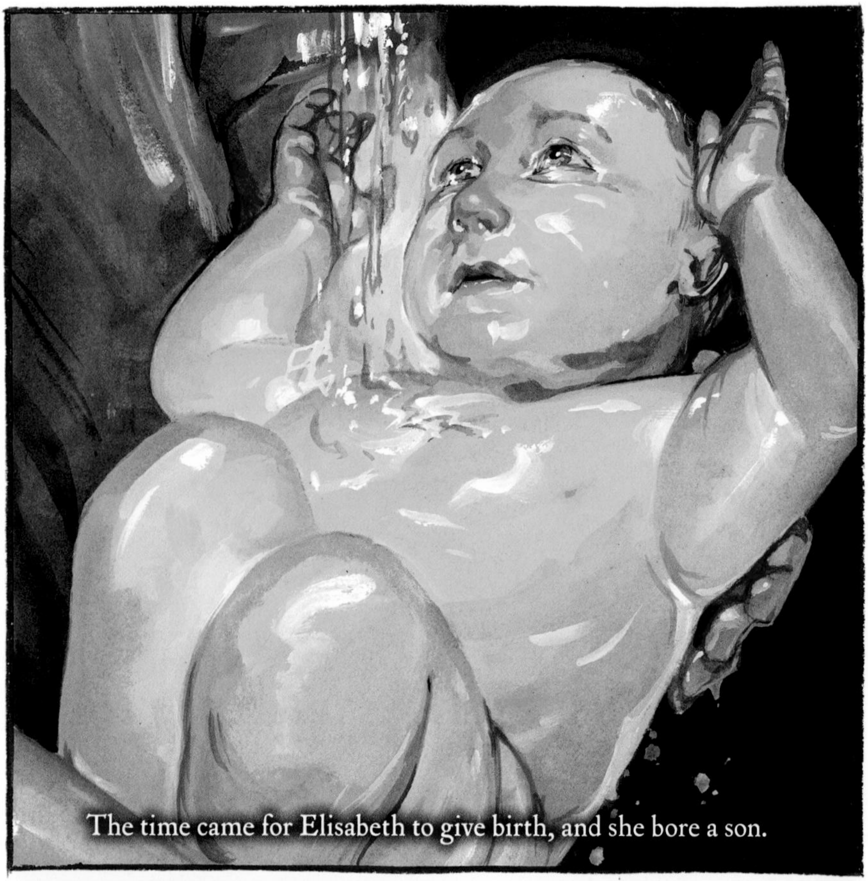
The time came for Elisabeth to give birth, and she bore a son.

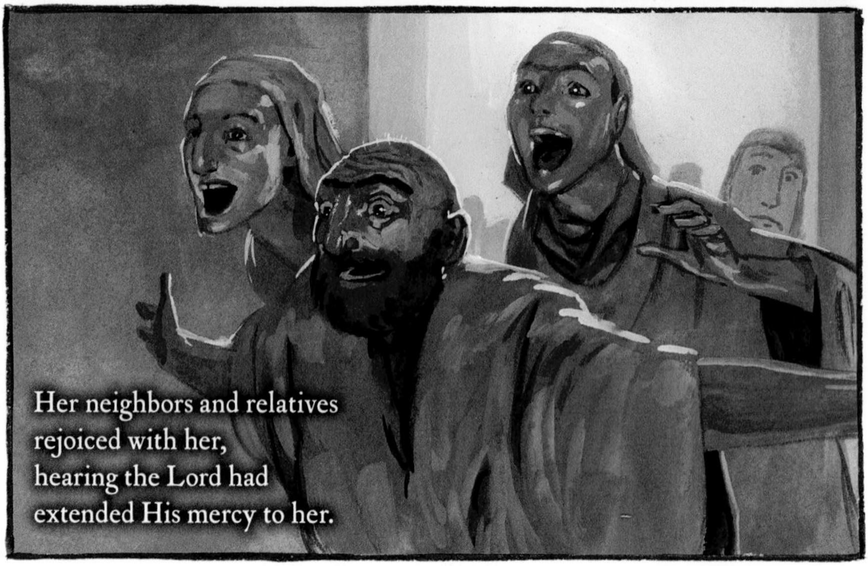
Her neighbors and relatives
rejoiced with her,
hearing the Lord had
extended His mercy to her.

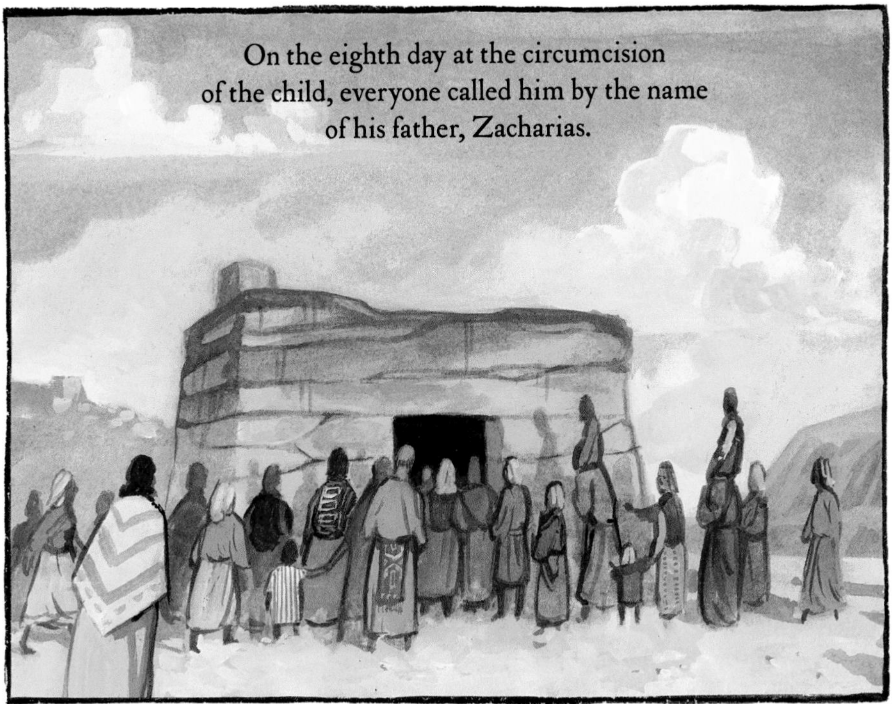
On the eighth day at the circumcision of the child, everyone called him by the name of his father, Zacharias.

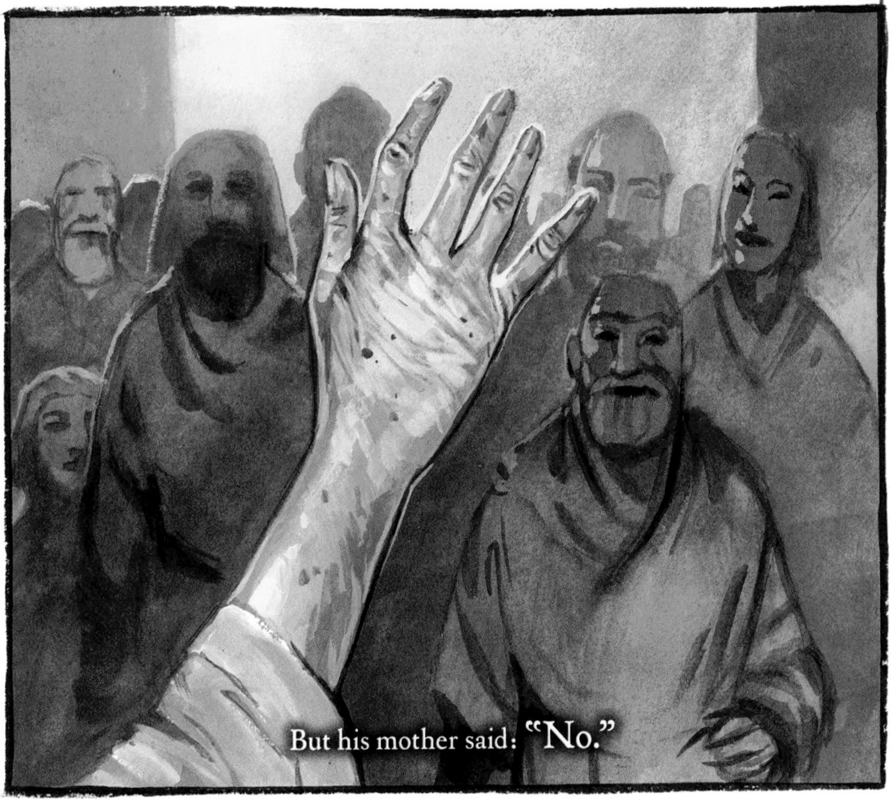
But his mother said: "No."

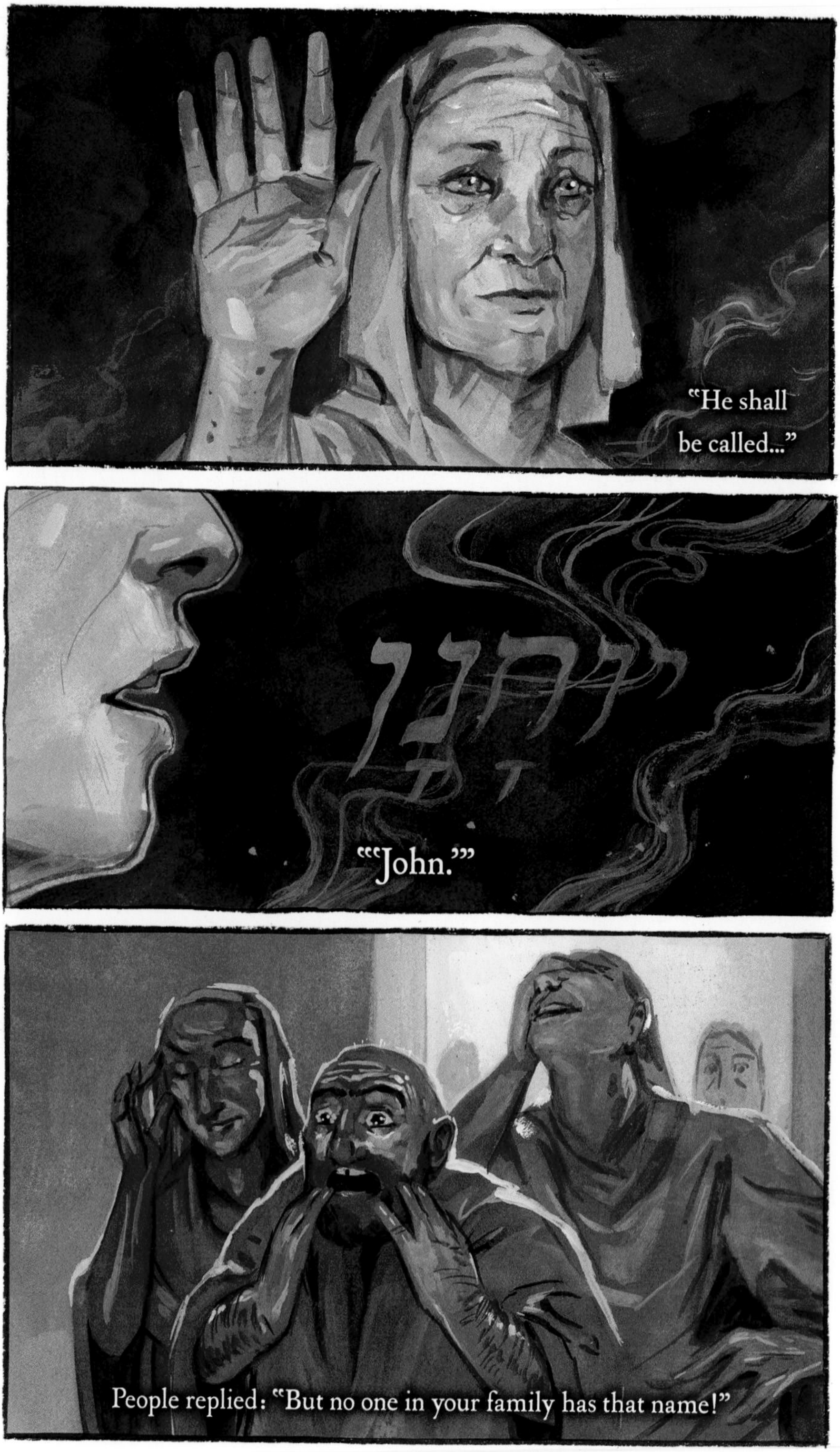
“He shall
be called...”
יוחנן
“‘John.’”
People replied: “But no one in your family has that name!”

So they motioned to his father to see what he wanted to name him.

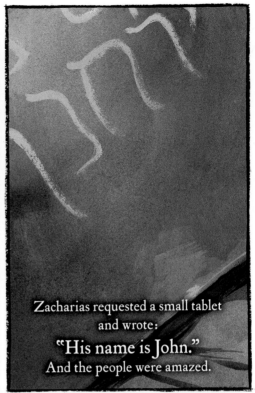

Zacharias requested a small tablet and wrote:

"His name is John."

And the people were amazed.

At that same instant his mouth opened, his tongue loosed...

...and he **blessed** God.

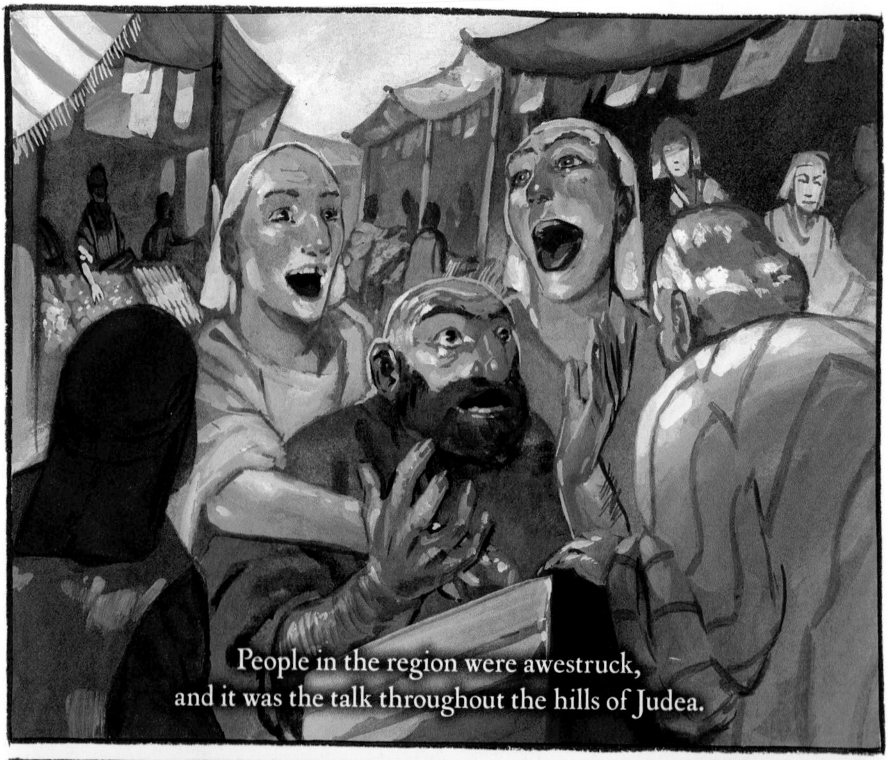
People in the region were awestruck,
and it was the talk throughout the hills of Judea.

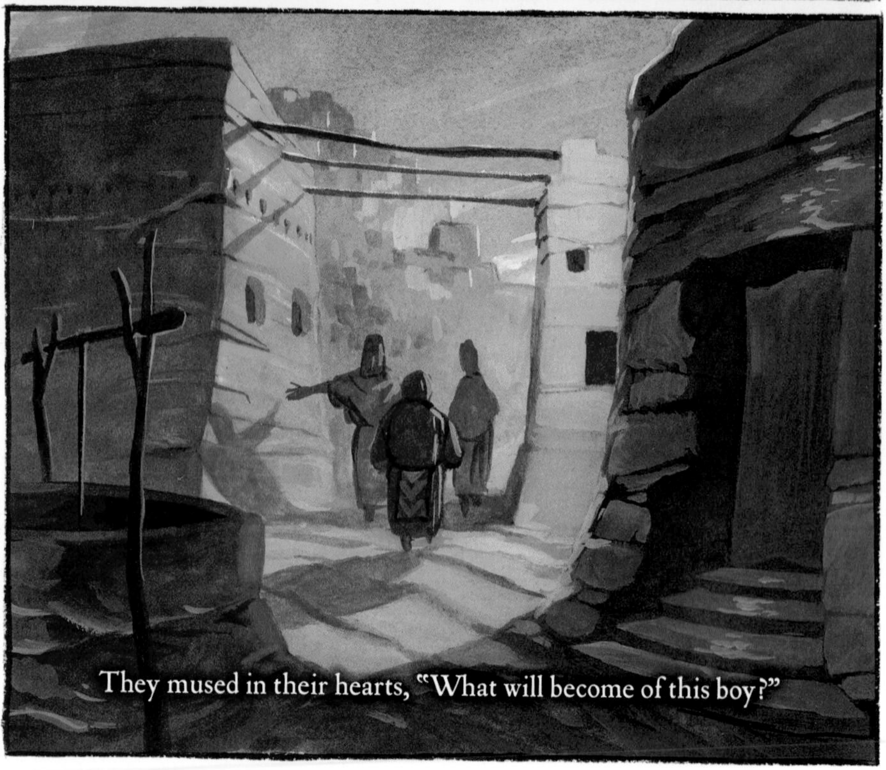
They mused in their hearts, "What will become of this boy?"

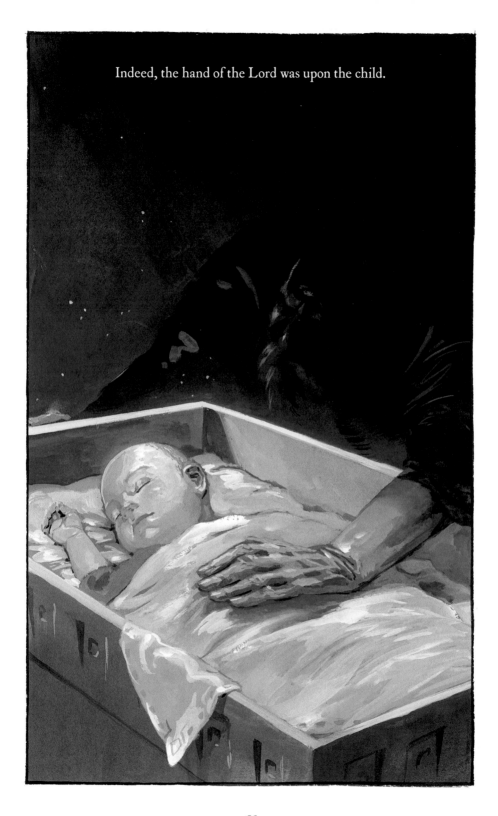

Indeed, the hand of the Lord was upon the child.

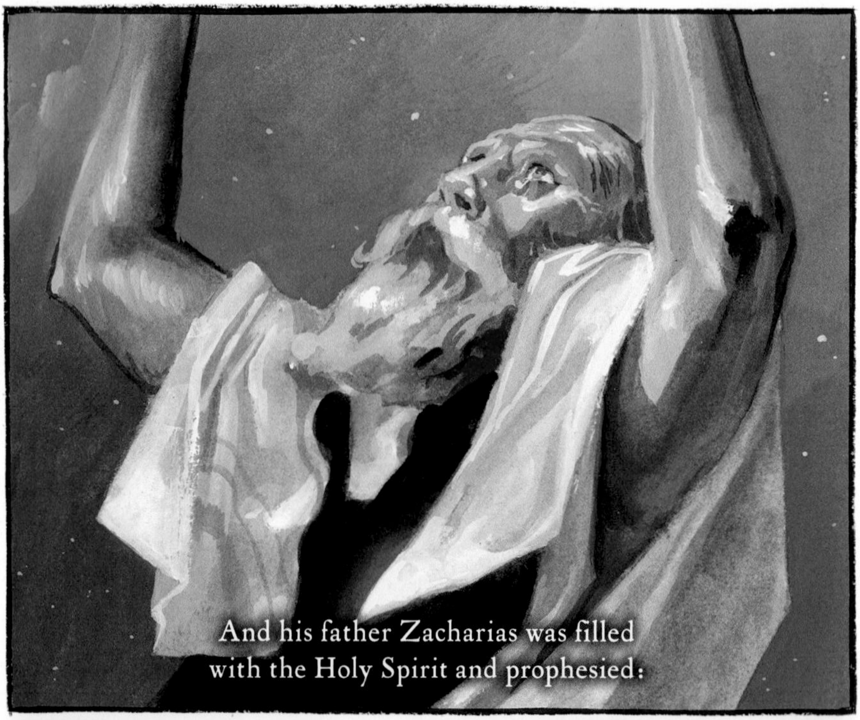
And his father Zacharias was filled
with the Holy Spirit and prophesied:

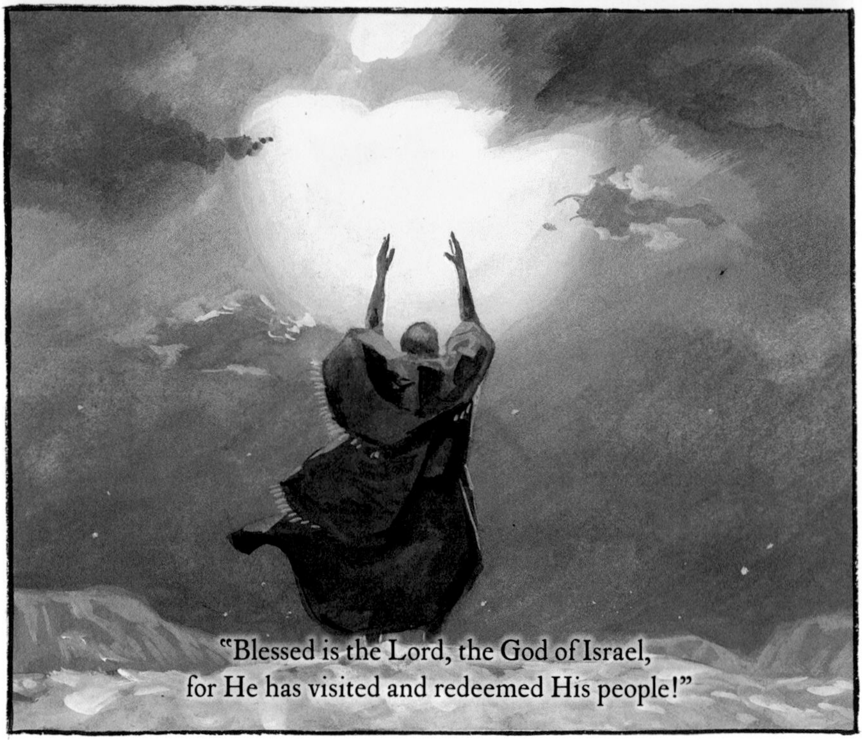
"Blessed is the Lord, the God of Israel,
for He has visited and redeemed His people!"

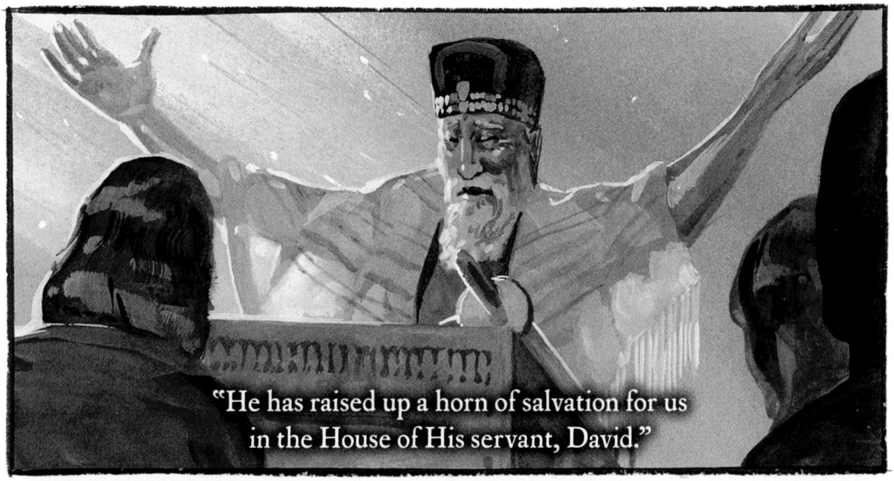
"He has raised up a horn of salvation for us in the House of His servant, David."

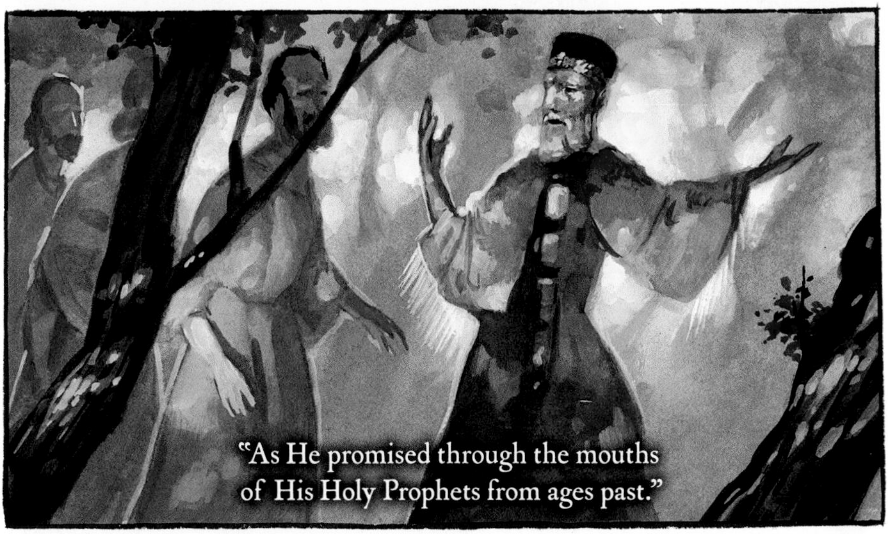
"As He promised through the mouths of His Holy Prophets from ages past."

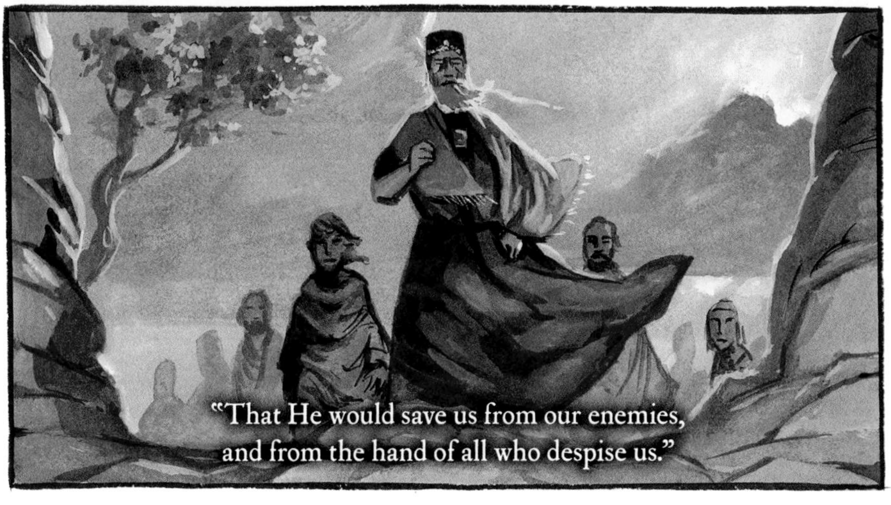
"That He would save us from our enemies, and from the hand of all who despise us."

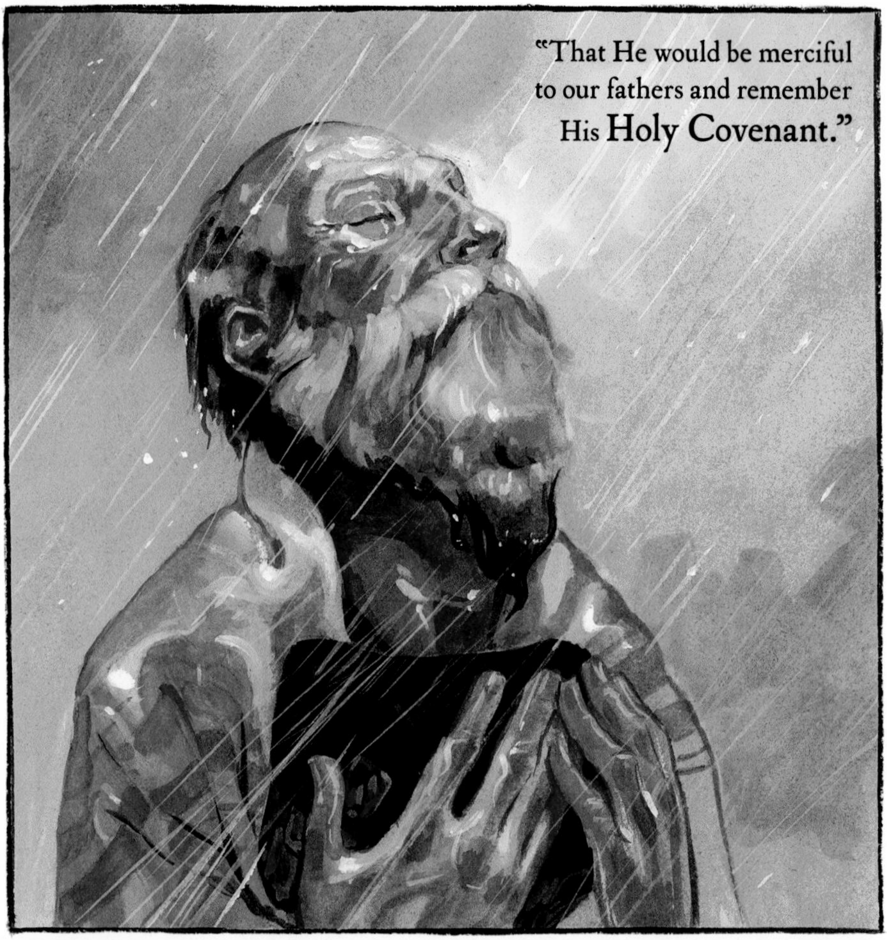
"That He would be merciful to our fathers and remember His Holy Covenant."

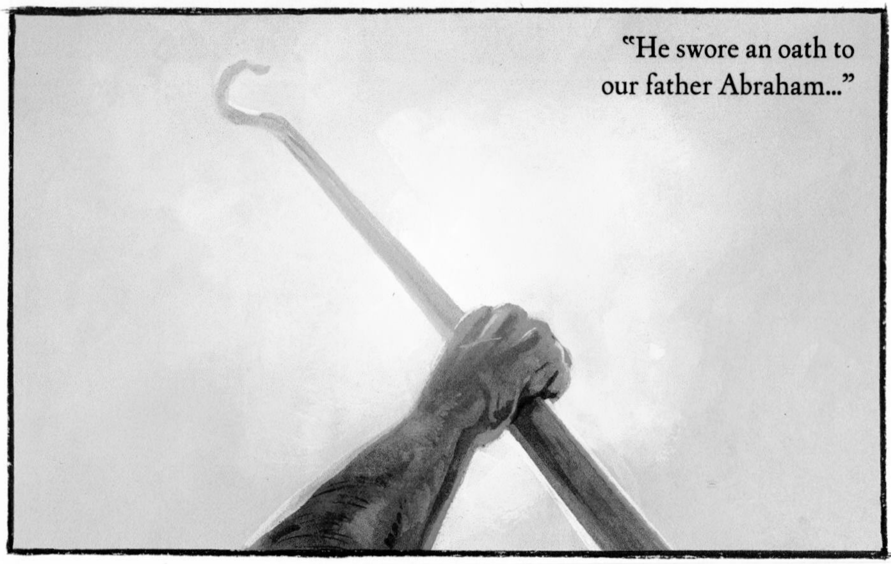
"He swore an oath to our father Abraham..."

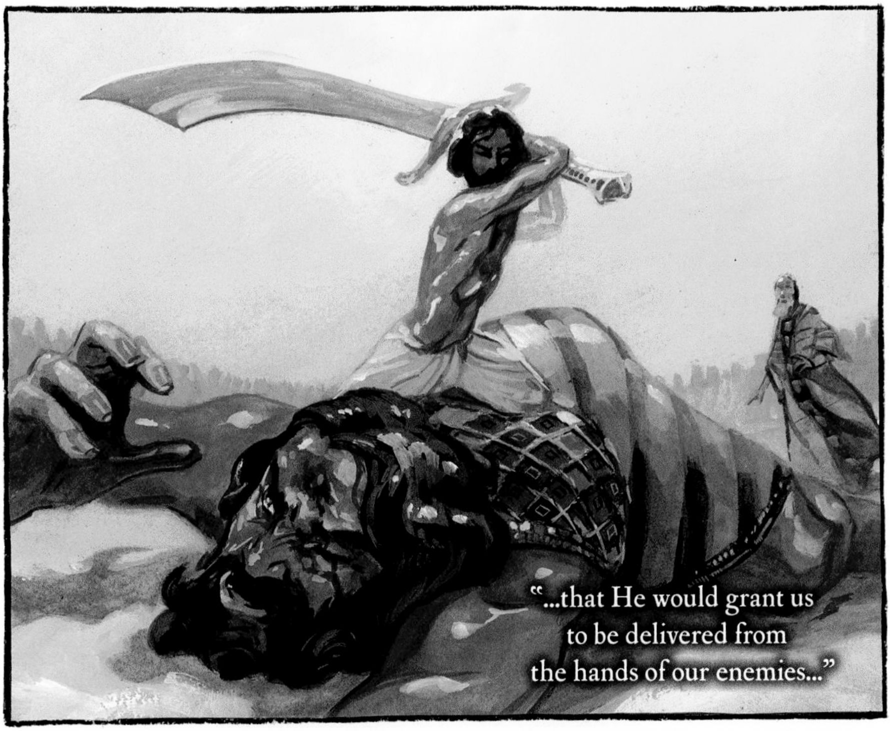
"...that He would grant us
to be delivered from
the hands of our enemies..."

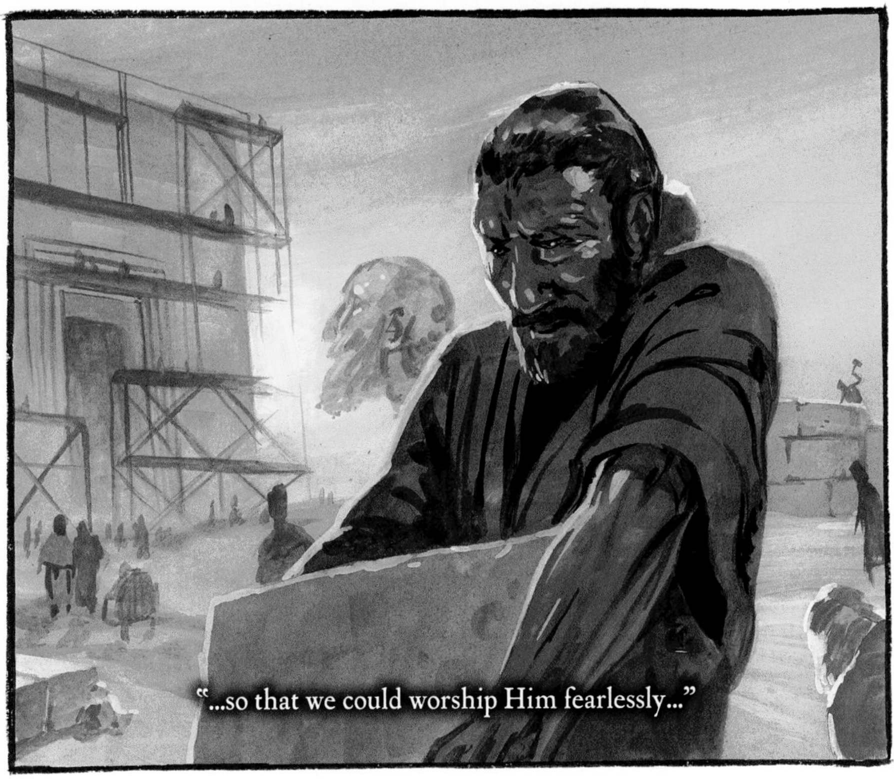
"...so that we could worship Him fearlessly..."

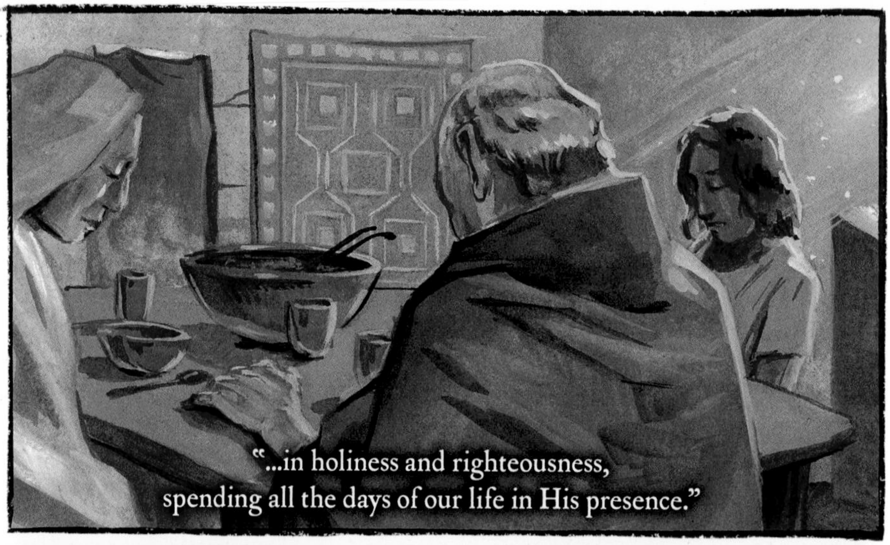
"...in holiness and righteousness,
spending all the days of our life in His presence."

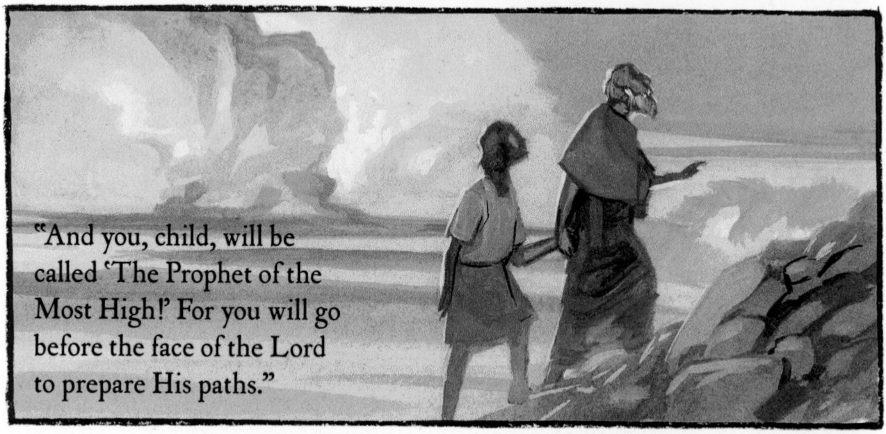
"And you, child, will be
called 'The Prophet of the
Most High!' For you will go
before the face of the Lord
to prepare His paths."

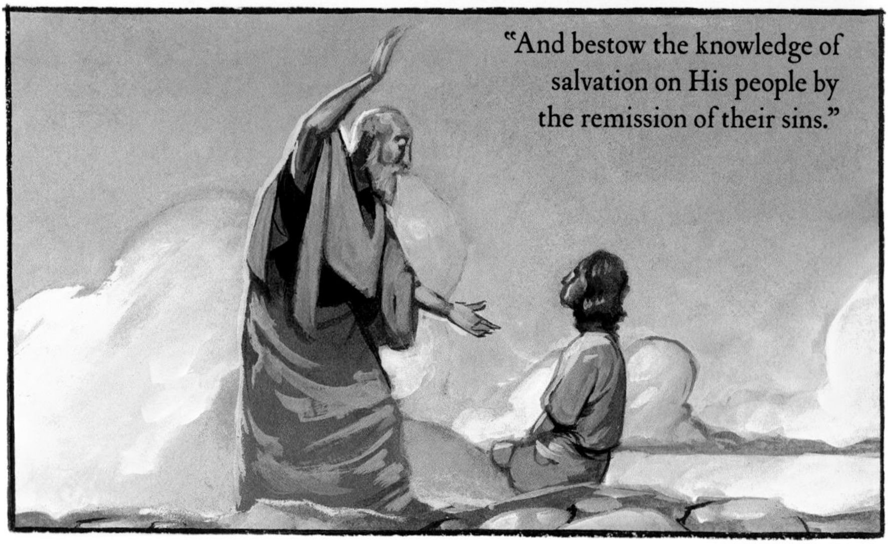
"And bestow the knowledge of
salvation on His people by
the remission of their sins."

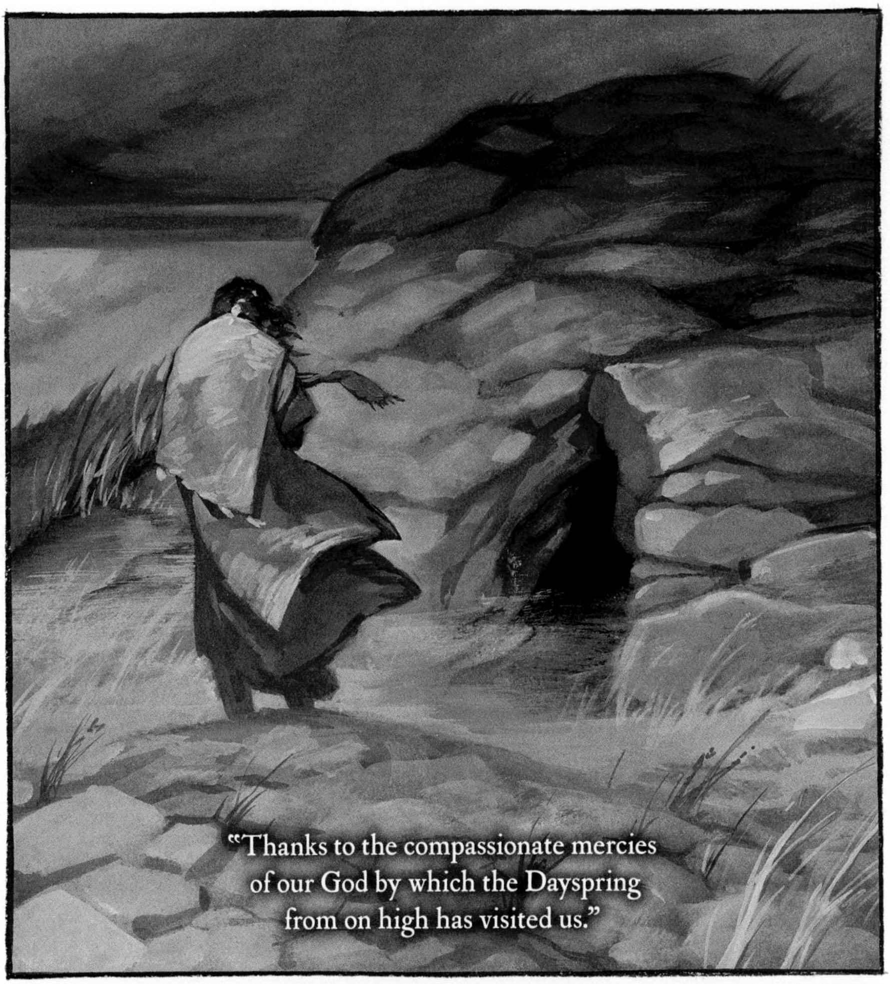
"Thanks to the compassionate mercies of our God by which the Dayspring from on high has visited us."

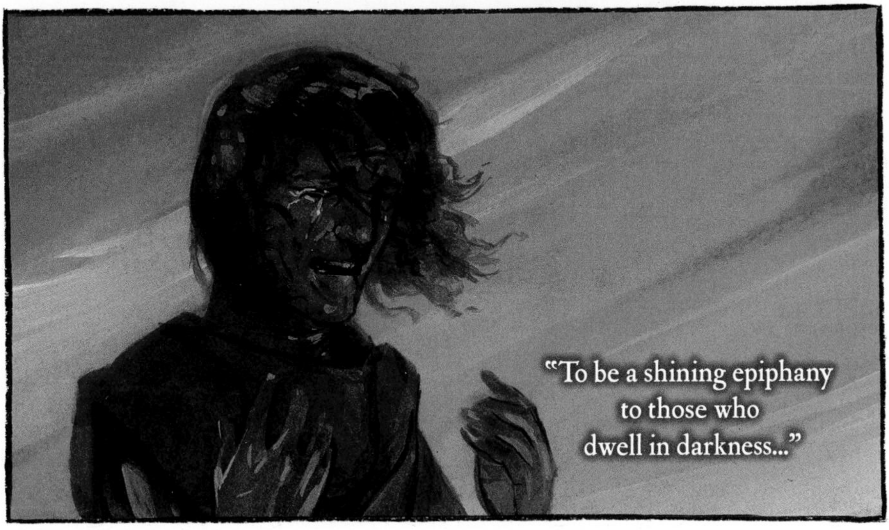
"To be a shining epiphany to those who dwell in darkness..."

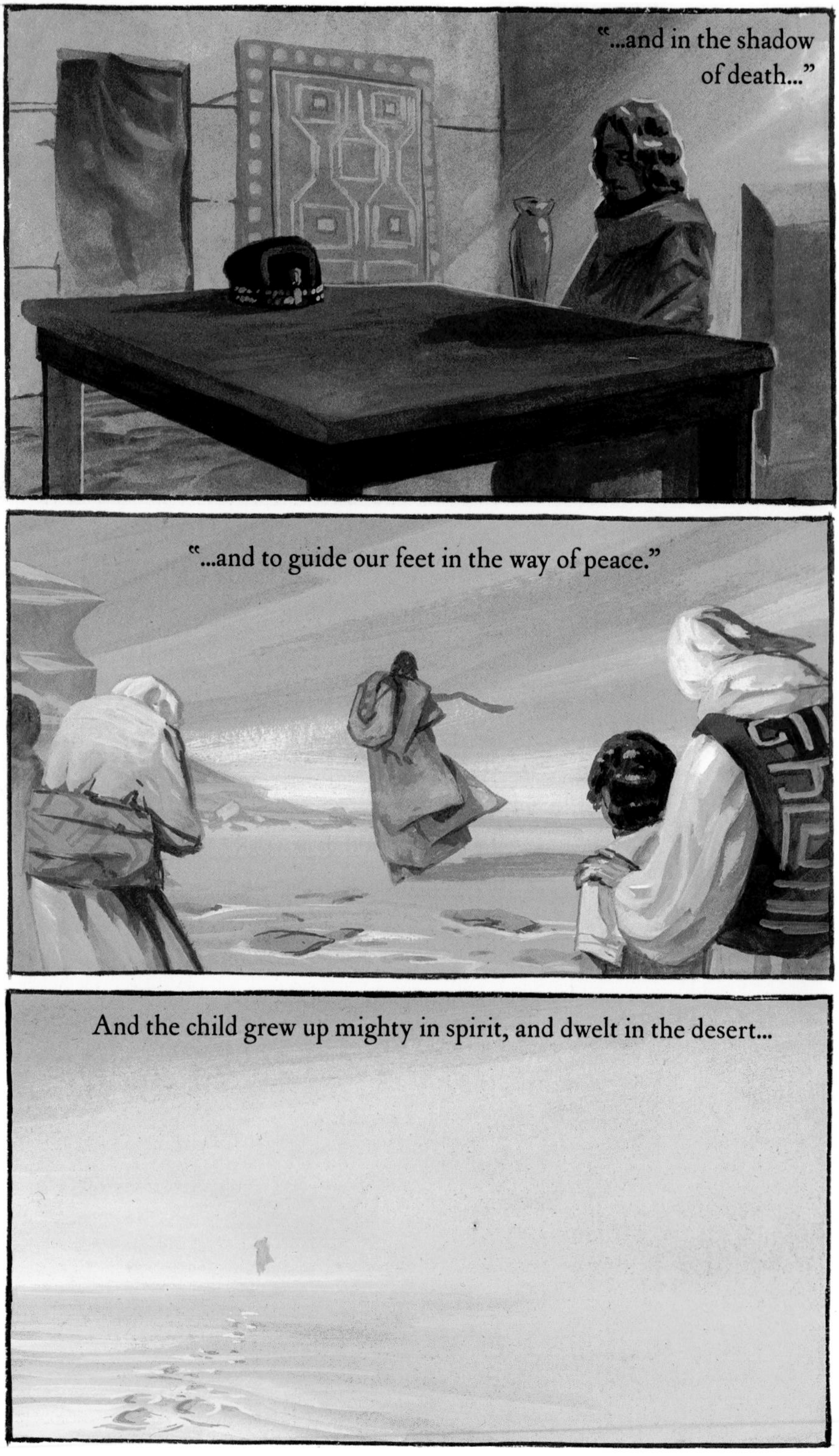
"...and in the shadow of death..."
"...and to guide our feet in the way of peace."
And the child grew up mighty in spirit, and dwelt in the desert...

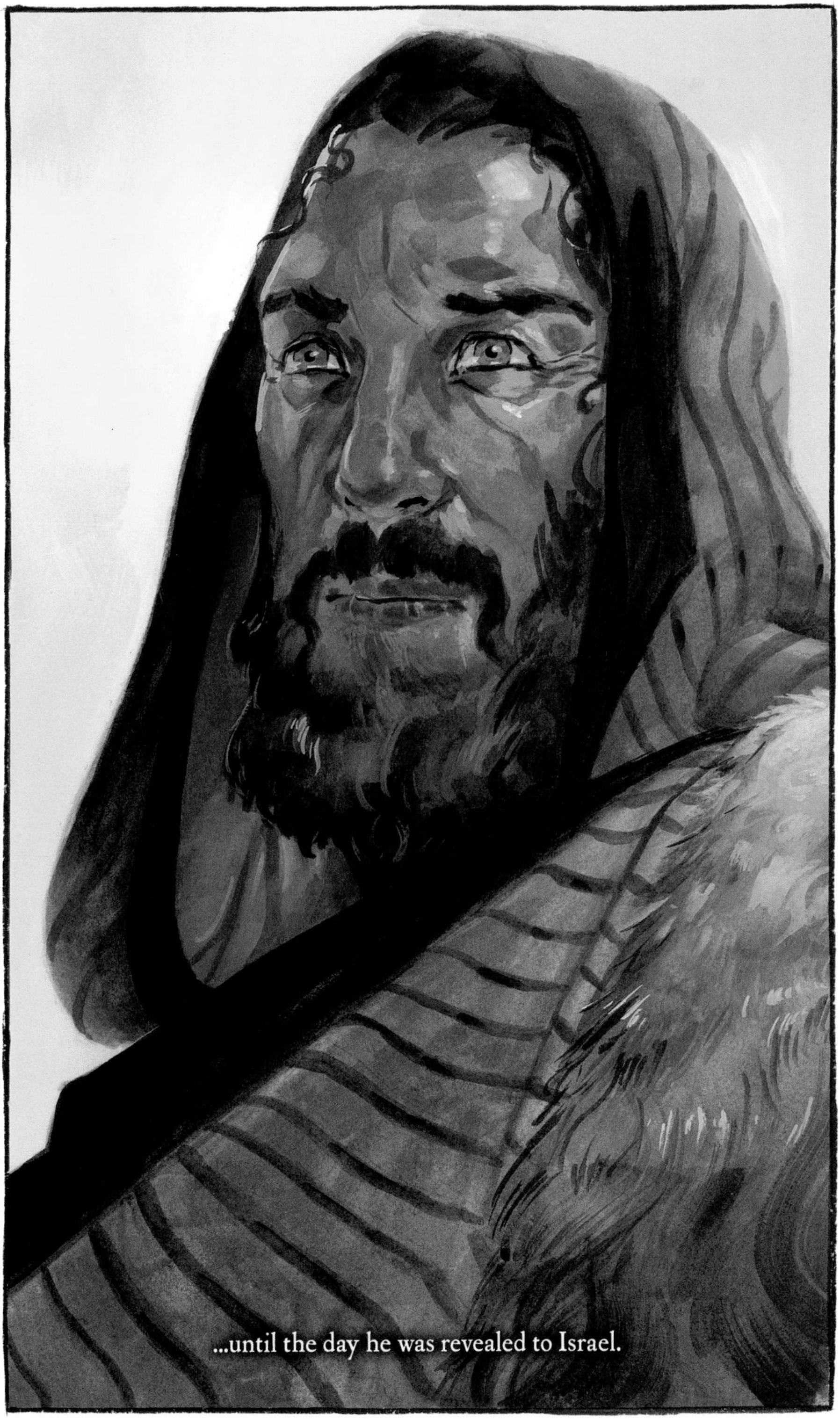
...until the day he was revealed to Israel.

BIRTH OF JESUS

MATTHEW 1:1,18–25; LUKE 2:1–20

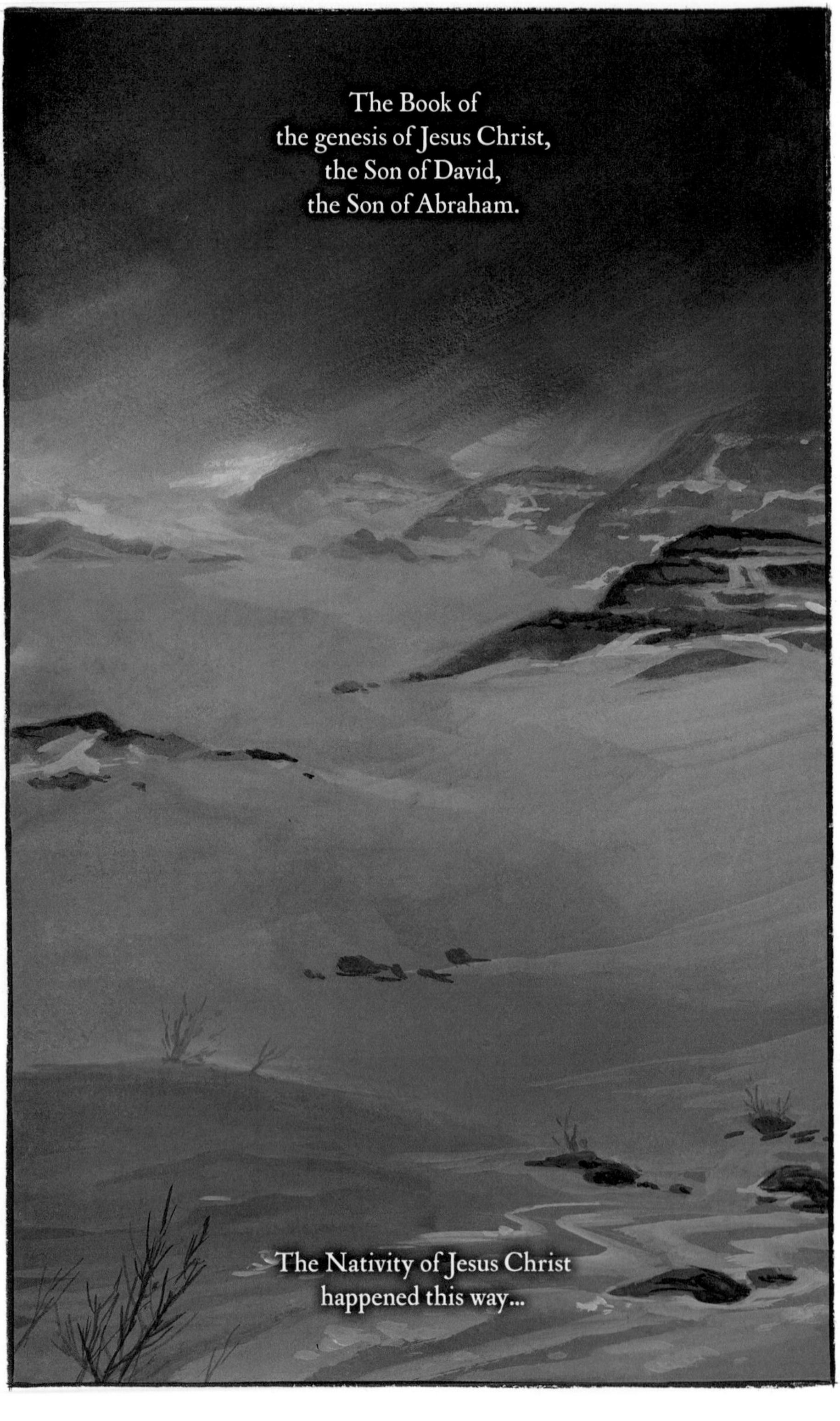
The Book of
the genesis of Jesus Christ,
the Son of David,
the Son of Abraham.
The Nativity of Jesus Christ
happened this way...

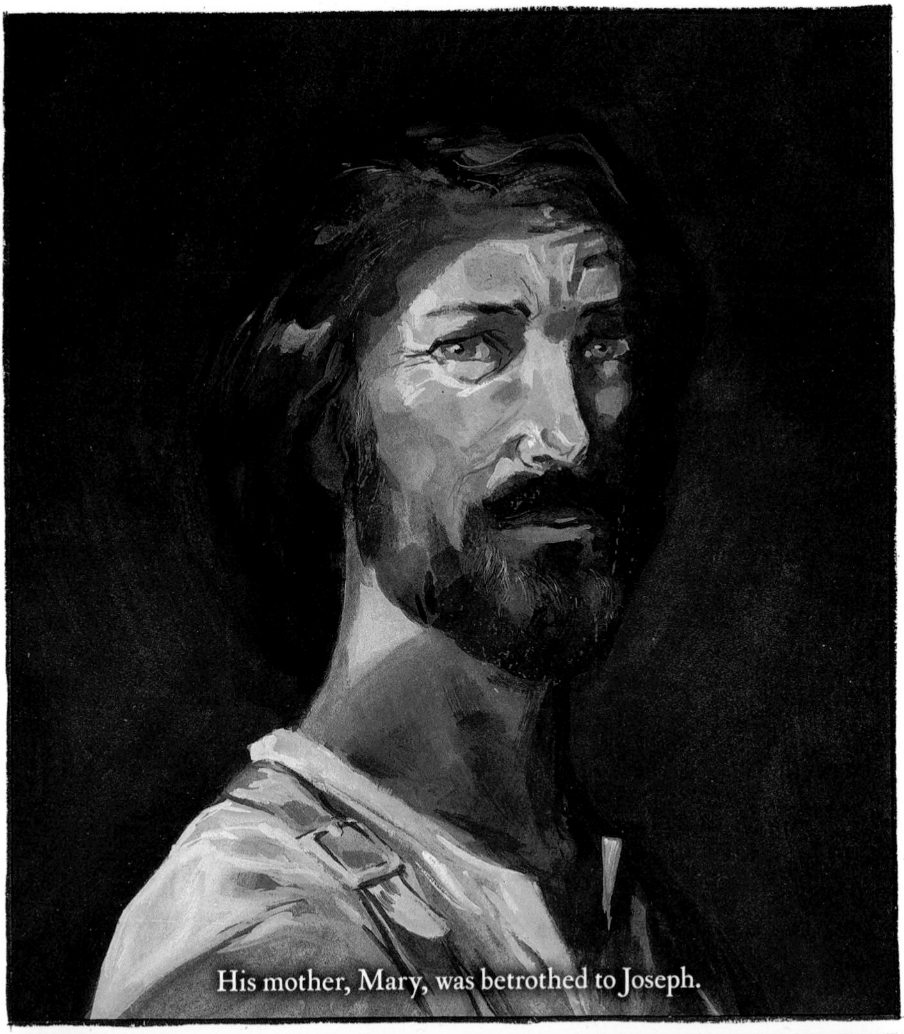
His mother, Mary, was betrothed to Joseph.

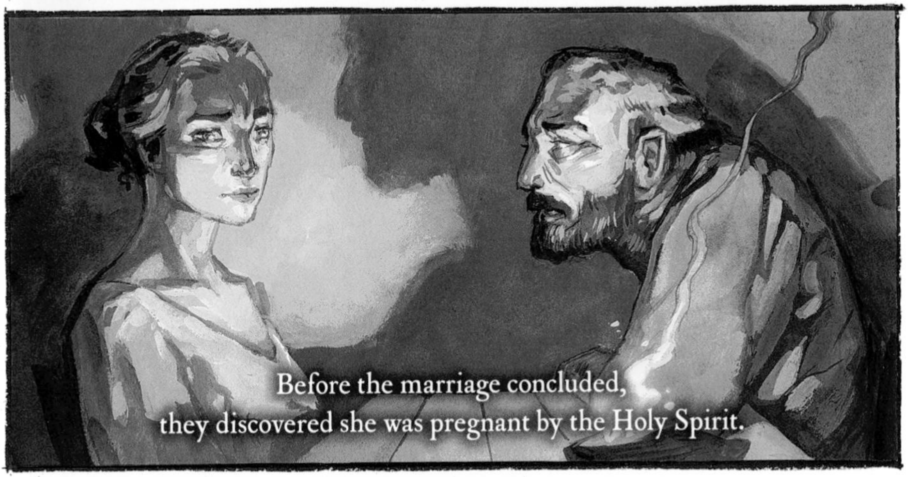
Before the marriage concluded,
they discovered she was pregnant by the Holy Spirit.

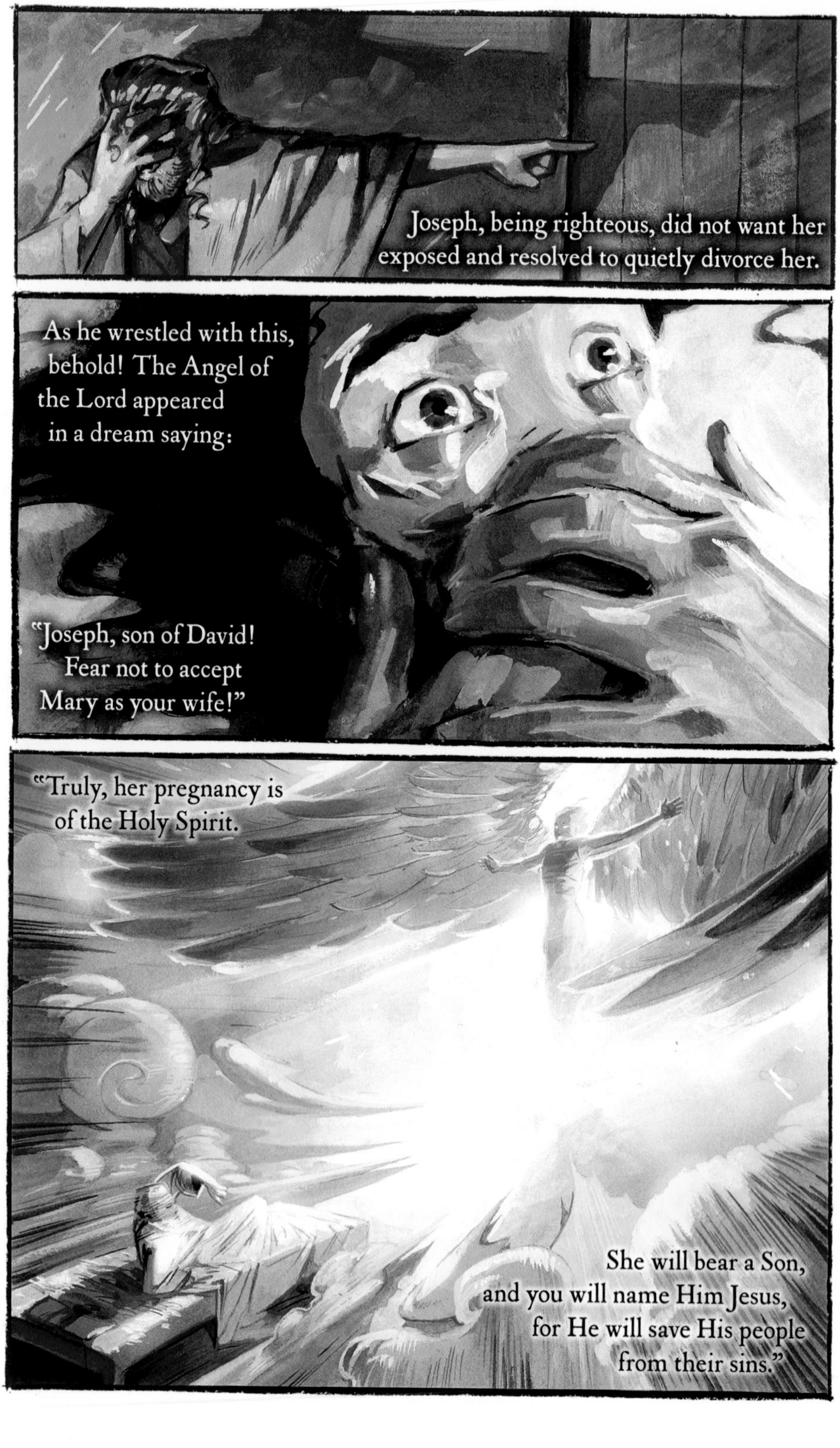
Joseph, being righteous, did not want her exposed and resolved to quietly divorce her.
As he wrestled with this, behold! The Angel of the Lord appeared in a dream saying:
"Joseph, son of David! Fear not to accept Mary as your wife!"
"Truly, her pregnancy is of the Holy Spirit.
She will bear a Son, and you will name Him Jesus, for He will save His people from their sins."

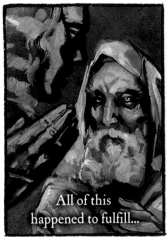

All of this
happened to fulfill...

...the word of the Lord
spoken through the Prophet.

"Behold! A Virgin will conceive and give birth to a Son.
And they will call His Name 'Emmanuel.'
Which means 'God is with us.'"

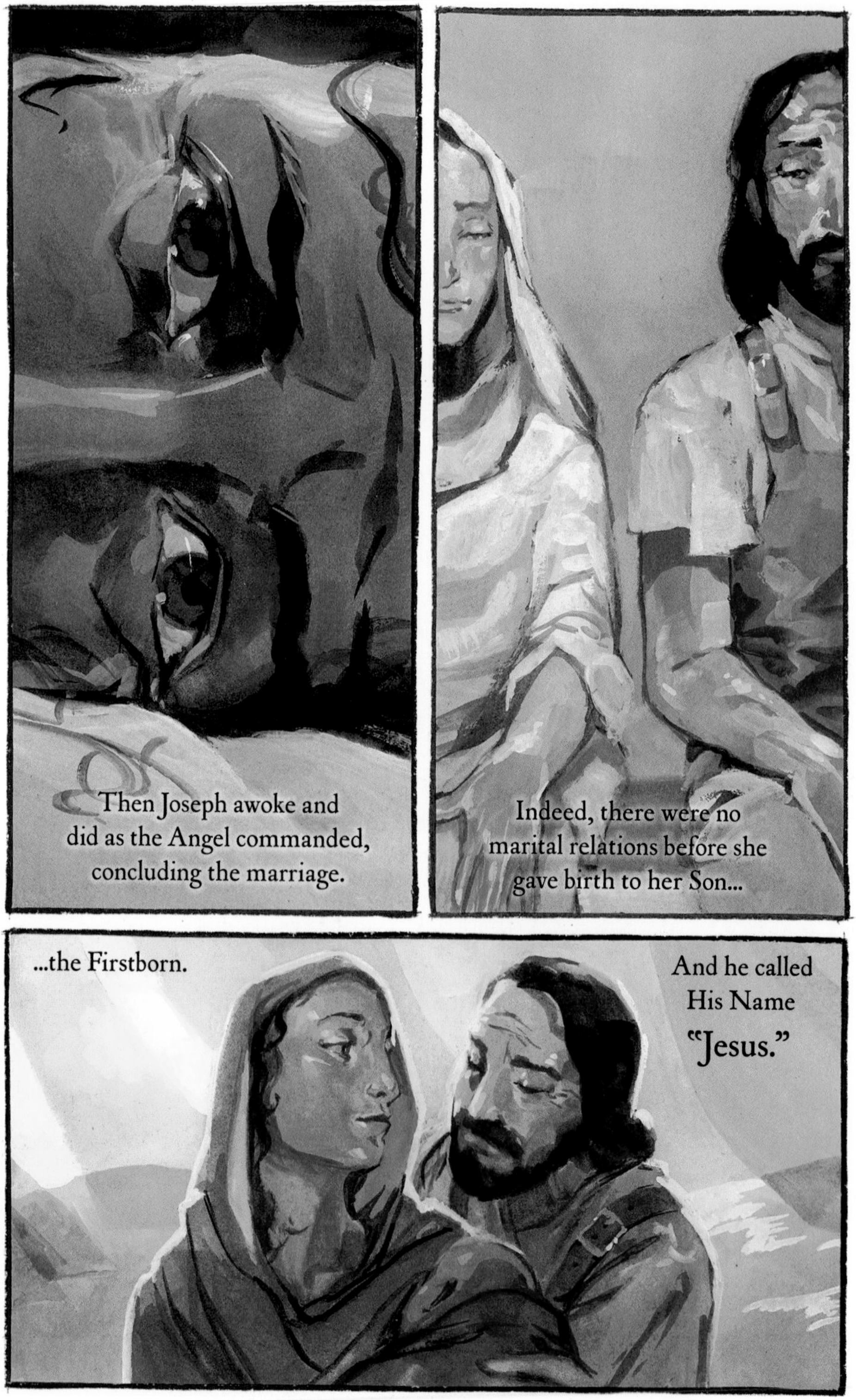
Then Joseph awoke and did as the Angel commanded, concluding the marriage.
Indeed, there were no marital relations before she gave birth to her Son...
...the Firstborn.
And he called His Name "Jesus."

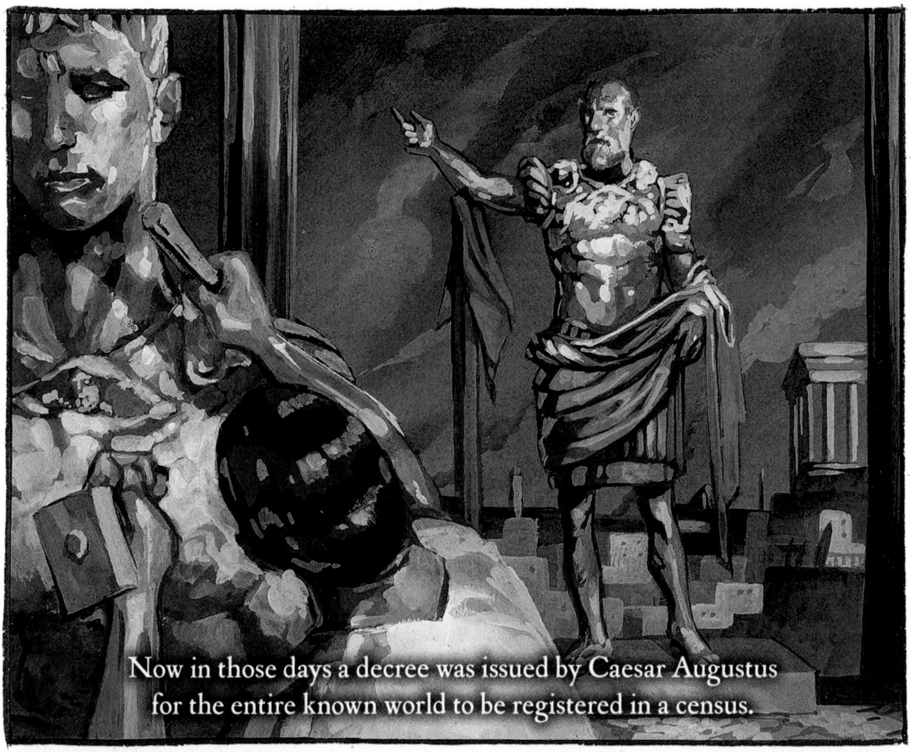
Now in those days a decree was issued by Caesar Augustus for the entire known world to be registered in a census.

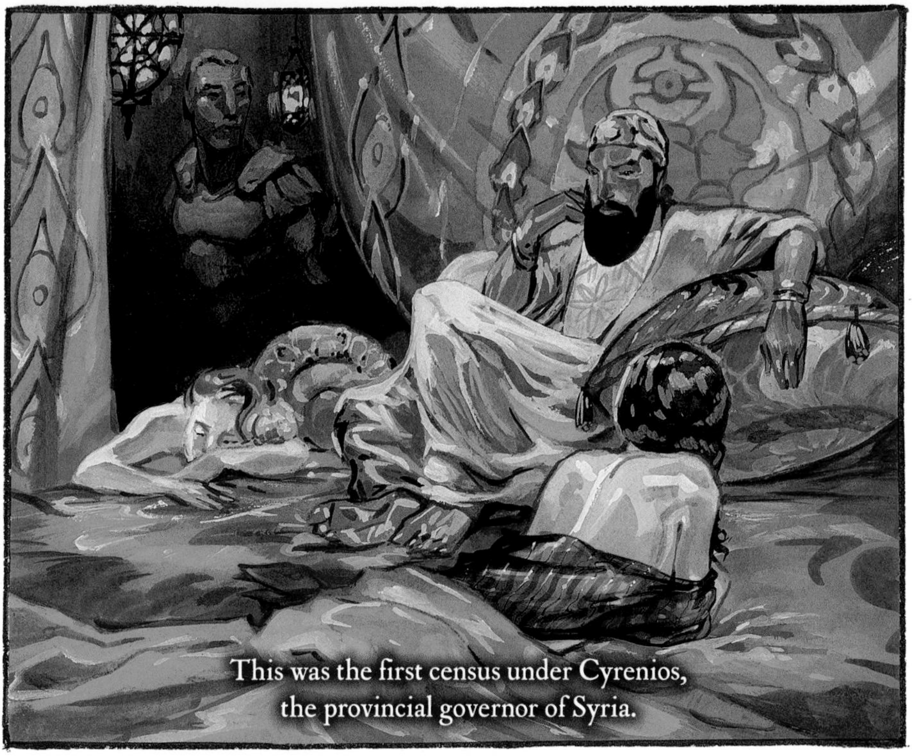
This was the first census under Cyrenios, the provincial governor of Syria.

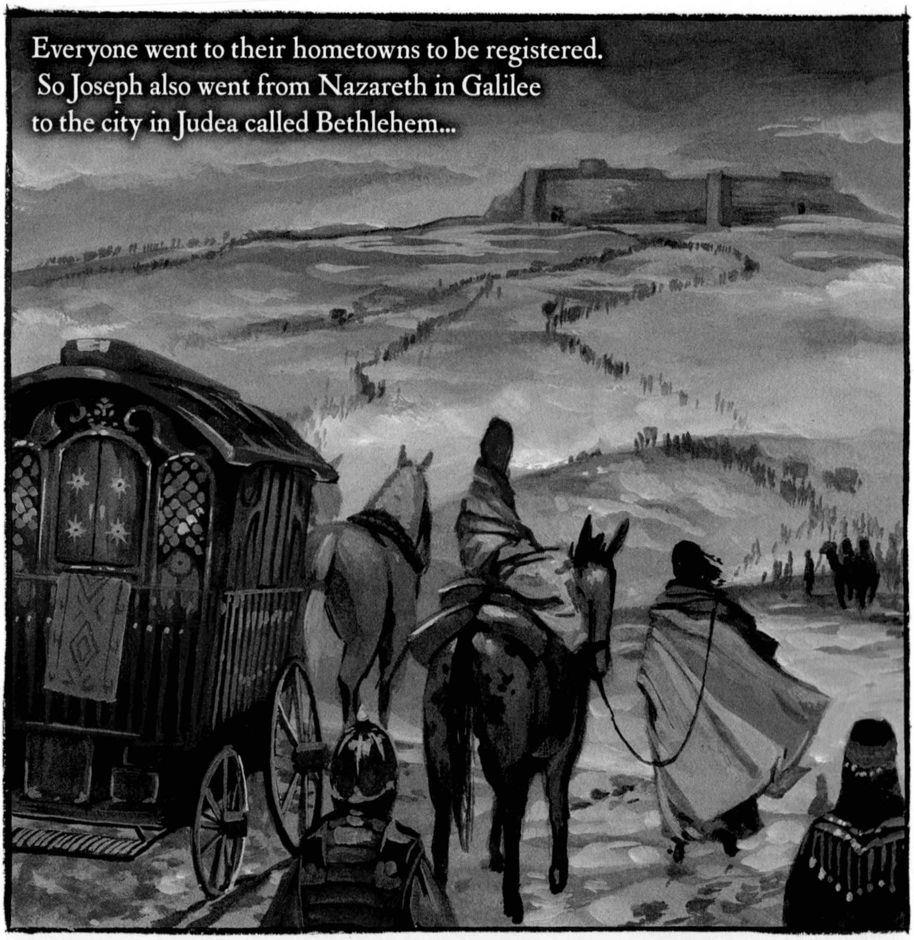
Everyone went to their hometowns to be registered.
So Joseph also went from Nazareth in Galilee
to the city in Judea called Bethlehem...

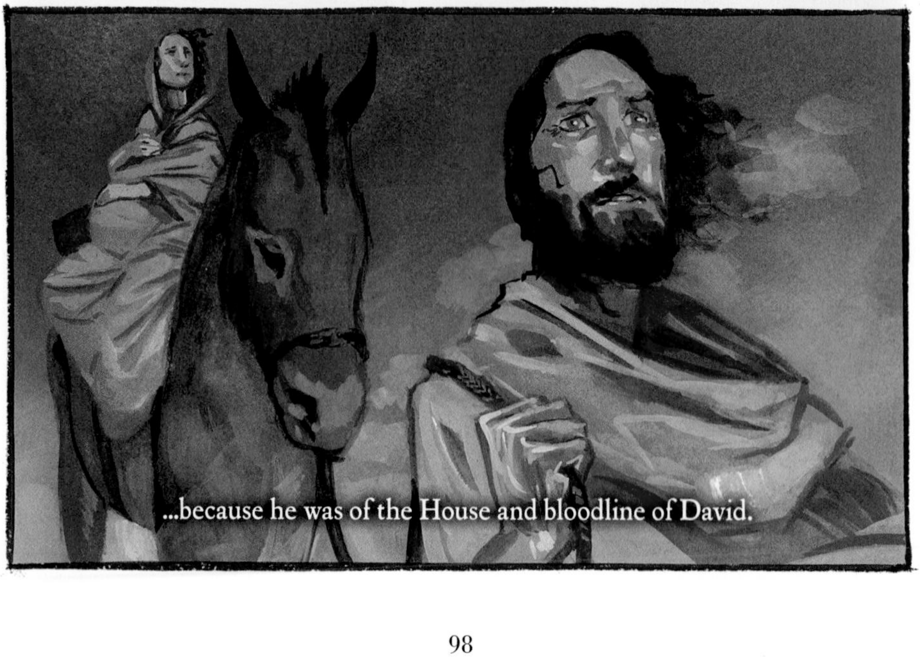
...because he was of the House and bloodline of David.

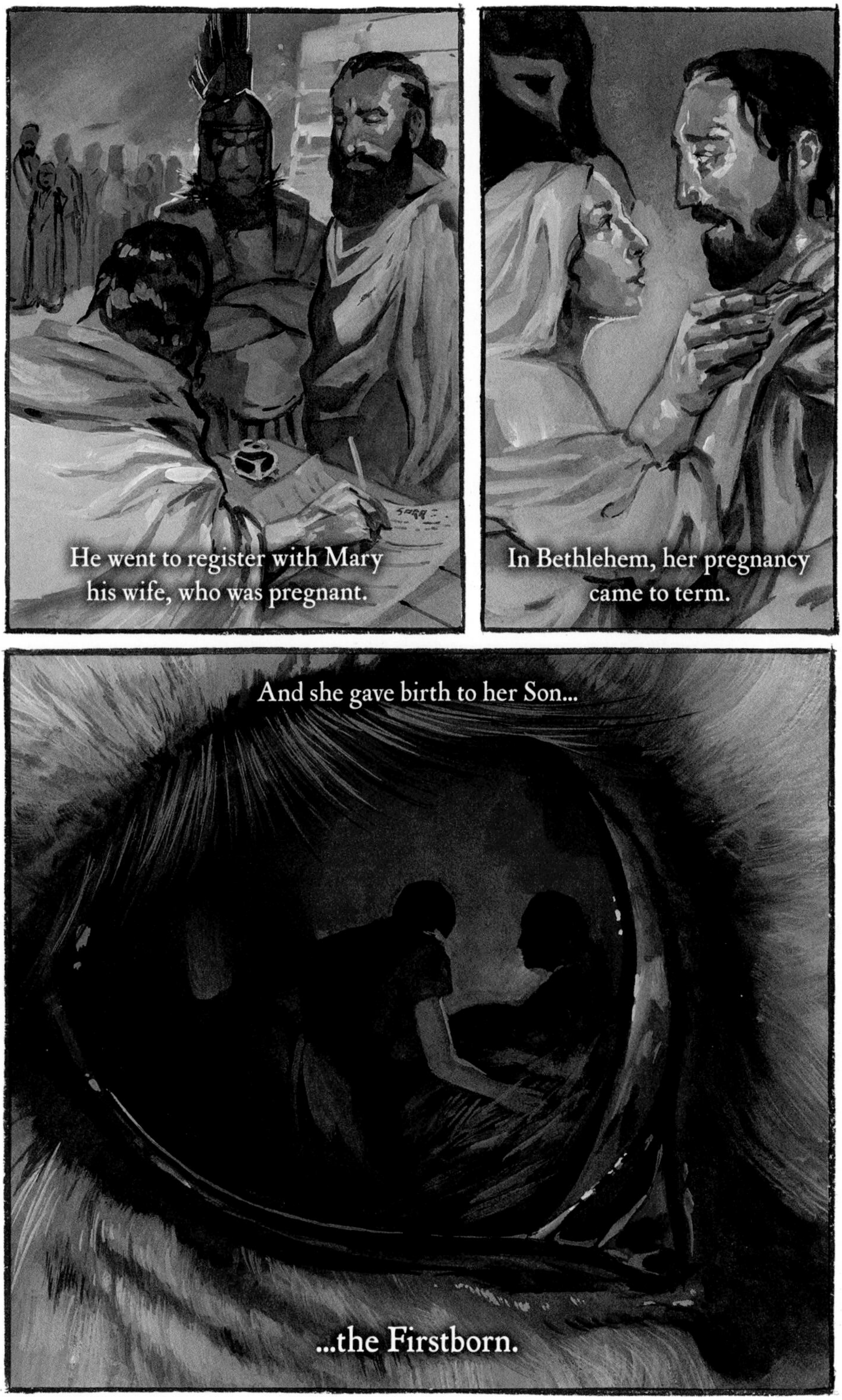
He went to register with Mary his wife, who was pregnant.
In Bethlehem, her pregnancy came to term.
And she gave birth to her Son...
...the Firstborn.

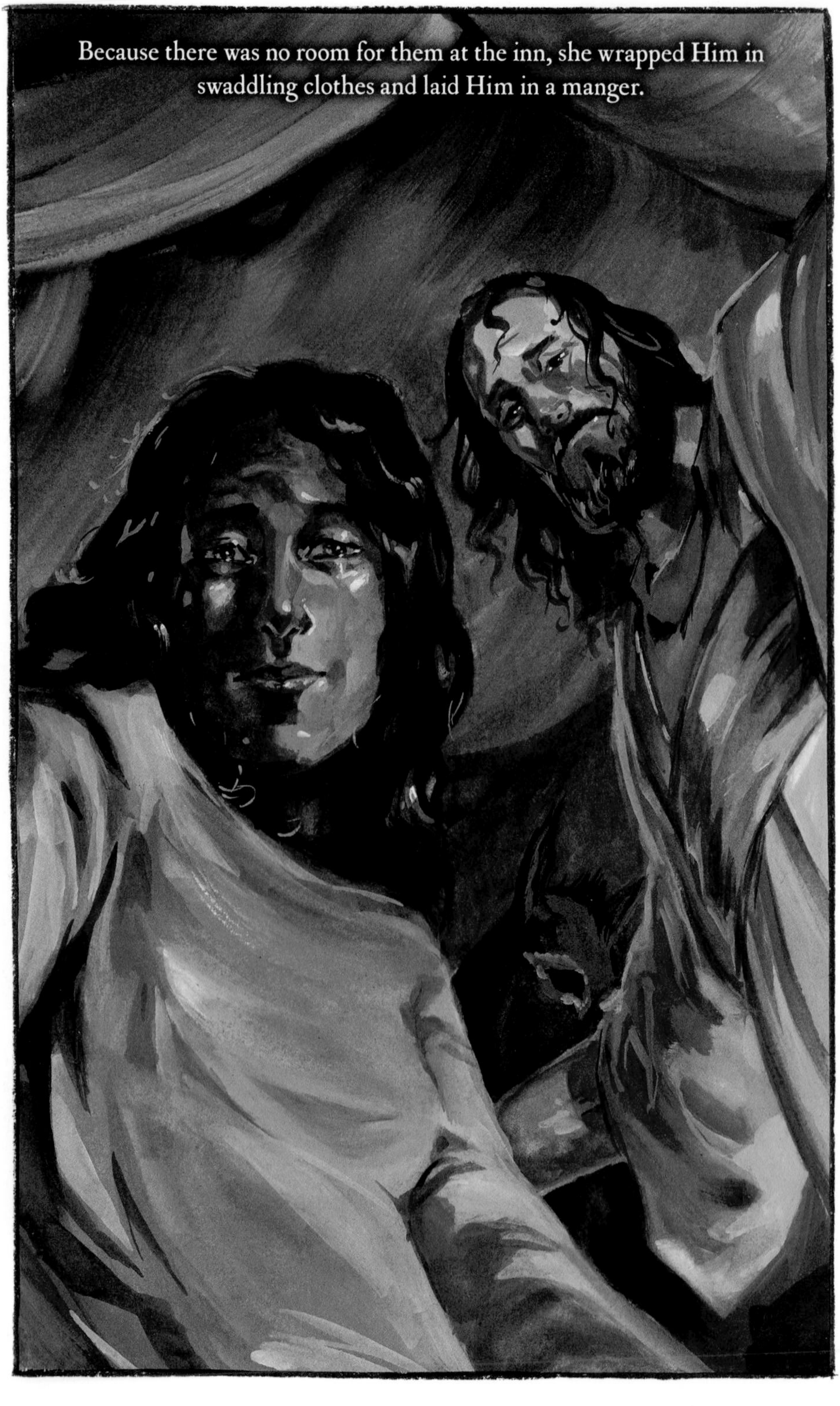
Because there was no room for them at the inn, she wrapped Him in swaddling clothes and laid Him in a manger.

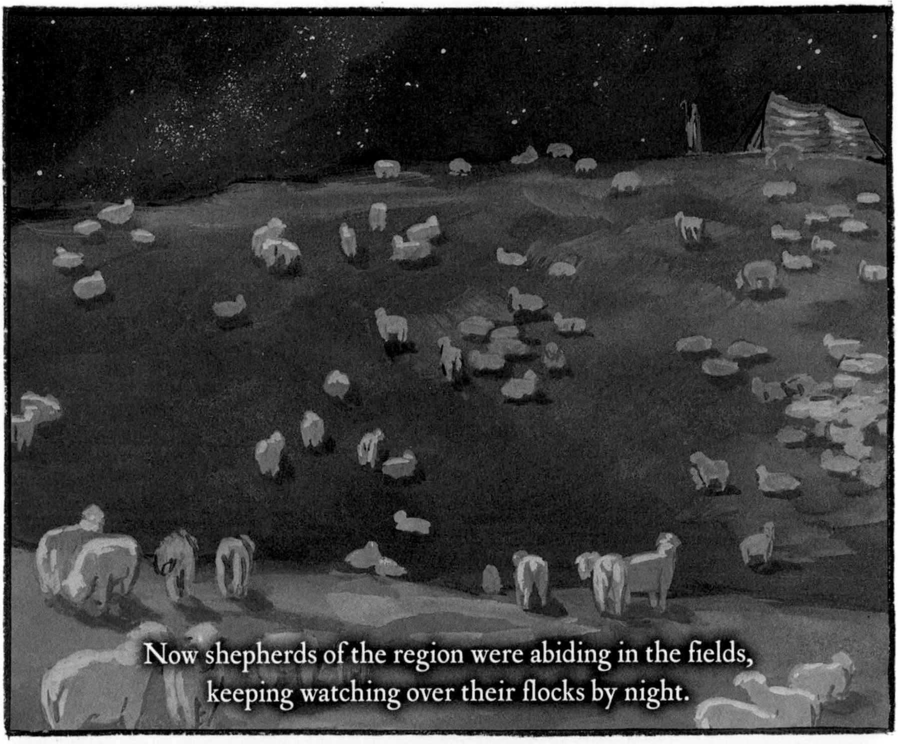
Now shepherds of the region were abiding in the fields, keeping watching over their flocks by night.

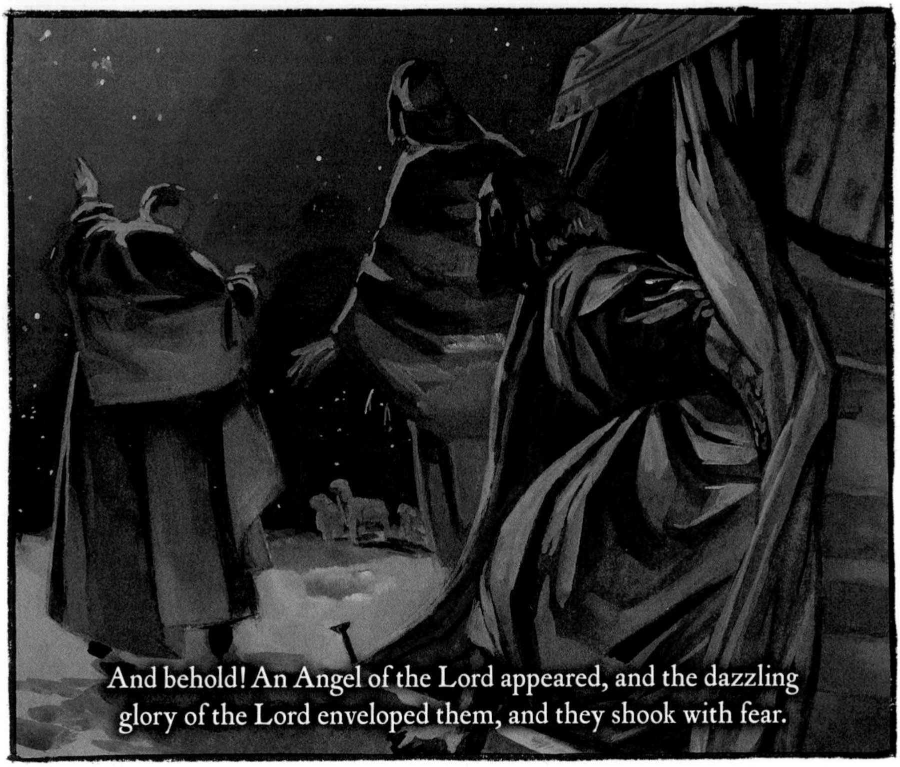
And behold! An Angel of the Lord appeared, and the dazzling glory of the Lord enveloped them, and they shook with fear.

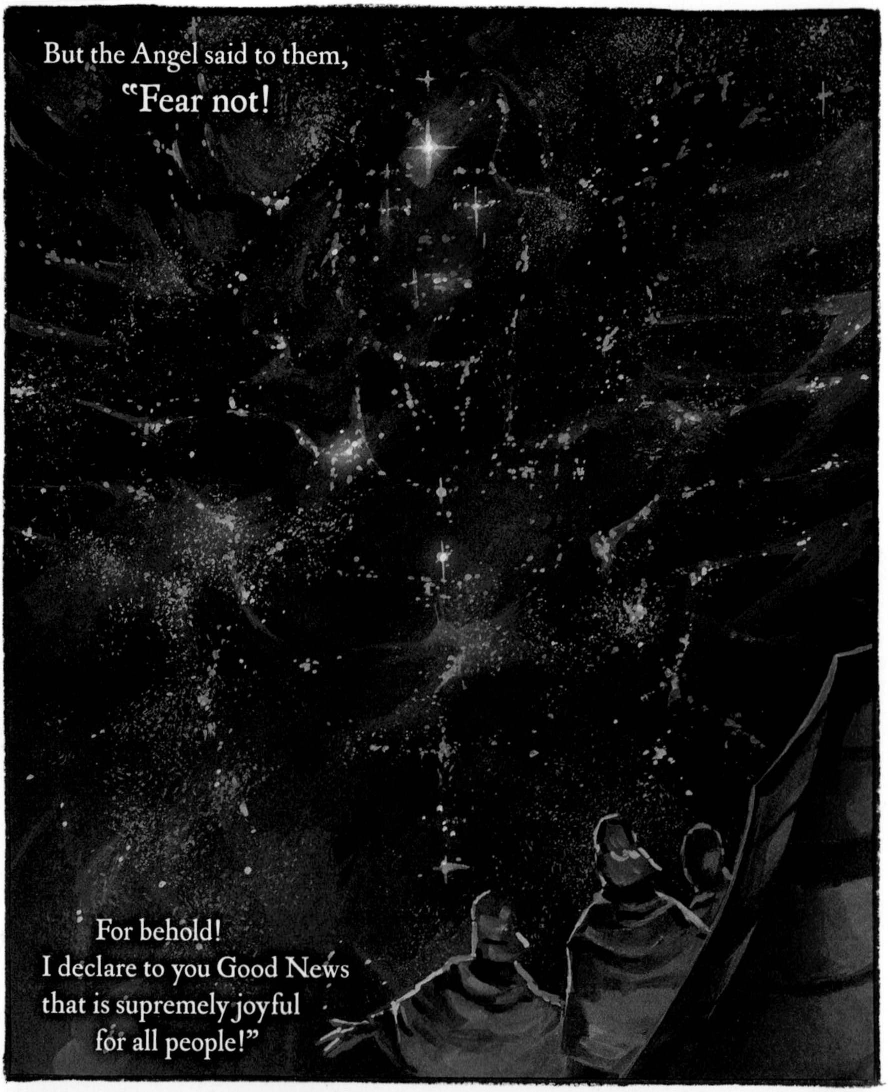
But the Angel said to them,
"Fear not!
For behold!
I declare to you Good News
that is supremely joyful
for all people!"

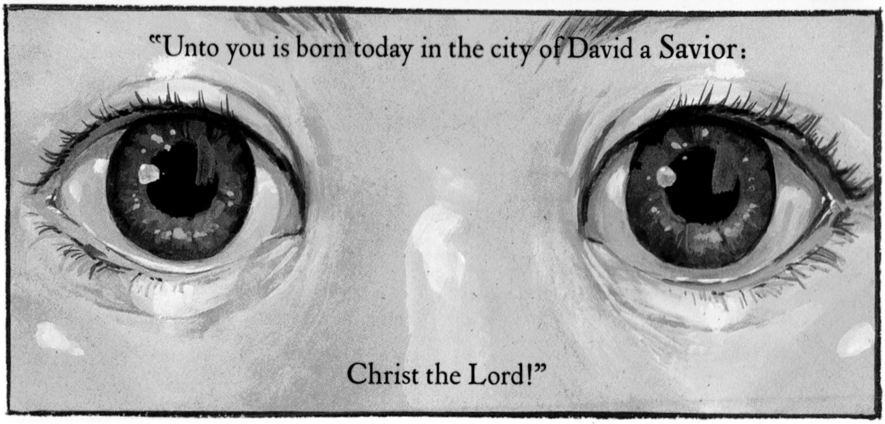
"Unto you is born today in the city of David a Savior:
Christ the Lord!"

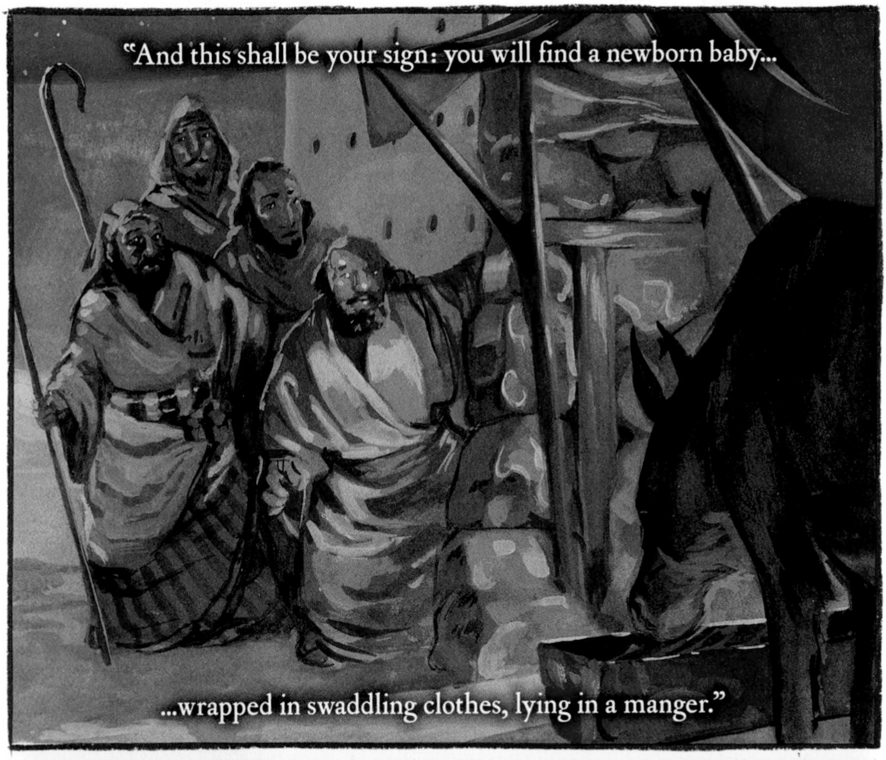
"And this shall be your sign: you will find a newborn baby...
...wrapped in swaddling clothes, lying in a manger."

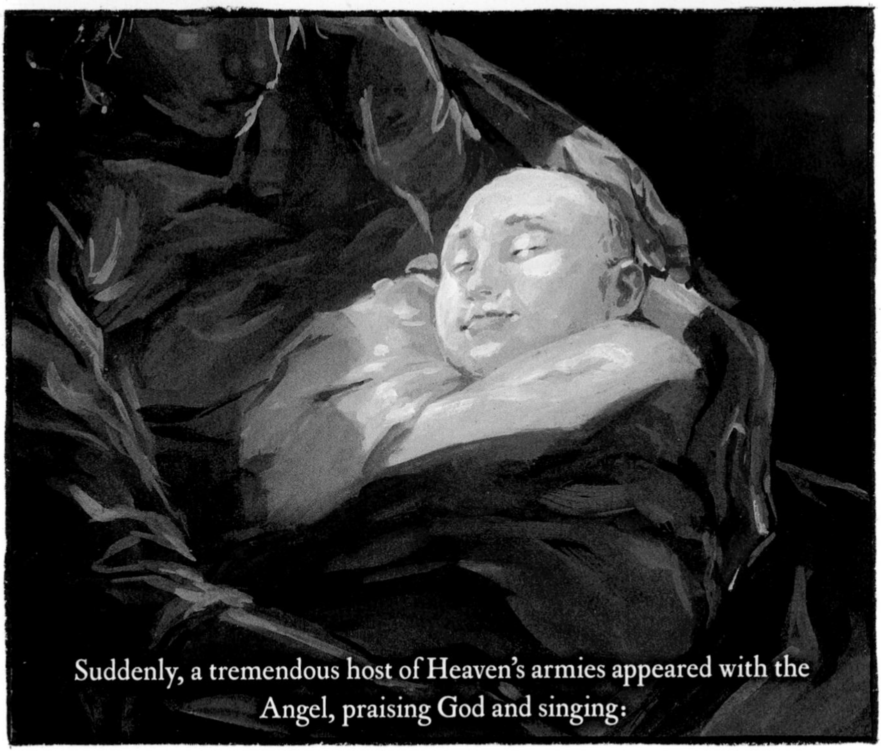
Suddenly, a tremendous host of Heaven's armies appeared with the Angel, praising God and singing:

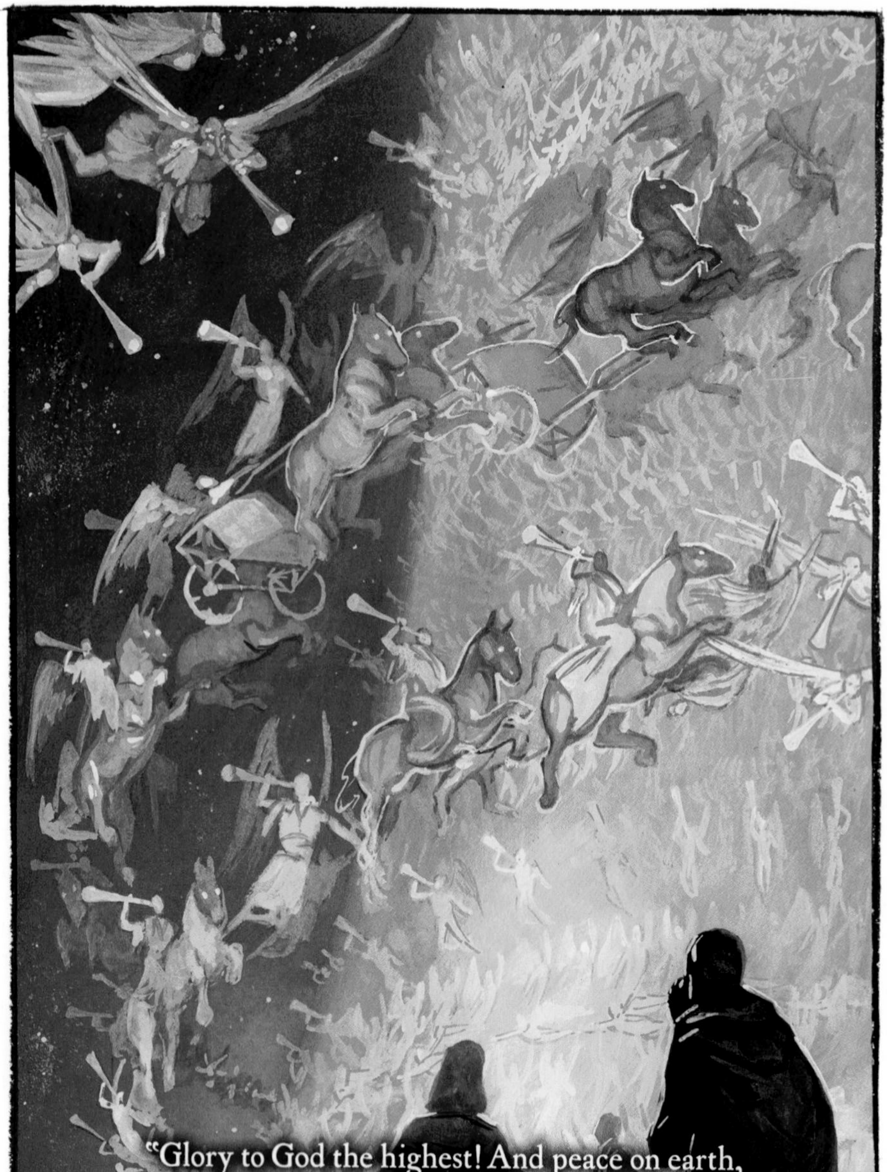
"Glory to God the highest! And peace on earth, good will to all humanity!"

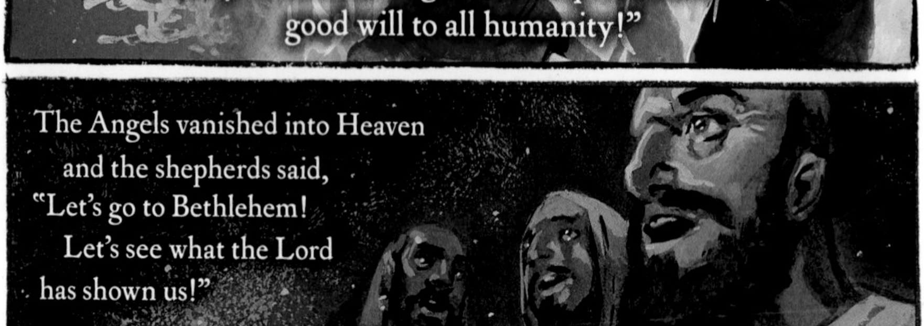
The Angels vanished into Heaven and the shepherds said, "Let's go to Bethlehem! Let's see what the Lord has shown us!"

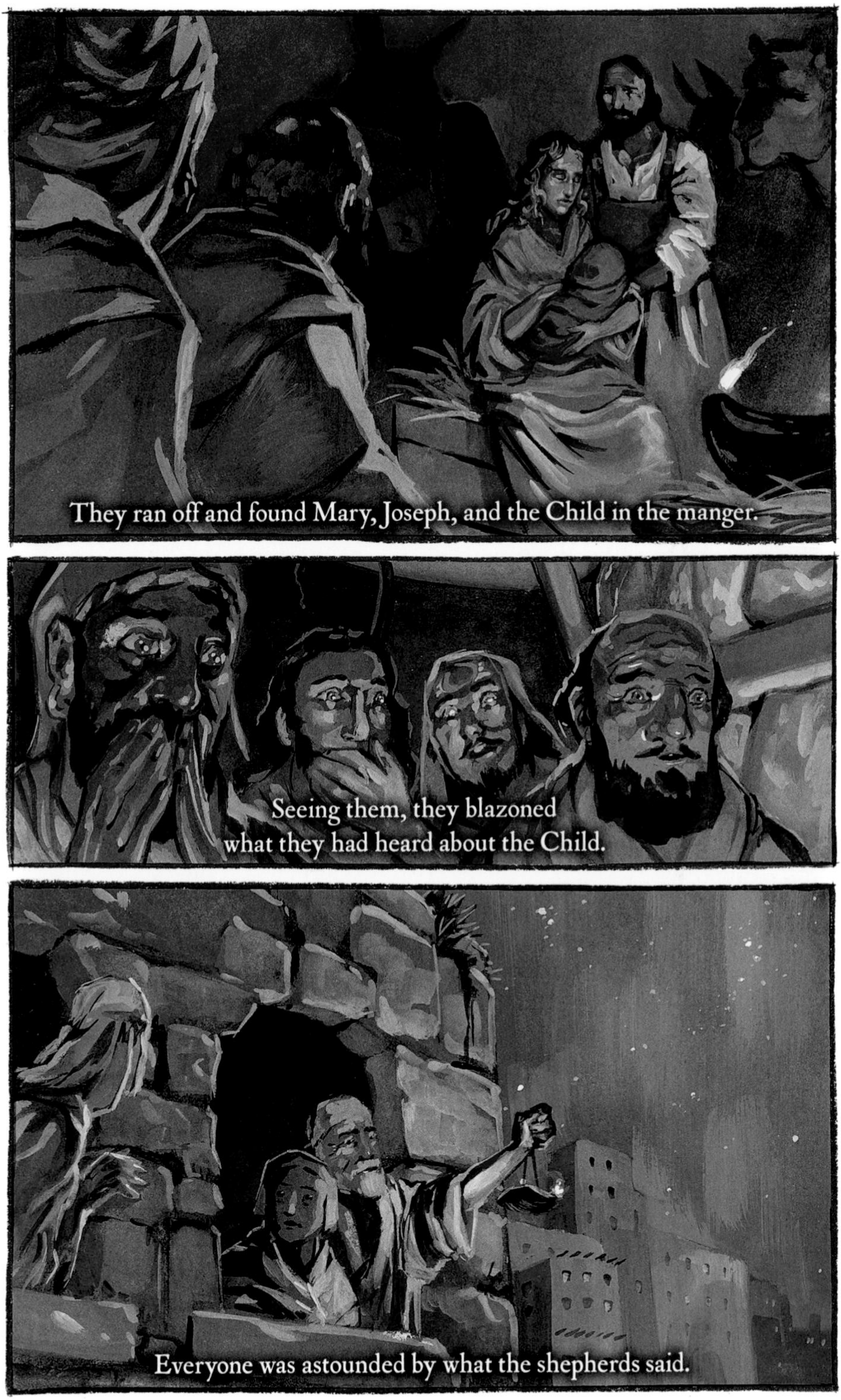
They ran off and found Mary, Joseph, and the Child in the manger.
Seeing them, they blazoned what they had heard about the Child.
Everyone was astounded by what the shepherds said.

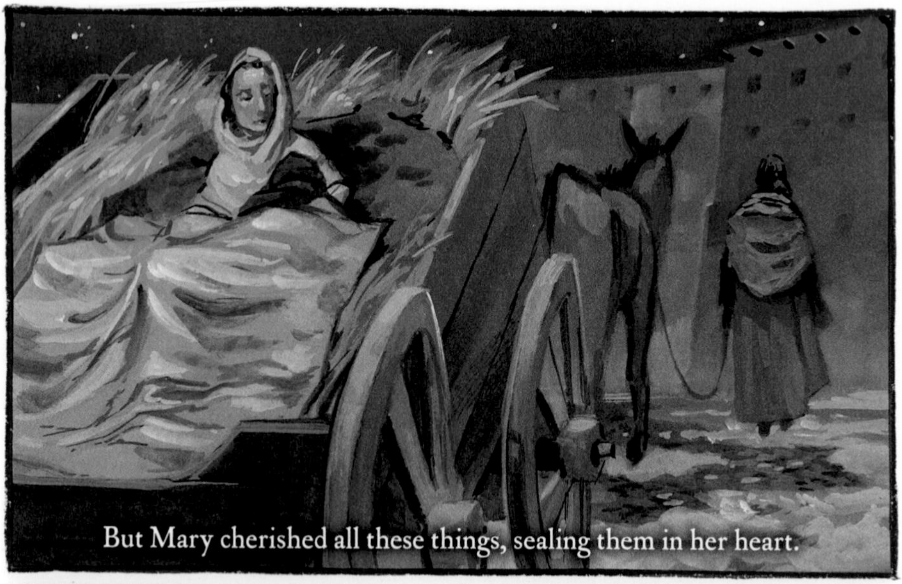
But Mary cherished all these things, sealing them in her heart.

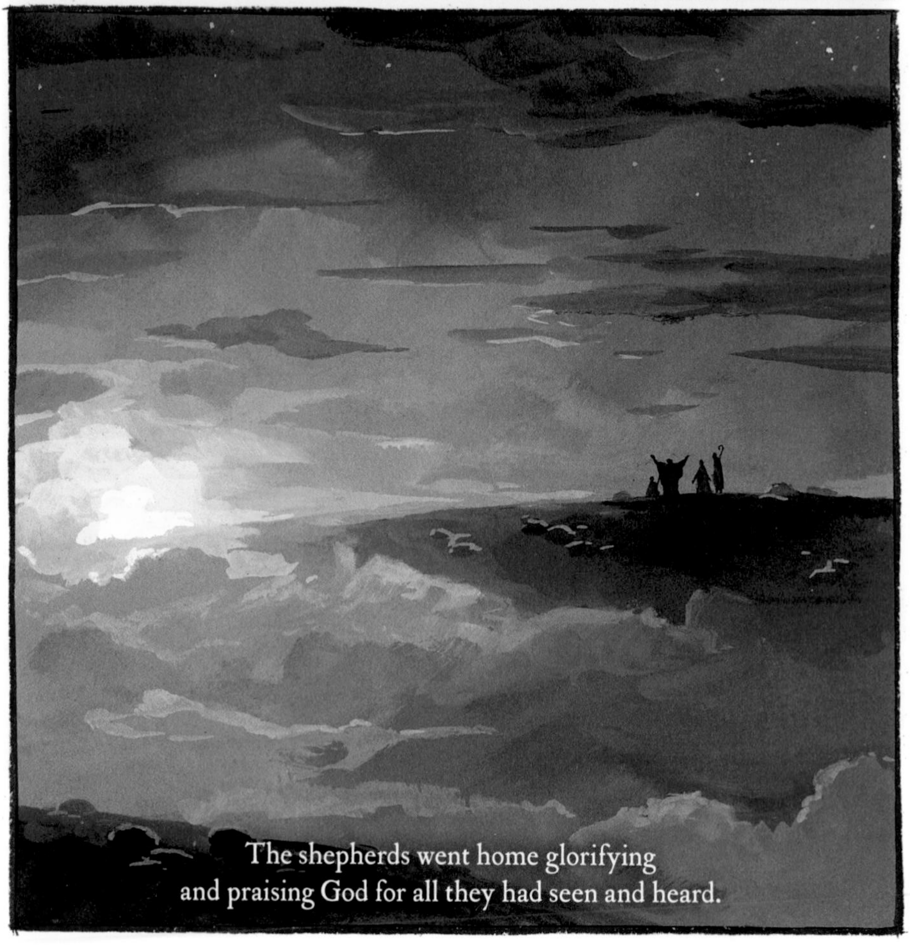
The shepherds went home glorifying
and praising God for all they had seen and heard.

Fulfillment of the Law

LUKE 2:21–38

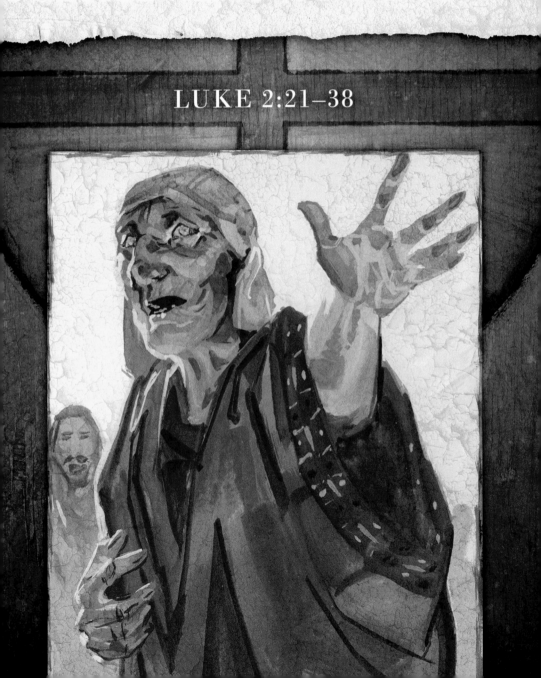

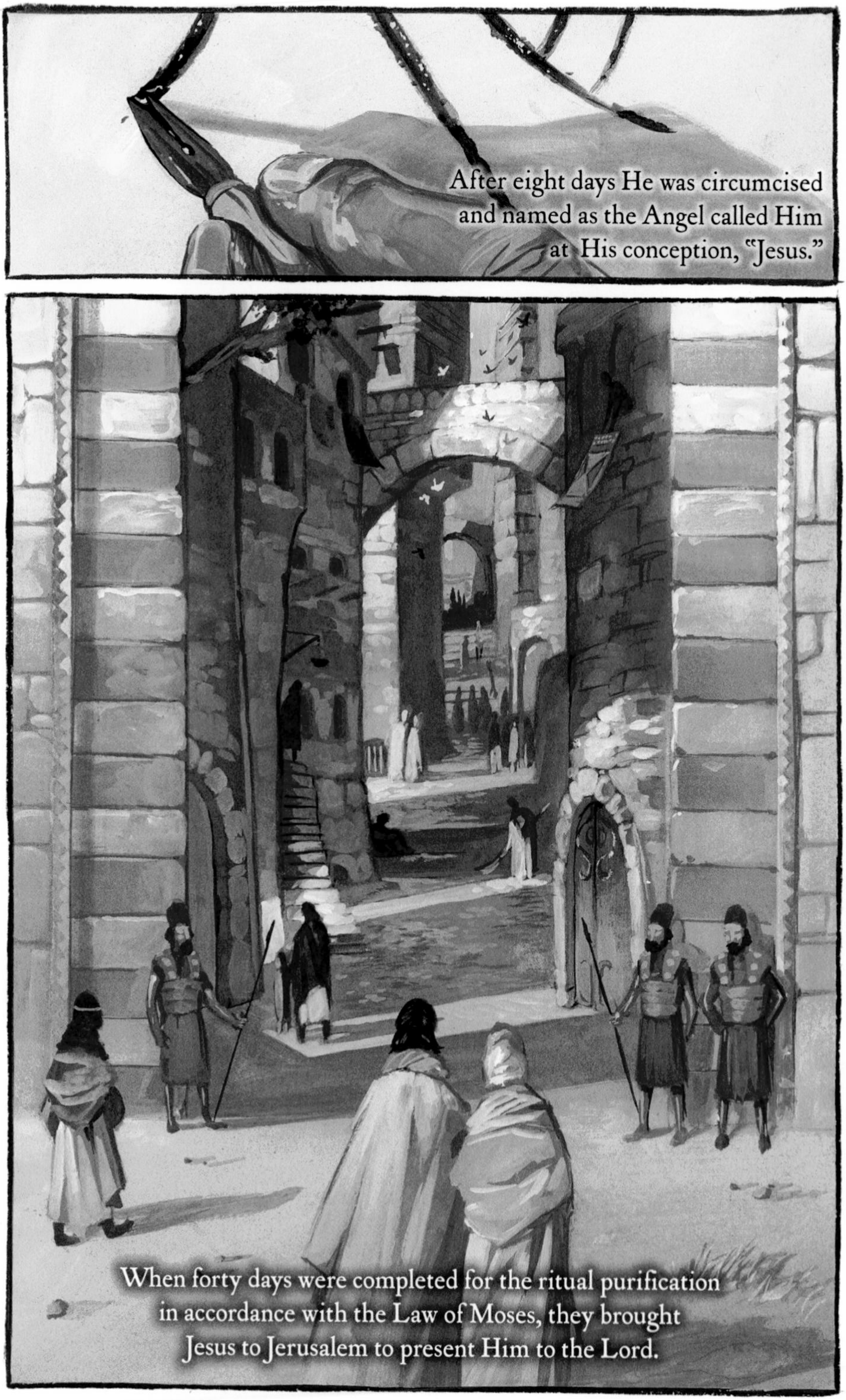
After eight days He was circumcised
and named as the Angel called Him
at His conception, "Jesus."
When forty days were completed for the ritual purification
in accordance with the Law of Moses, they brought
Jesus to Jerusalem to present Him to the Lord.

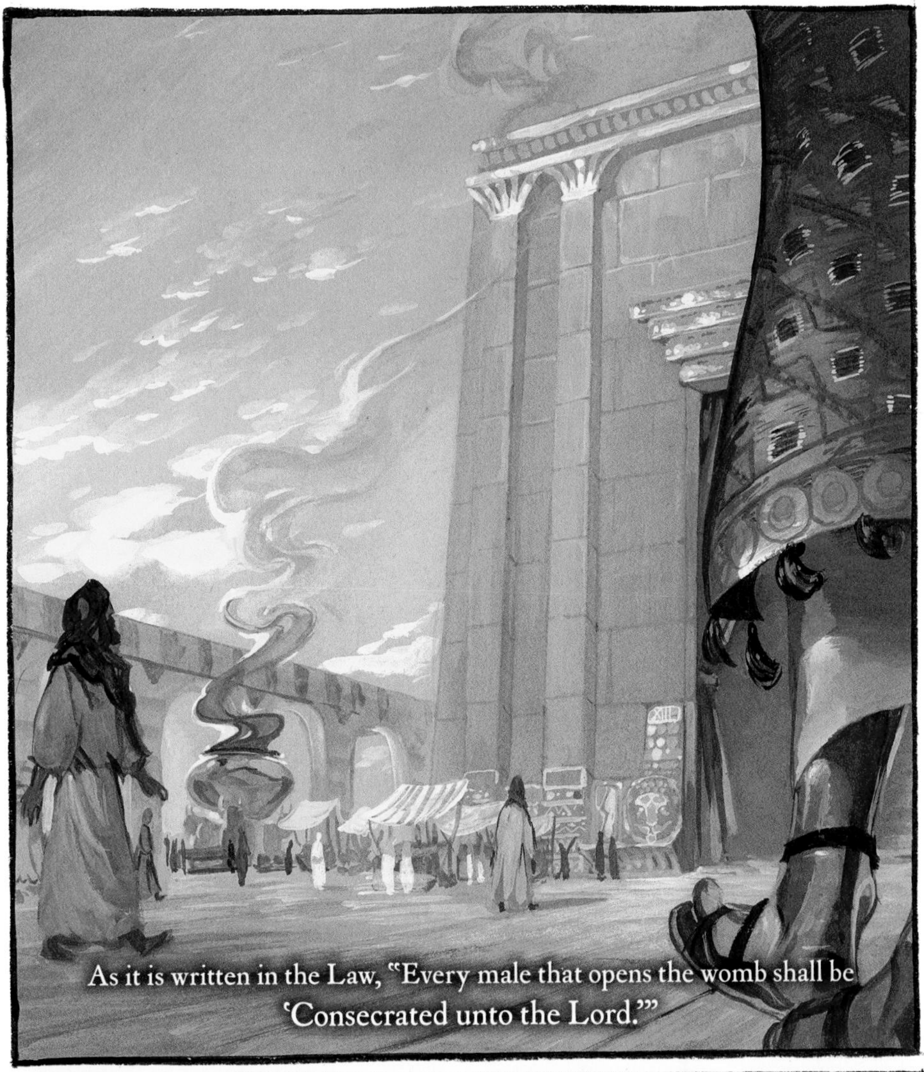
As it is written in the Law, "Every male that opens the womb shall be
'Consecrated unto the Lord.'"

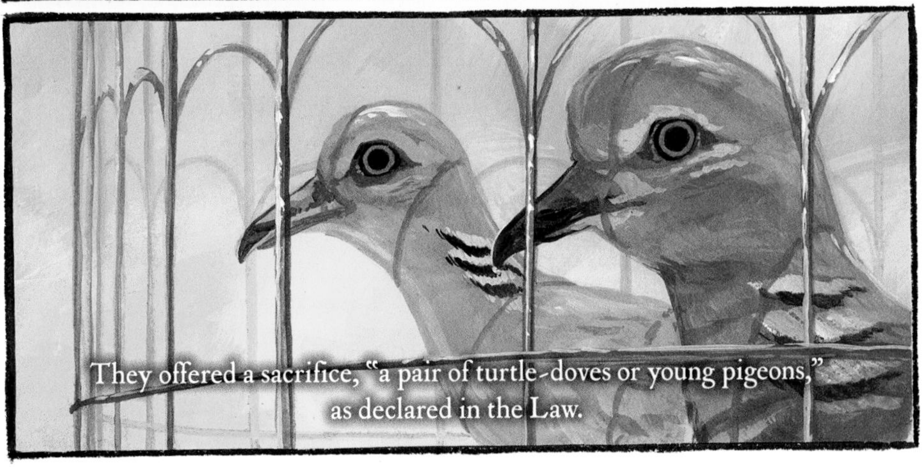
They offered a sacrifice, "a pair of turtle-doves or young pigeons,"
as declared in the Law.

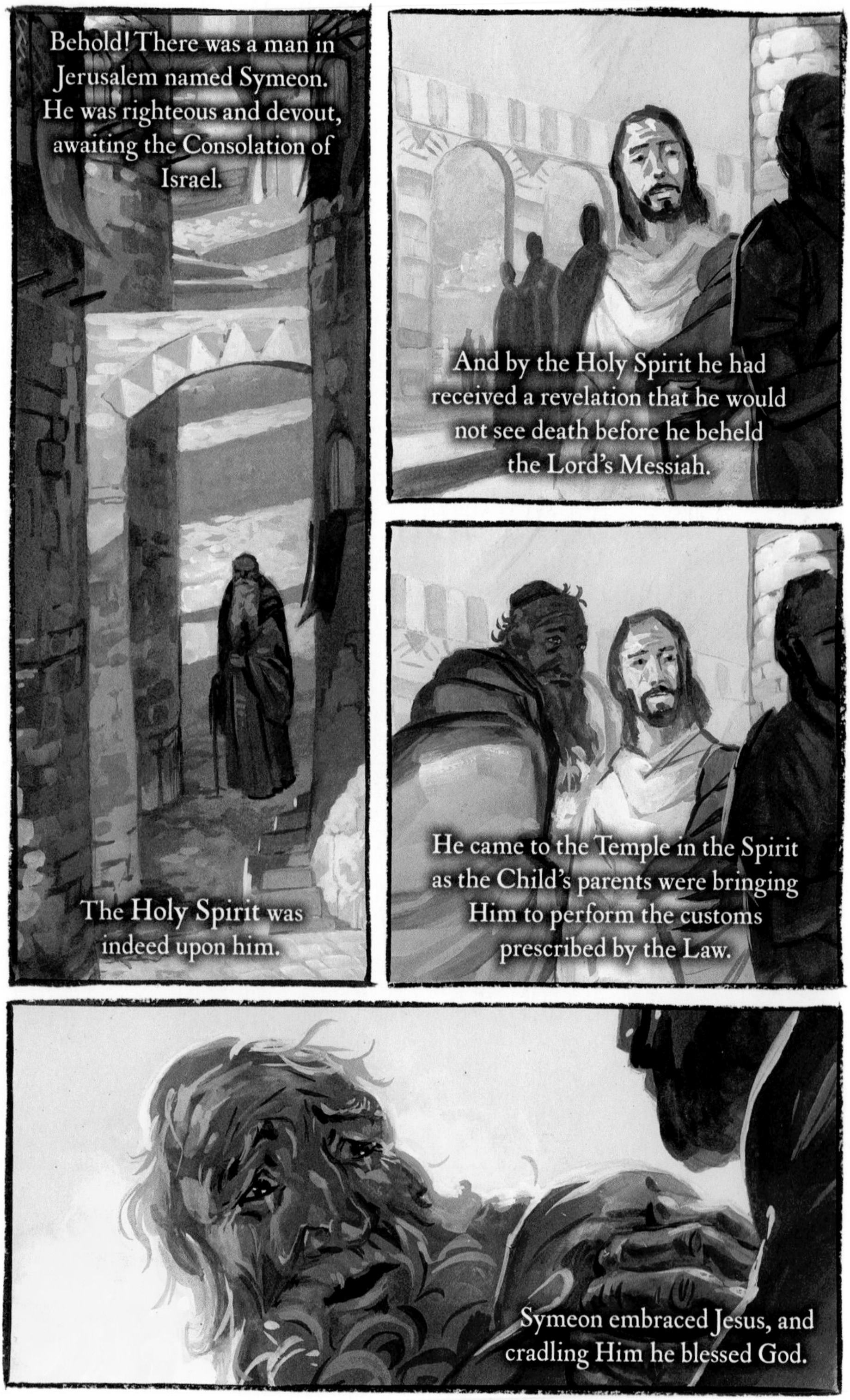
Behold! There was a man in Jerusalem named Symeon. He was righteous and devout, awaiting the Consolation of Israel.
The Holy Spirit was indeed upon him.
And by the Holy Spirit he had received a revelation that he would not see death before he beheld the Lord's Messiah.
He came to the Temple in the Spirit as the Child's parents were bringing Him to perform the customs prescribed by the Law.
Symeon embraced Jesus, and cradling Him he blessed God.

"Now, O Master, release Your servant in peace, as You promised, for my eyes have seen Your salvation, which You have prepared in the presence of all peoples, the light for the revelation of the Nations, and the glory of Your people, Israel!"

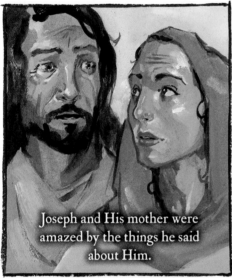

Joseph and His mother were amazed by the things he said about Him.

Symeon blessed them and said to Mary His Mother, "Behold, He is laid down for the fall and rising again of many in Israel, and as a sign of contradiction!"

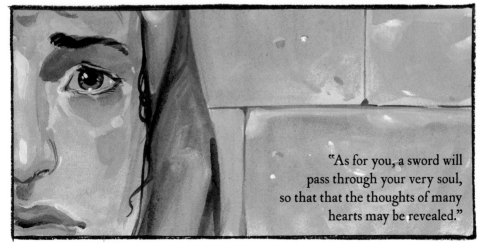

"As for you, a sword will pass through your very soul, so that that the thoughts of many hearts may be revealed."

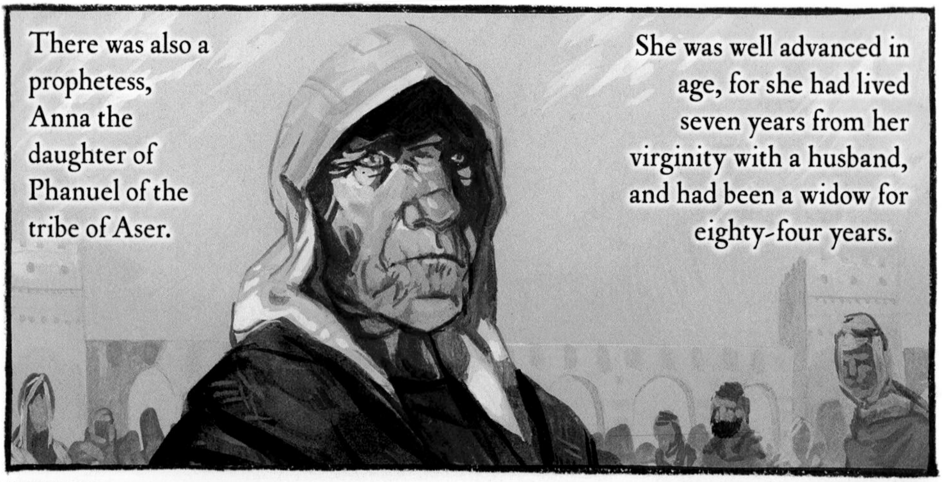
There was also a prophetess, Anna the daughter of Phanuel of the tribe of Aser.
She was well advanced in age, for she had lived seven years from her virginity with a husband, and had been a widow for eighty-four years.

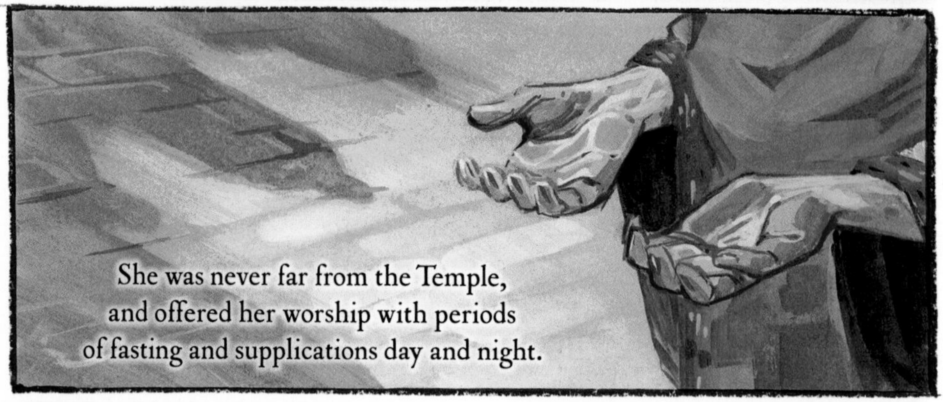
She was never far from the Temple, and offered her worship with periods of fasting and supplications day and night.

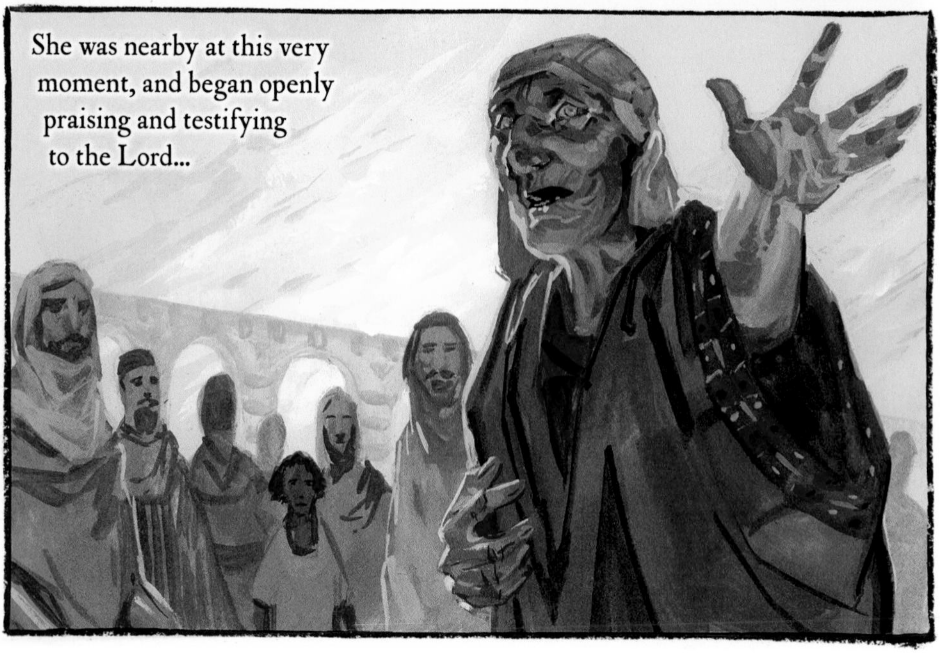
She was nearby at this very moment, and began openly praising and testifying to the Lord...

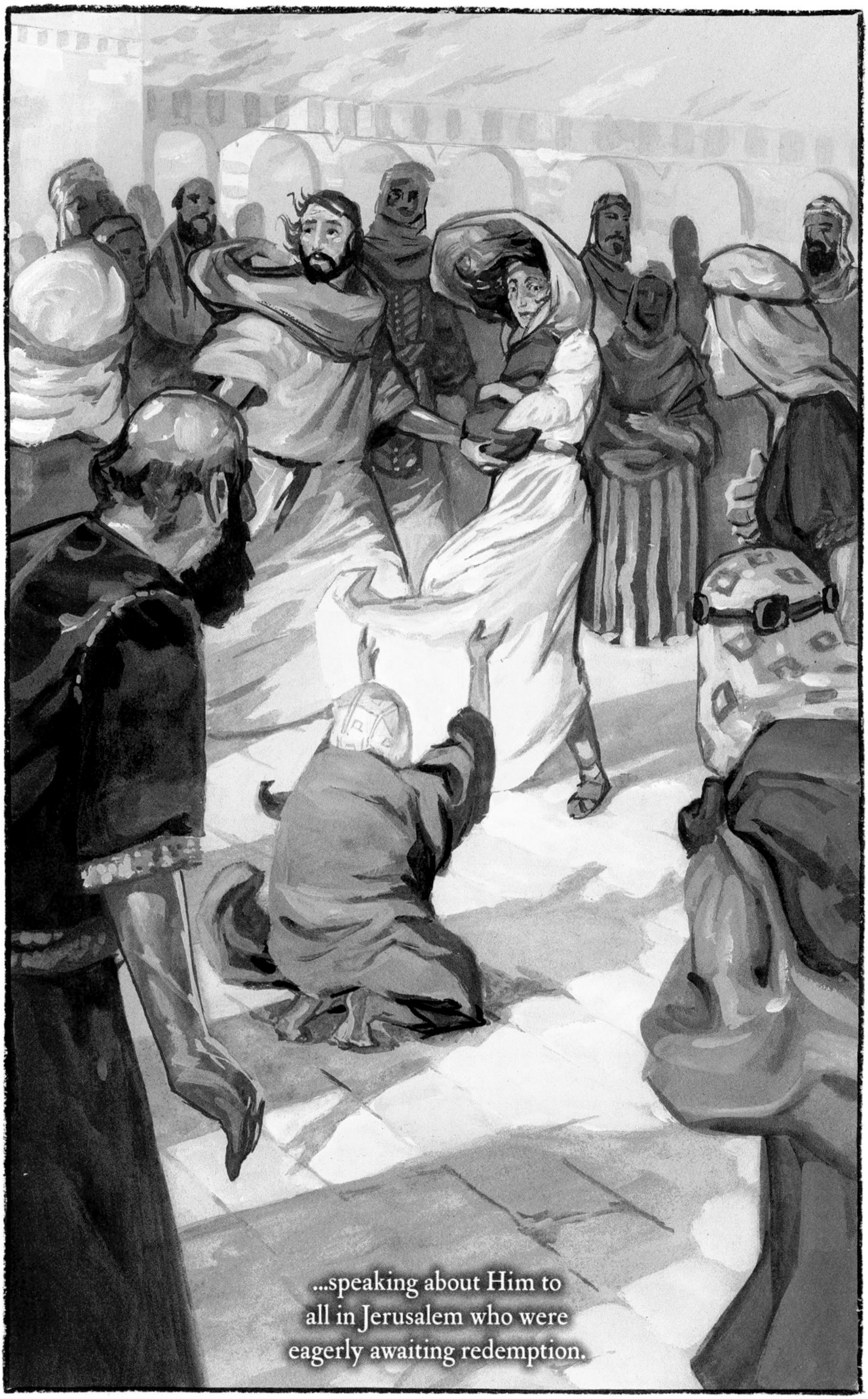
...speaking about Him to
all in Jerusalem who were
eagerly awaiting redemption.

ADORATION OF THE MAGI

MATTHEW 2:1–12

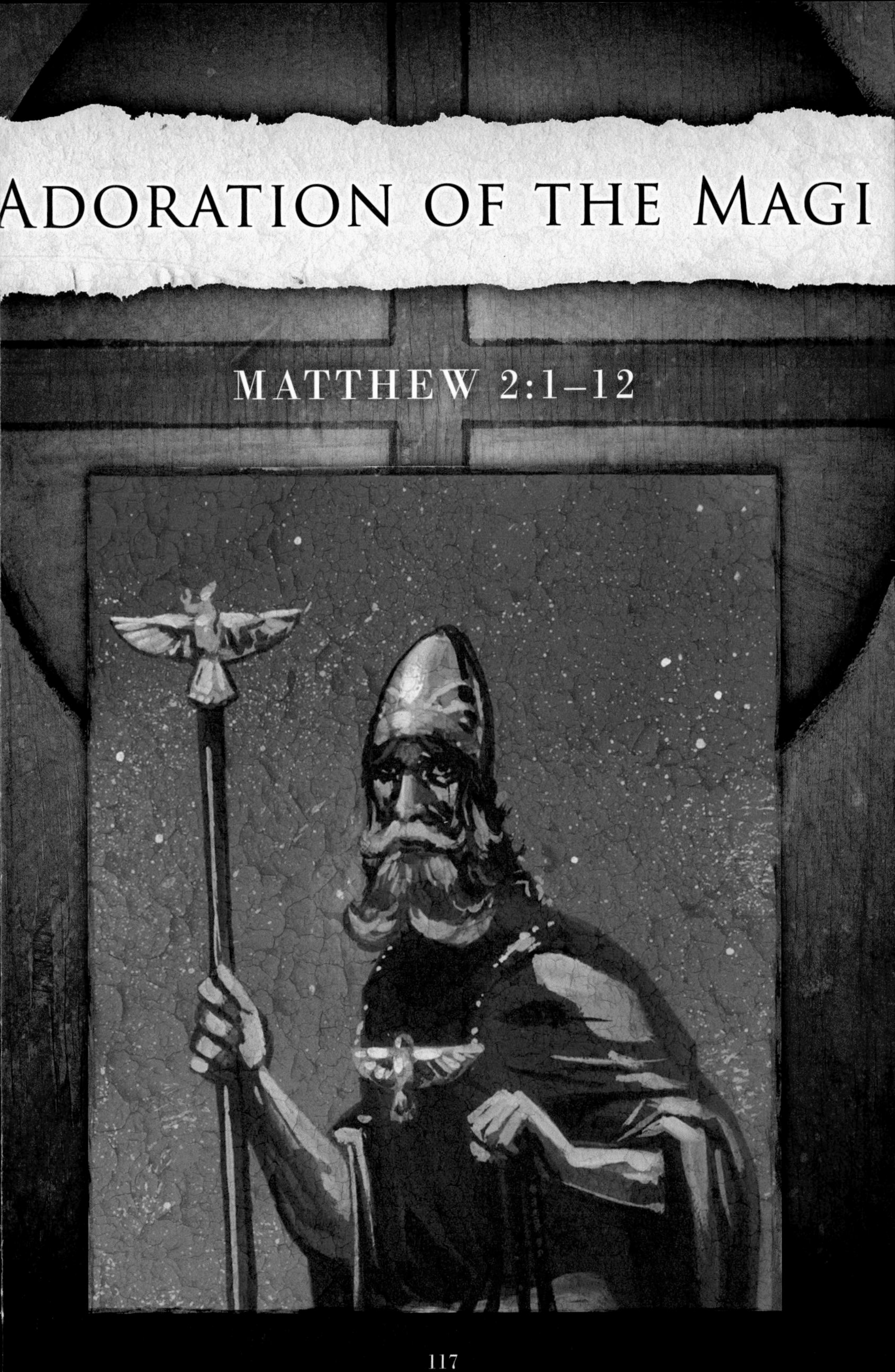

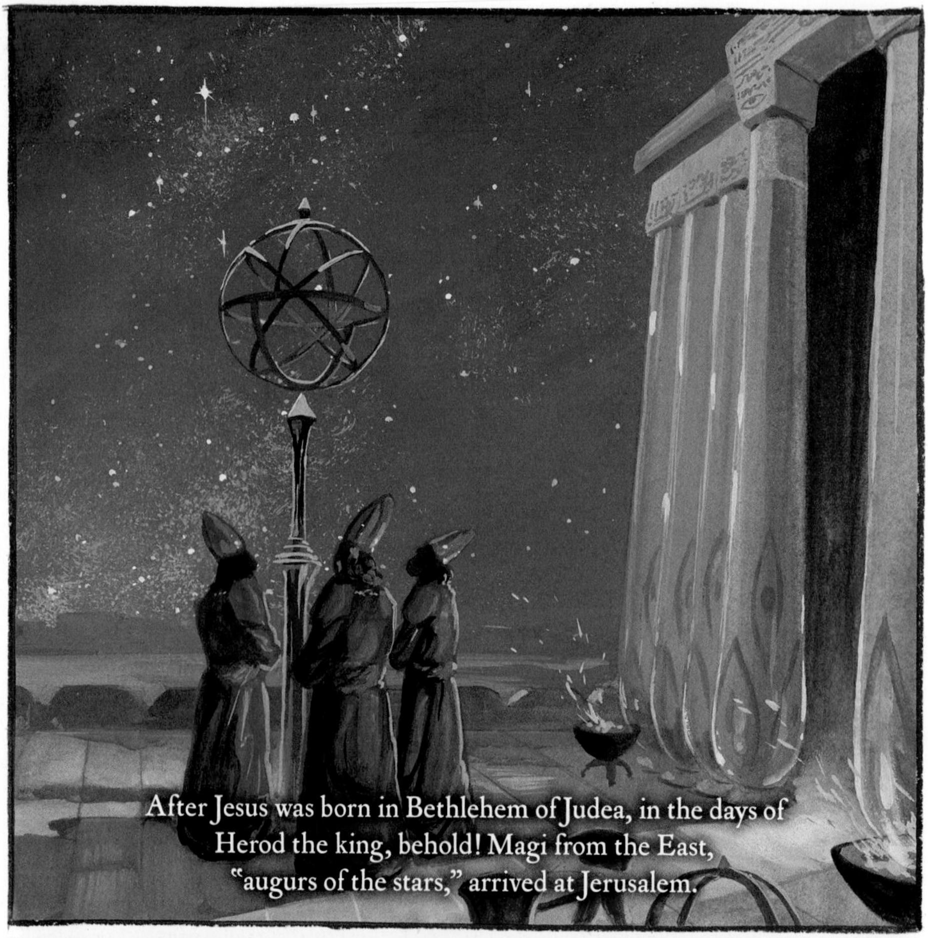
After Jesus was born in Bethlehem of Judea, in the days of Herod the king, behold! Magi from the East, "augurs of the stars," arrived at Jerusalem.

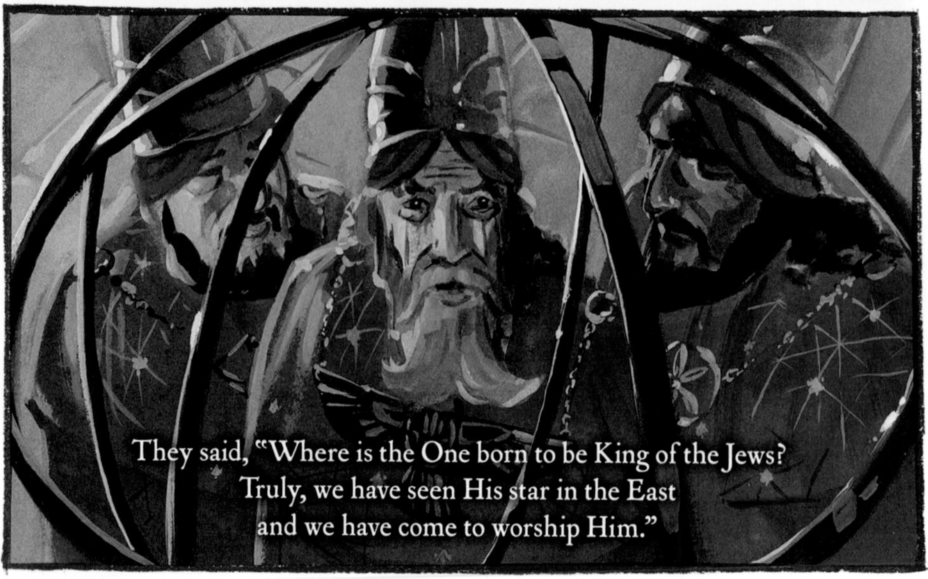
They said, "Where is the One born to be King of the Jews? Truly, we have seen His star in the East and we have come to worship Him."

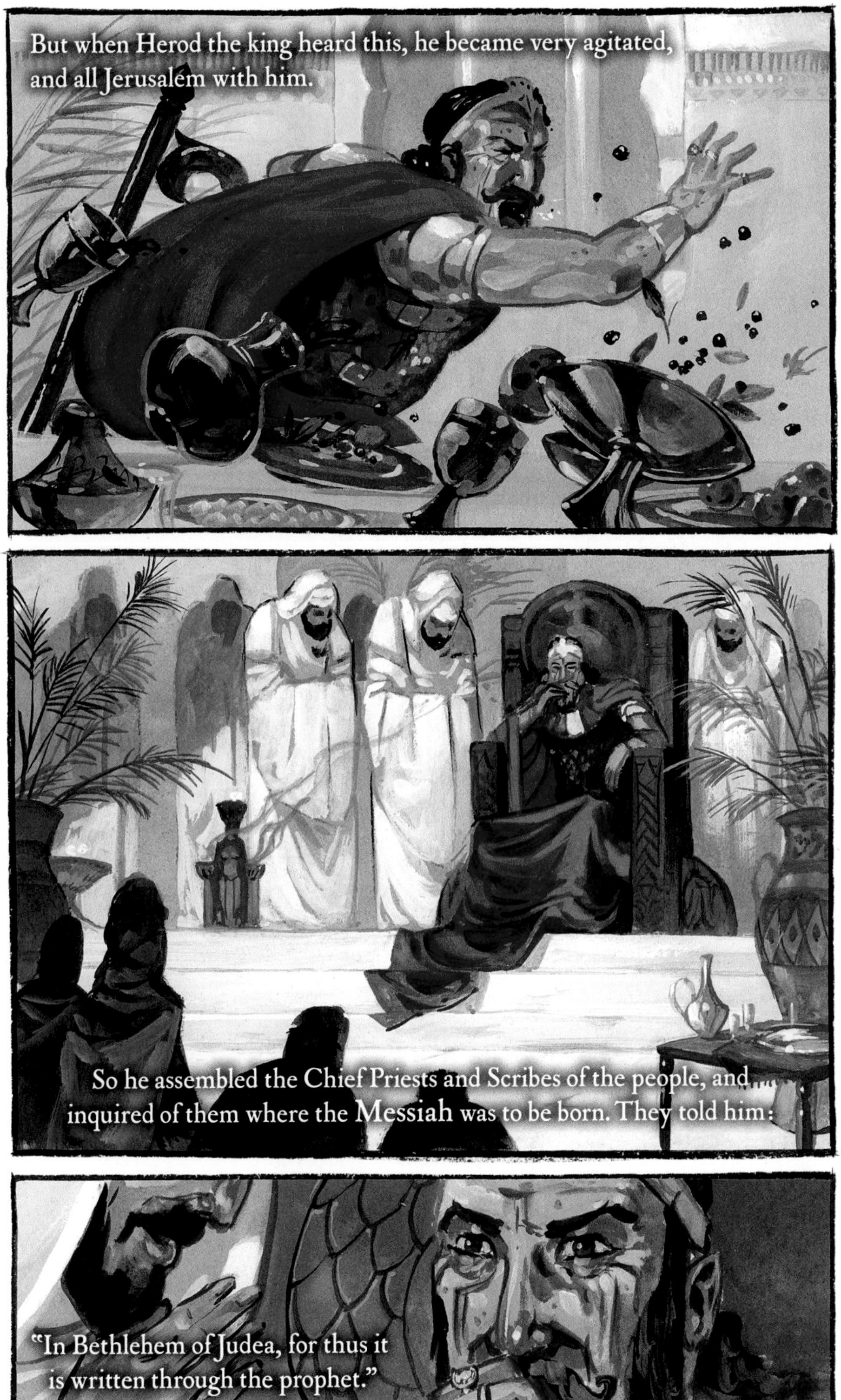
But when Herod the king heard this, he became very agitated, and all Jerusalem with him.
So he assembled the Chief Priests and Scribes of the people, and inquired of them where the Messiah was to be born. They told him:
"In Bethlehem of Judea, for thus it is written through the prophet."

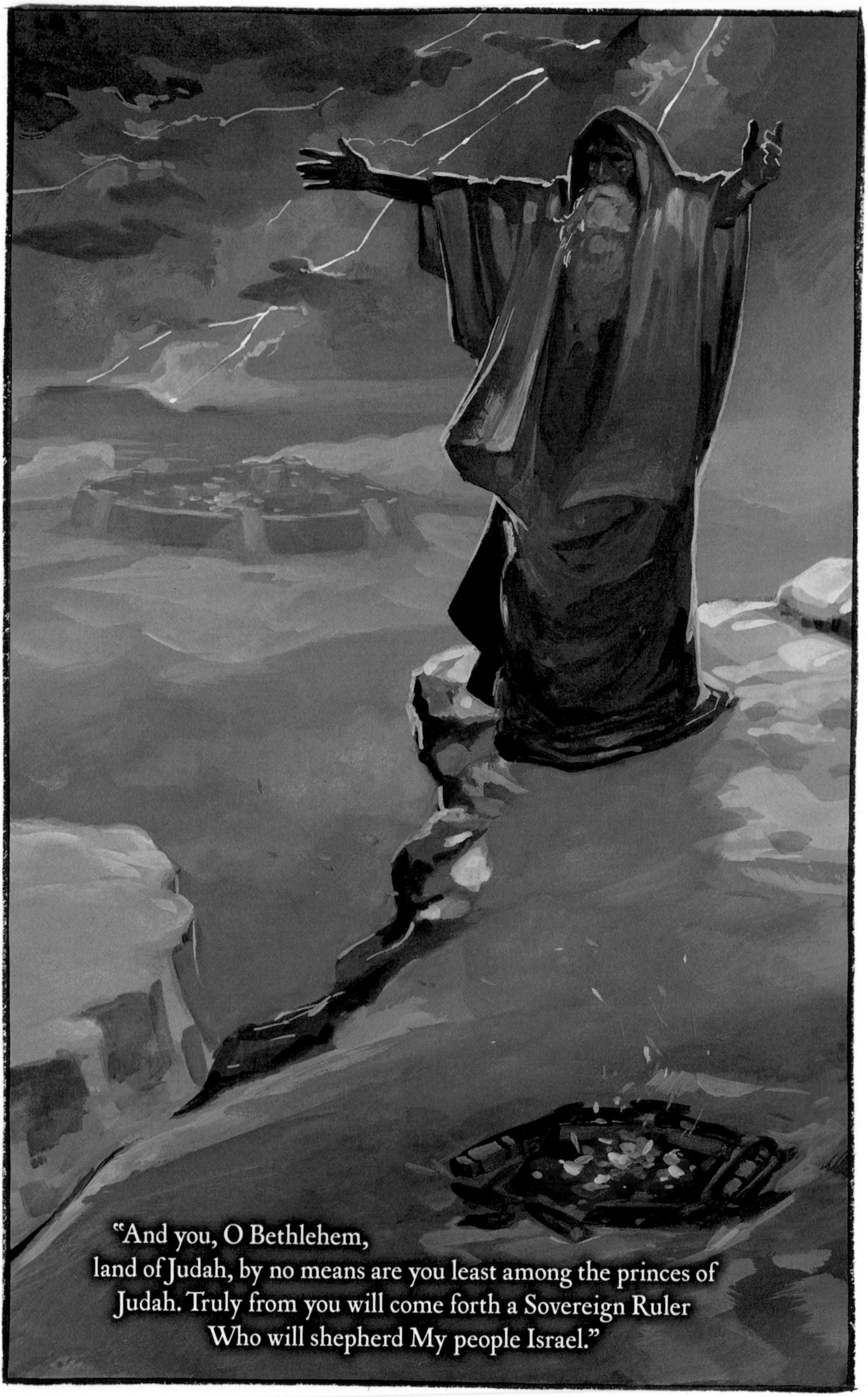
"And you, O Bethlehem,
land of Judah, by no means are you least among the princes of
Judah. Truly from you will come forth a Sovereign Ruler
Who will shepherd My people Israel."

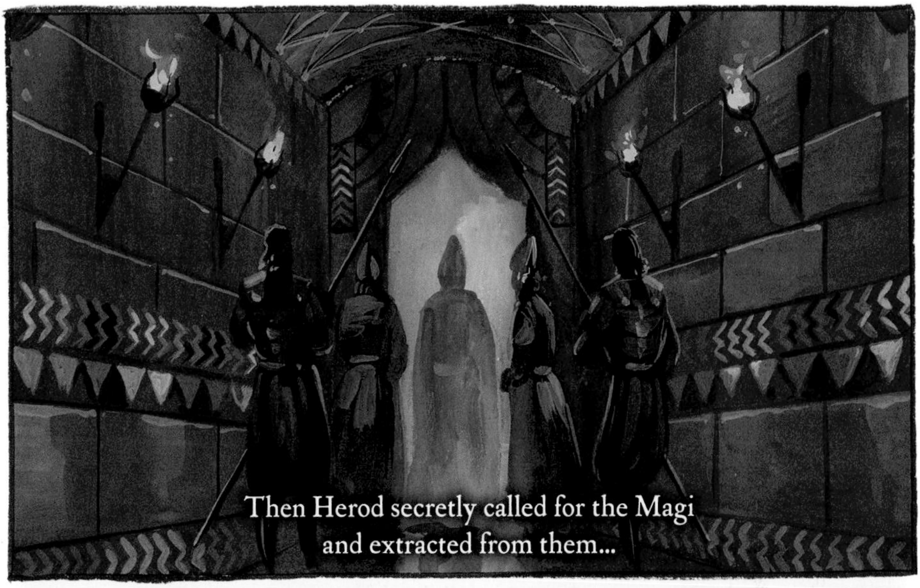
Then Herod secretly called for the Magi
and extracted from them...

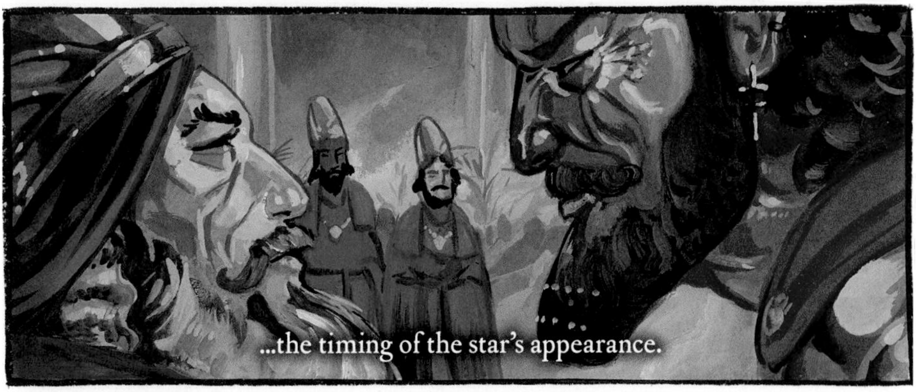
...the timing of the star's appearance.

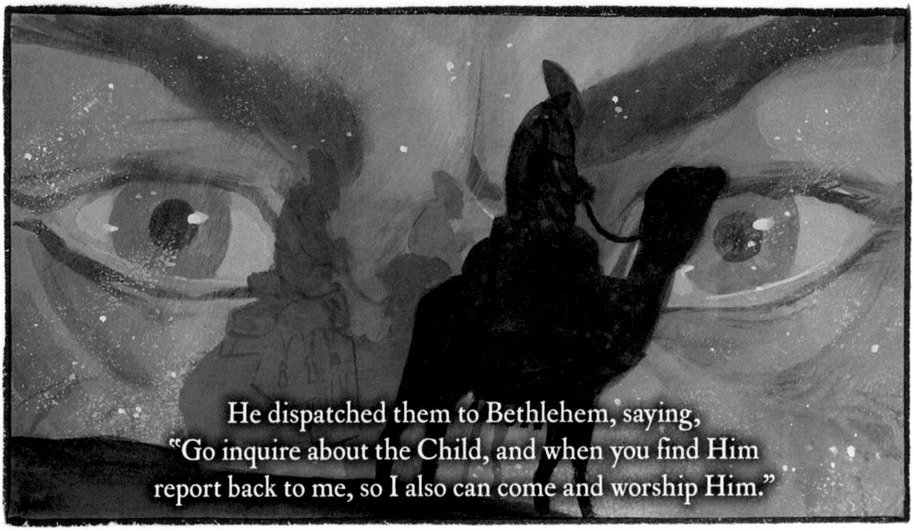
He dispatched them to Bethlehem, saying,
"Go inquire about the Child, and when you find Him
report back to me, so I also can come and worship Him."

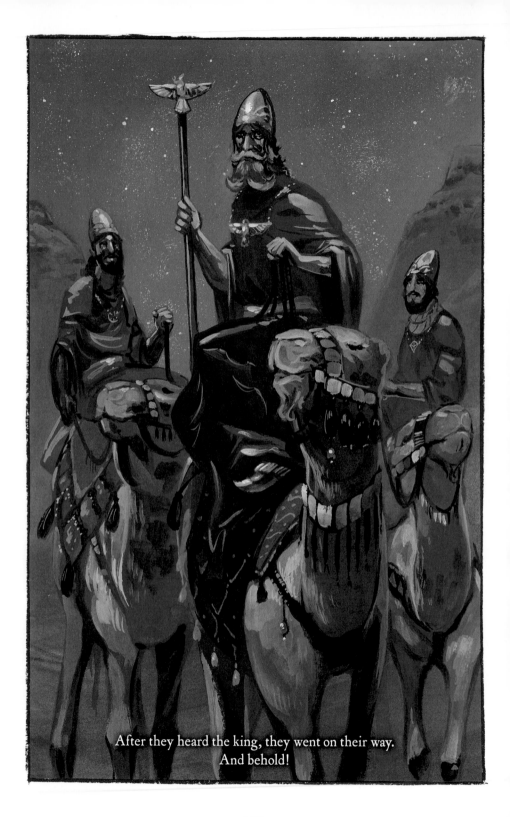

After they heard the king, they went on their way.
And behold!

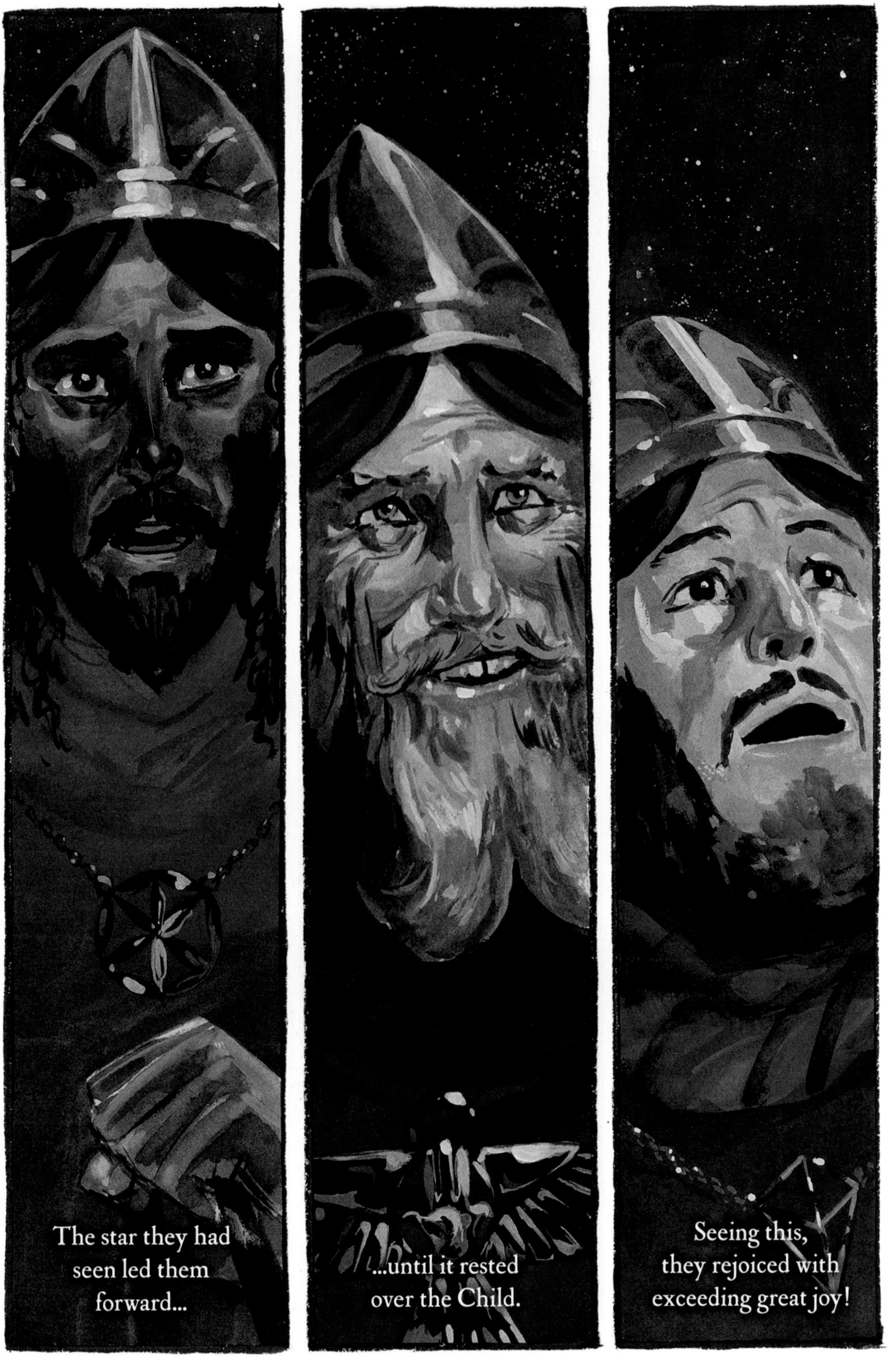
The star they had seen led them forward...
...until it rested over the Child.
Seeing this, they rejoiced with exceeding great joy!

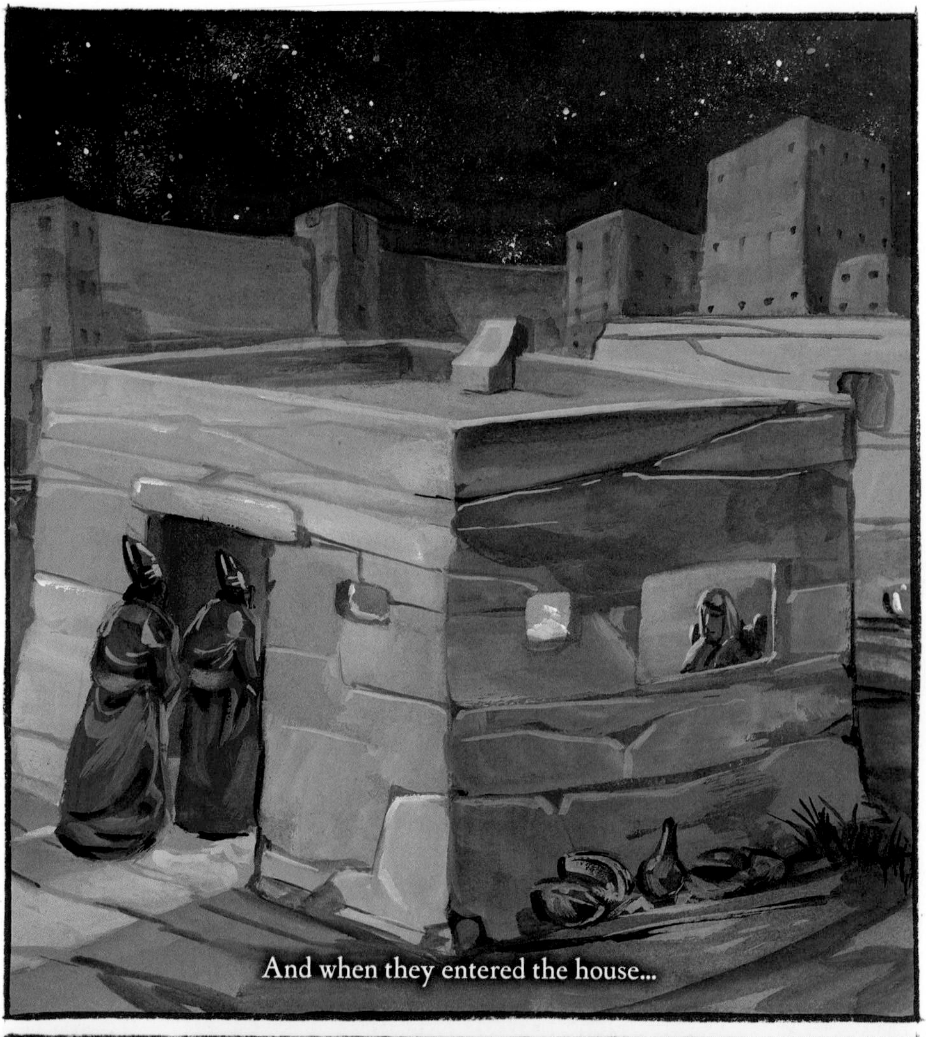
And when they entered the house...

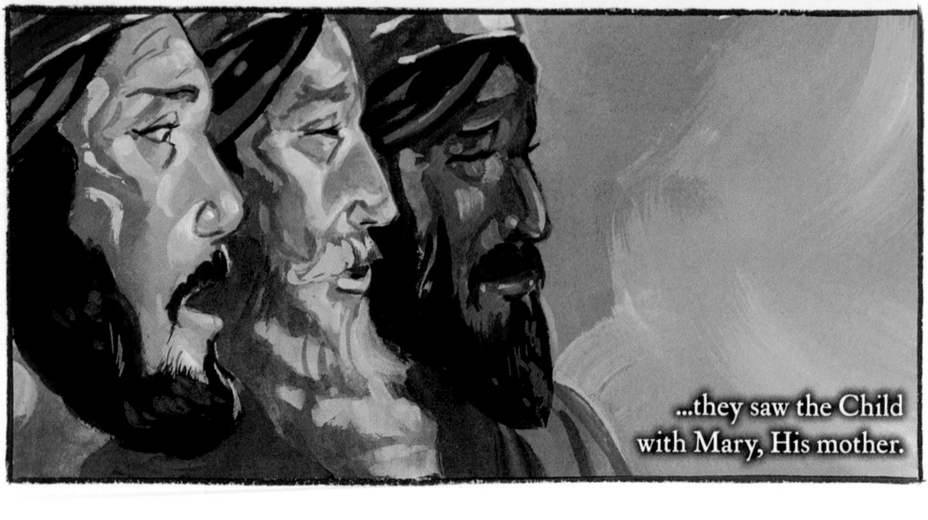
...they saw the Child
with Mary, His mother.

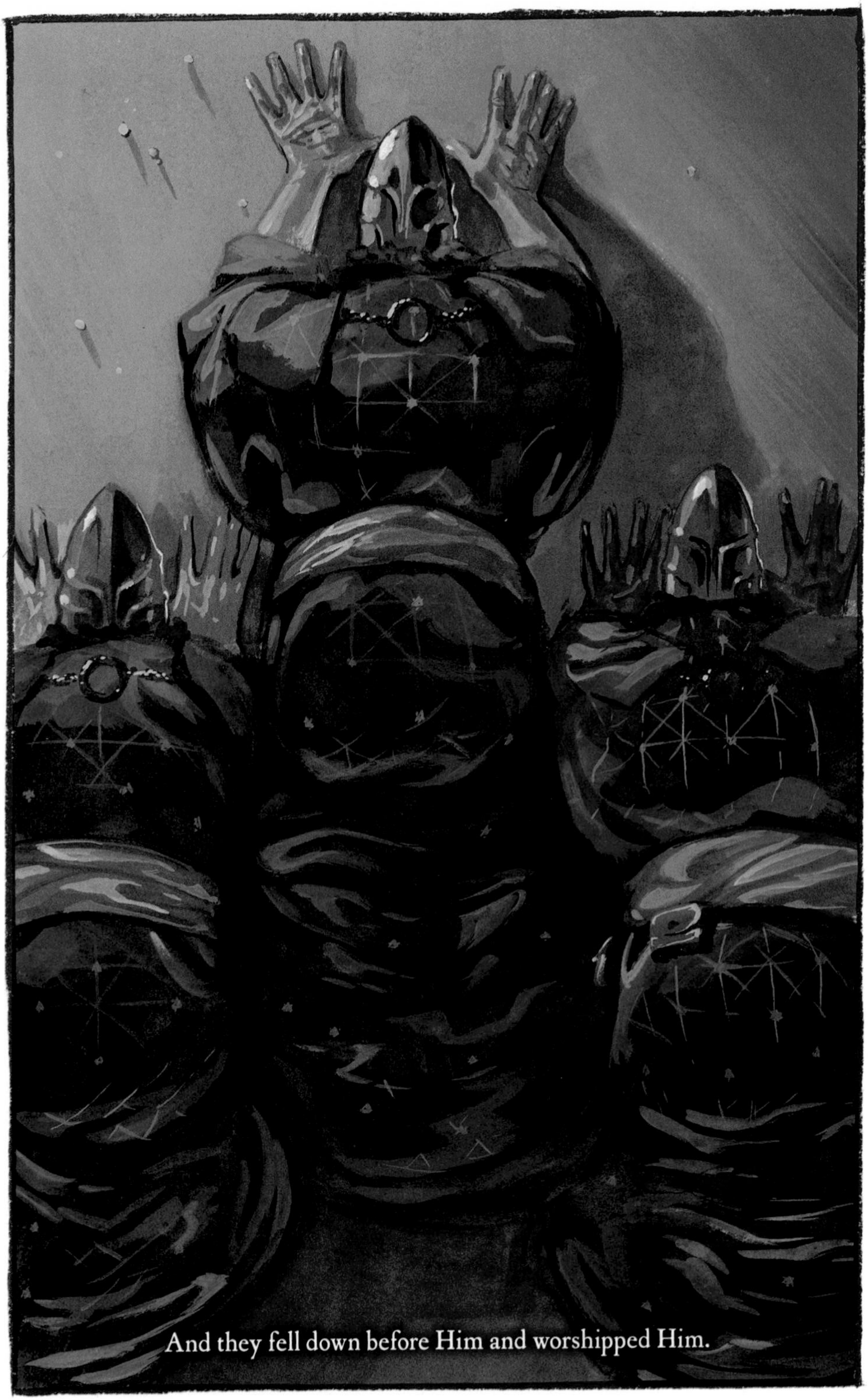
And they fell down before Him and worshipped Him.

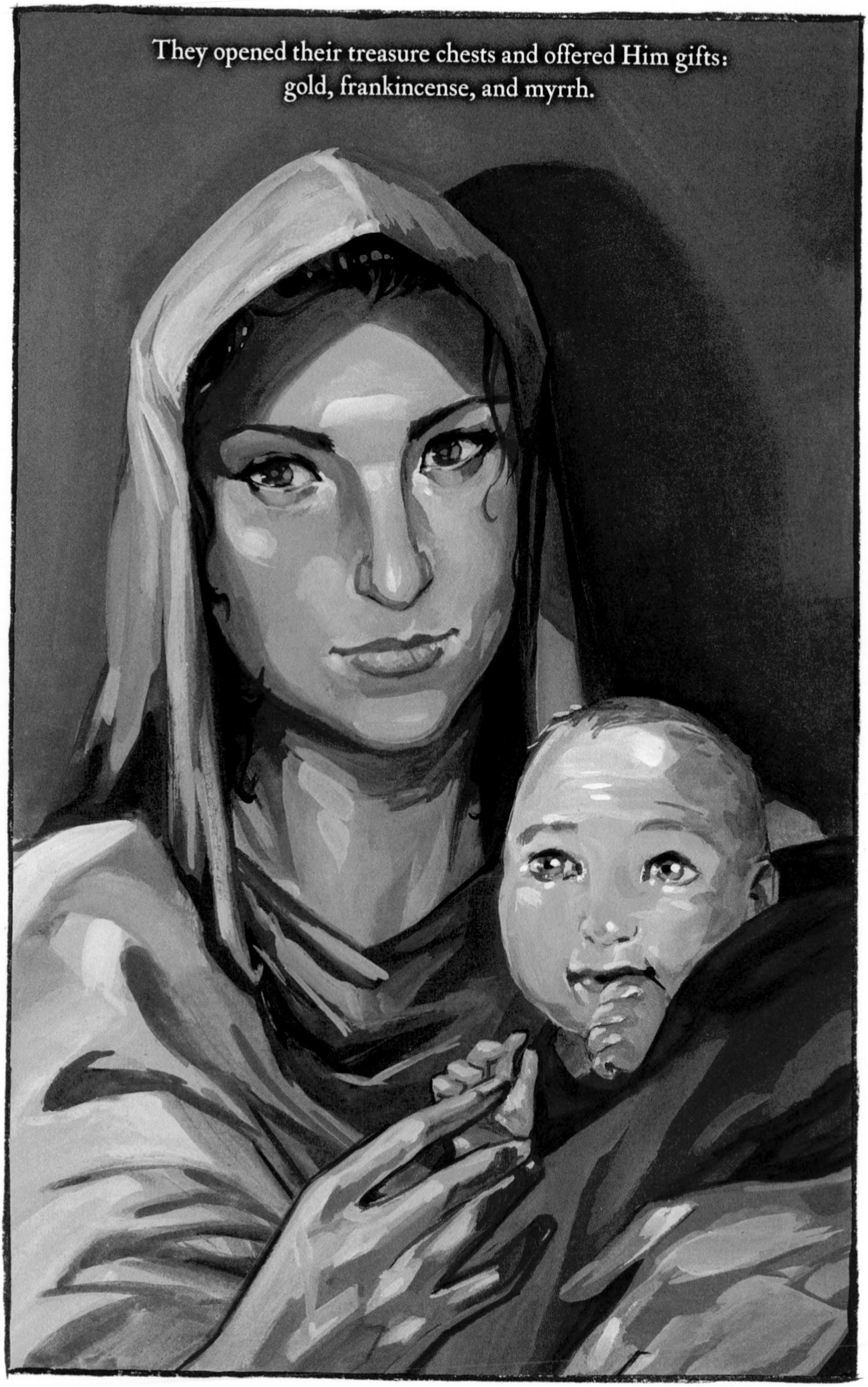
They opened their treasure chests and offered Him gifts: gold, frankincense, and myrrh.

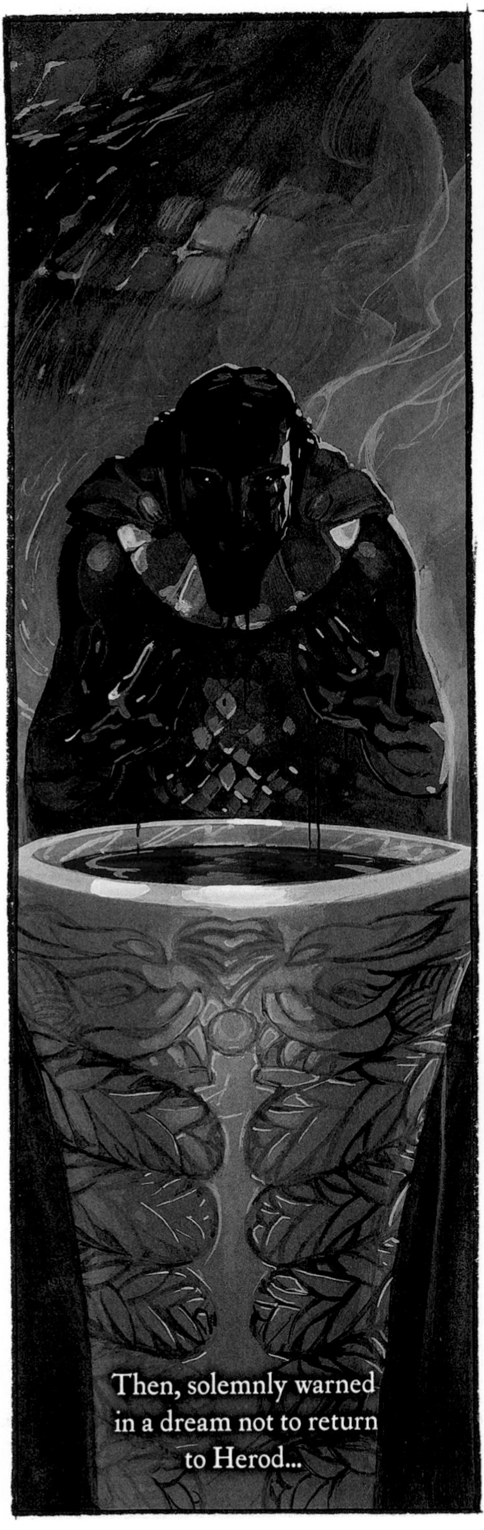
Then, solemnly warned in a dream not to return to Herod...

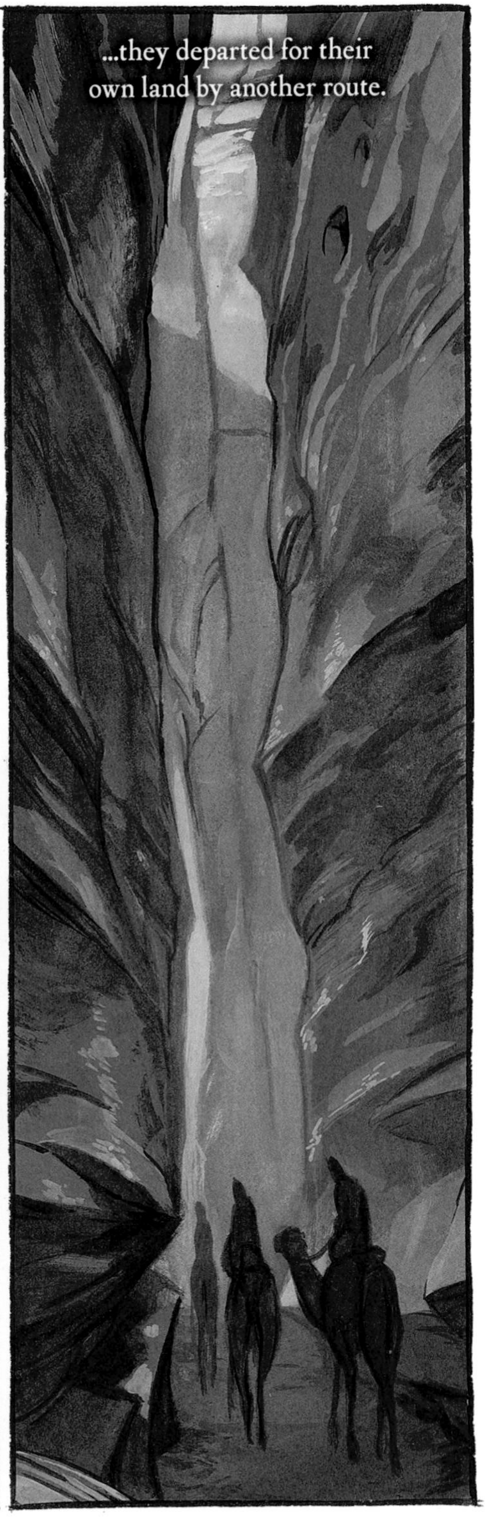
...they departed for their own land by another route.

FLIGHT TO EGYPT

MATTHEW 2:13–23

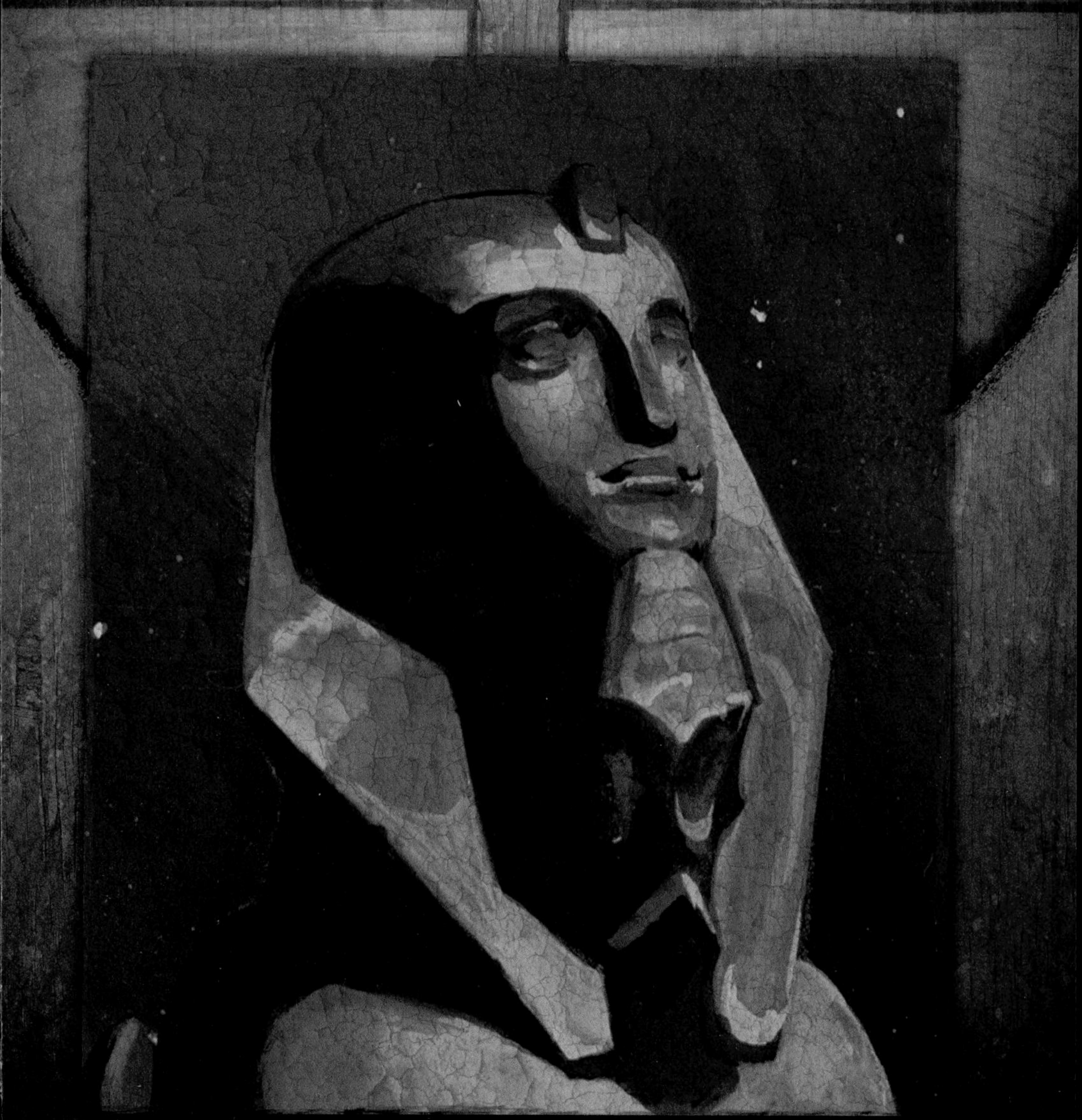

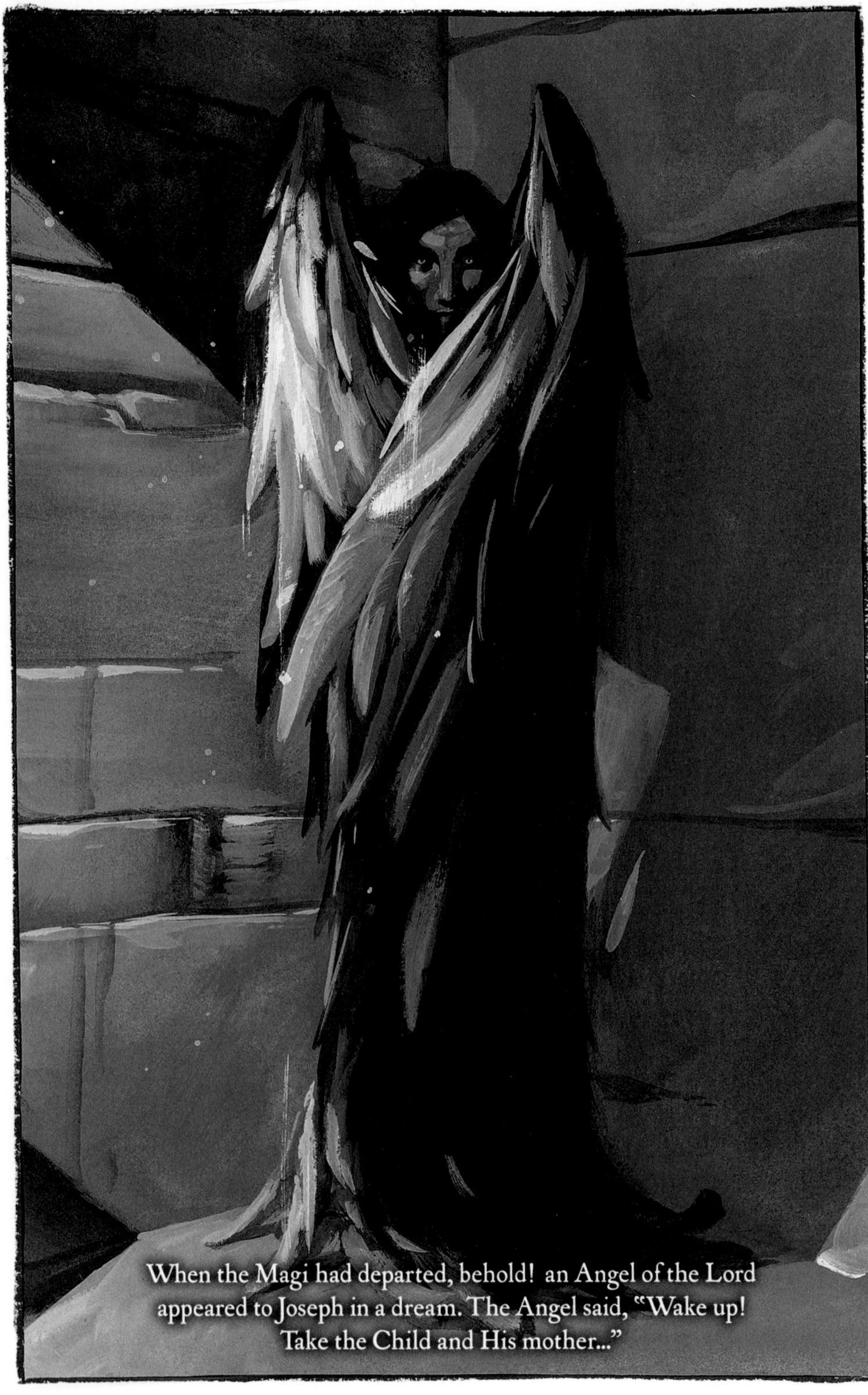
When the Magi had departed, behold! an Angel of the Lord appeared to Joseph in a dream. The Angel said, "Wake up! Take the Child and His mother..."

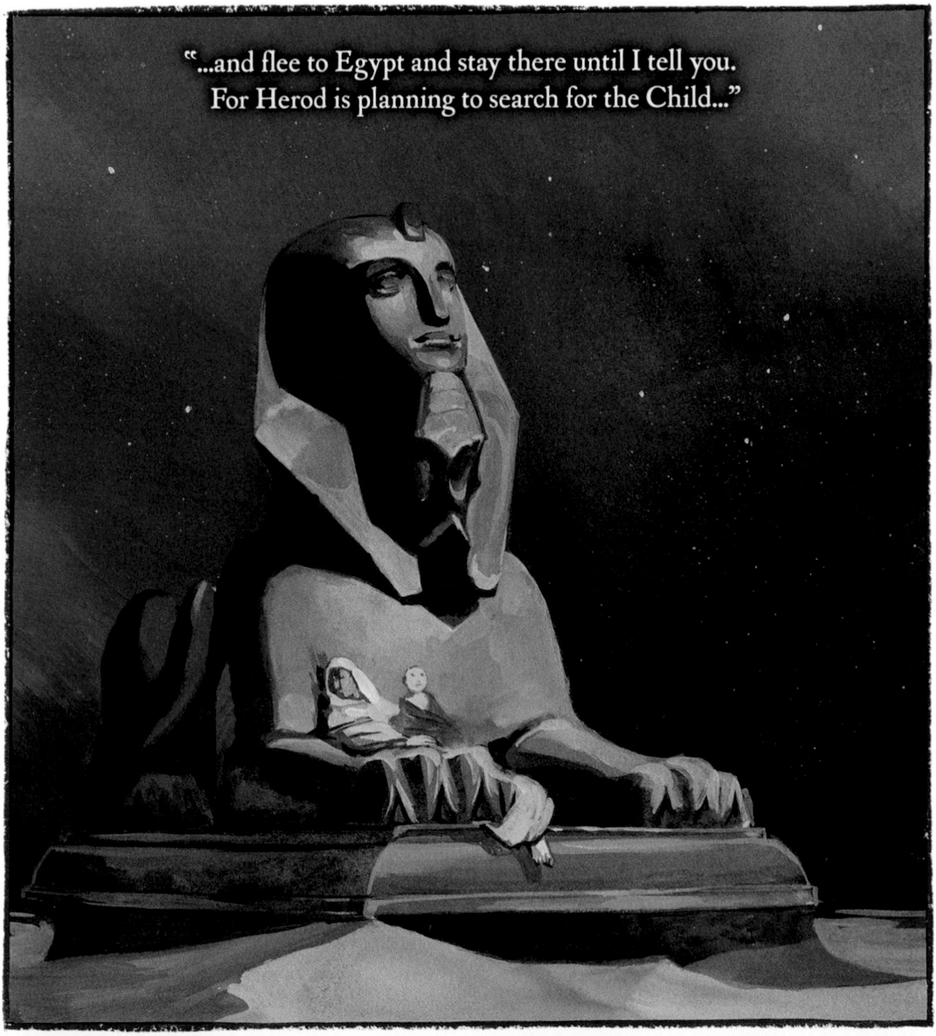
"...and flee to Egypt and stay there until I tell you. For Herod is planning to search for the Child..."

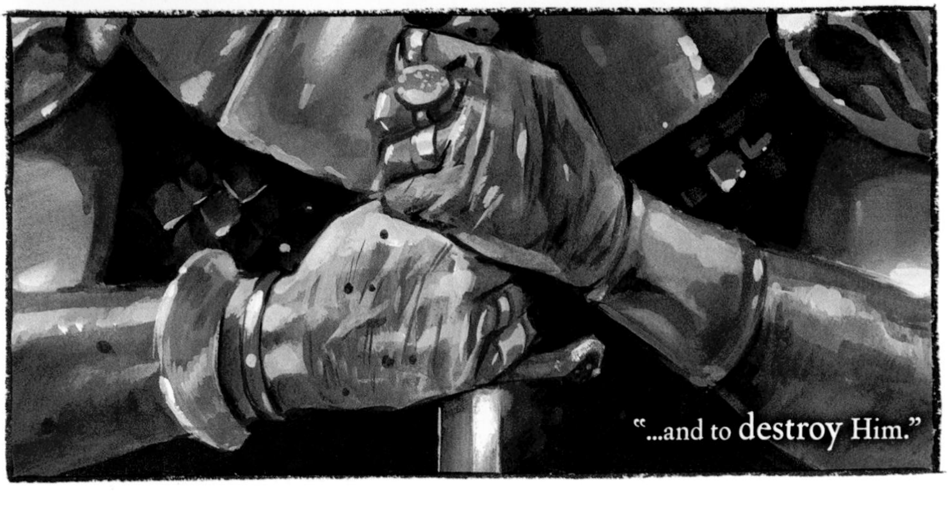
"...and to destroy Him."

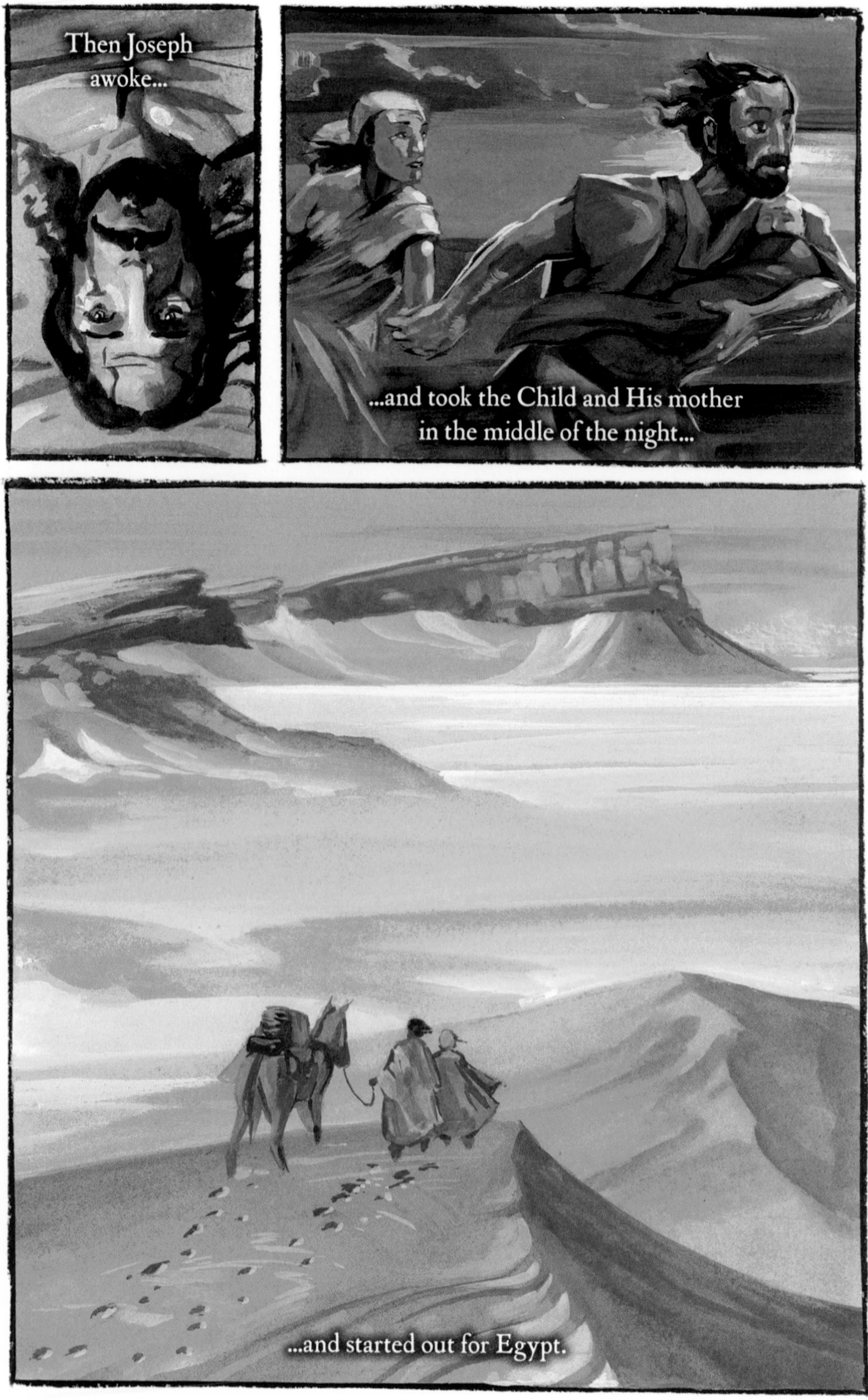
Then Joseph awoke...
...and took the Child and His mother in the middle of the night...
...and started out for Egypt.

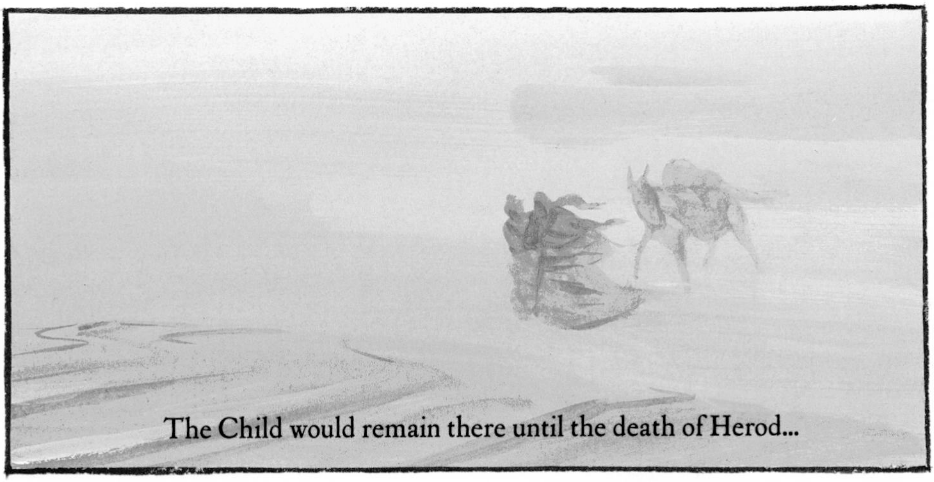
The Child would remain there until the death of Herod...

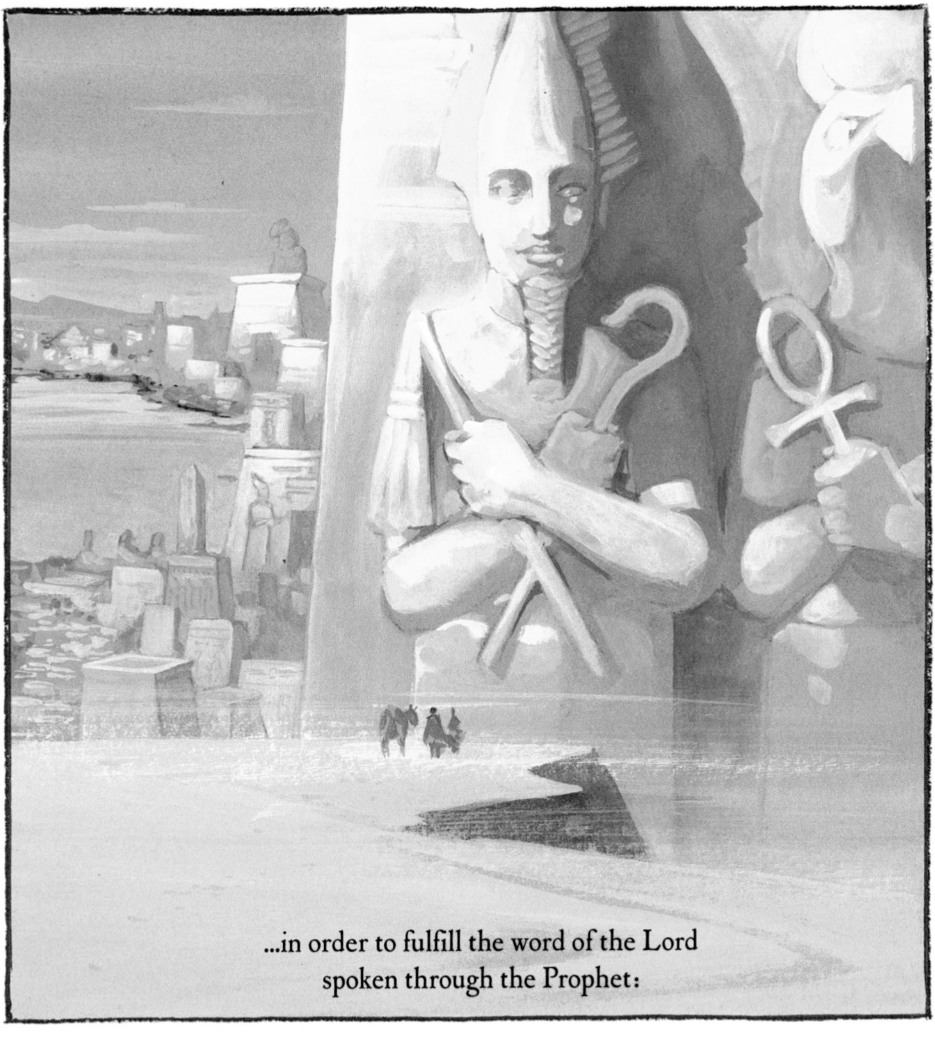
...in order to fulfill the word of the Lord
spoken through the Prophet:

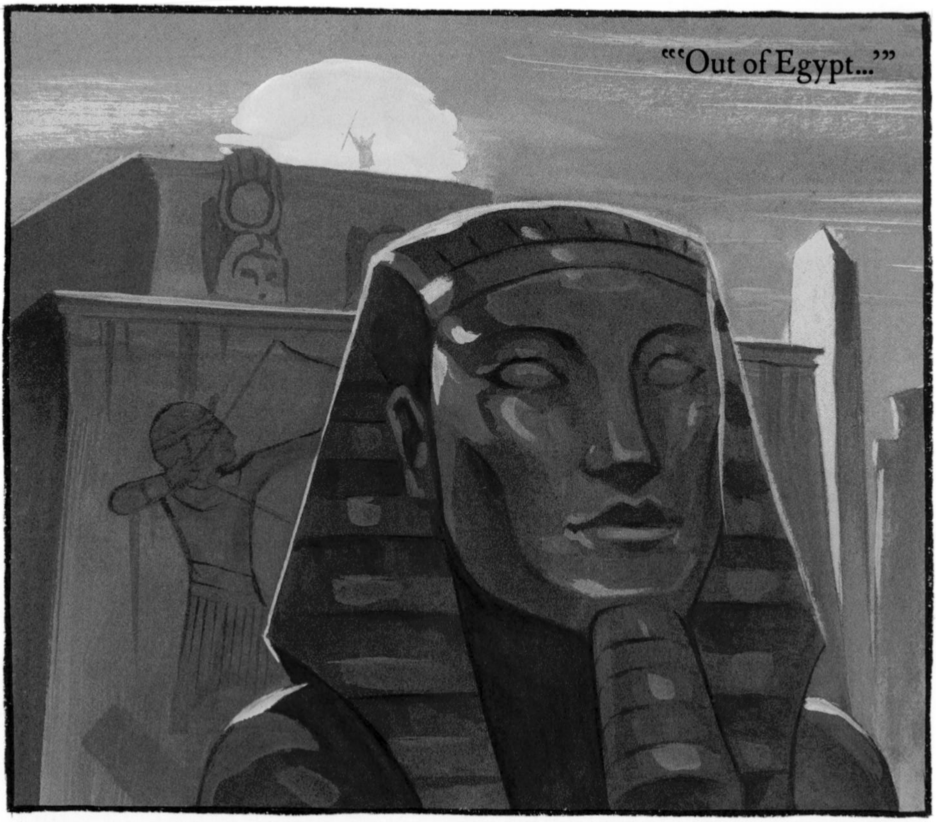
"'Out of Egypt...'"

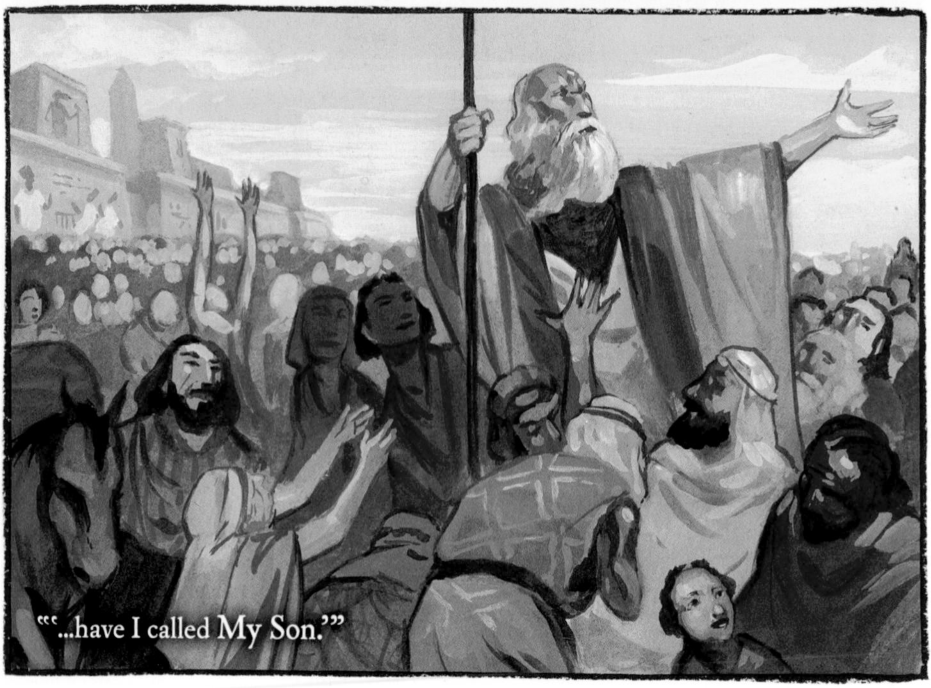
"'...have I called My Son.'"

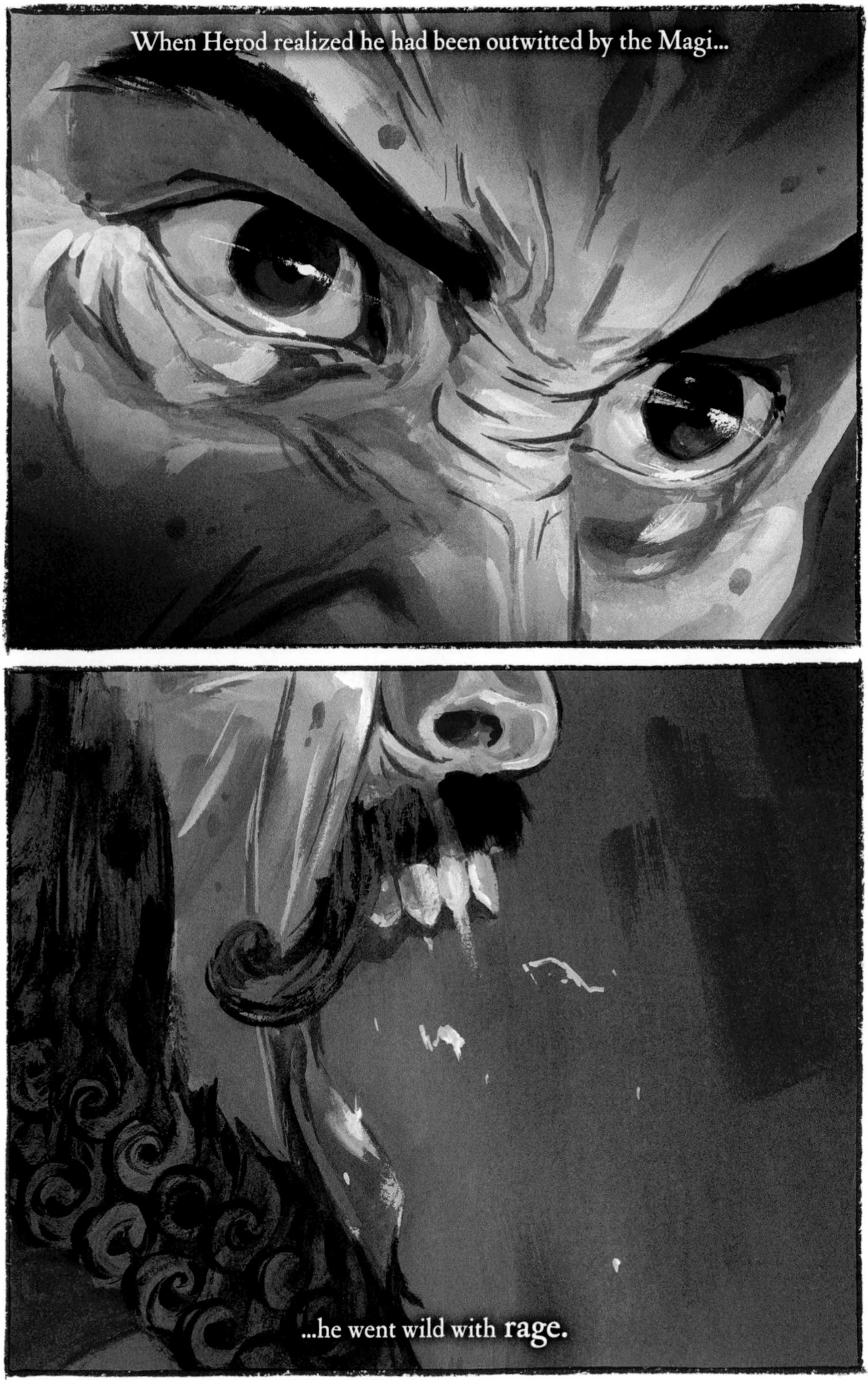
When Herod realized he had been outwitted by the Magi...
...he went wild with rage.

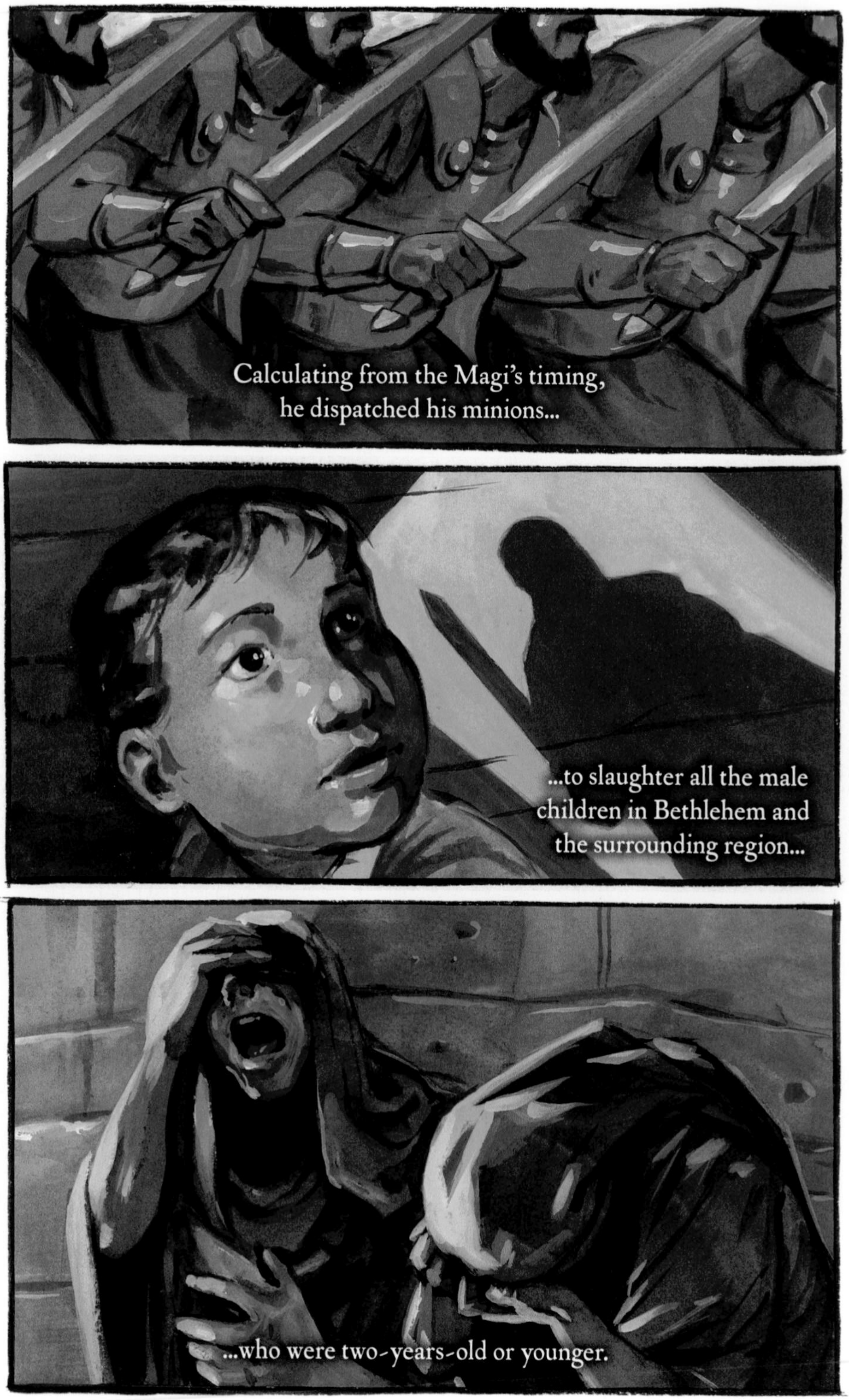
Calculating from the Magi's timing, he dispatched his minions...
...to slaughter all the male children in Bethlehem and the surrounding region...
...who were two-years-old or younger.

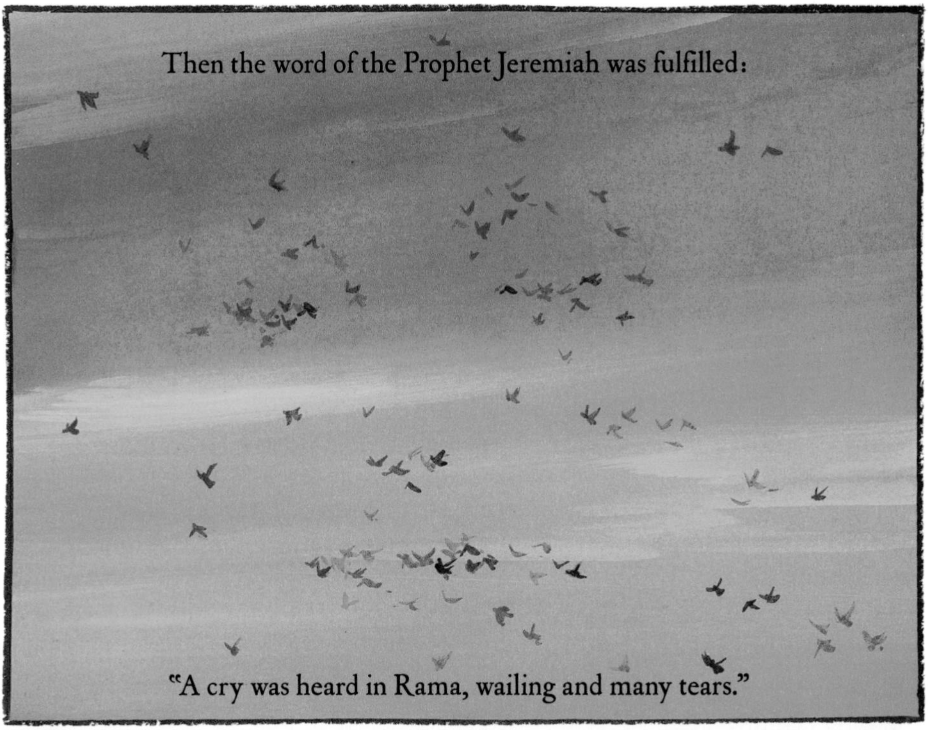
Then the word of the Prophet Jeremiah was fulfilled:
"A cry was heard in Rama, wailing and many tears."

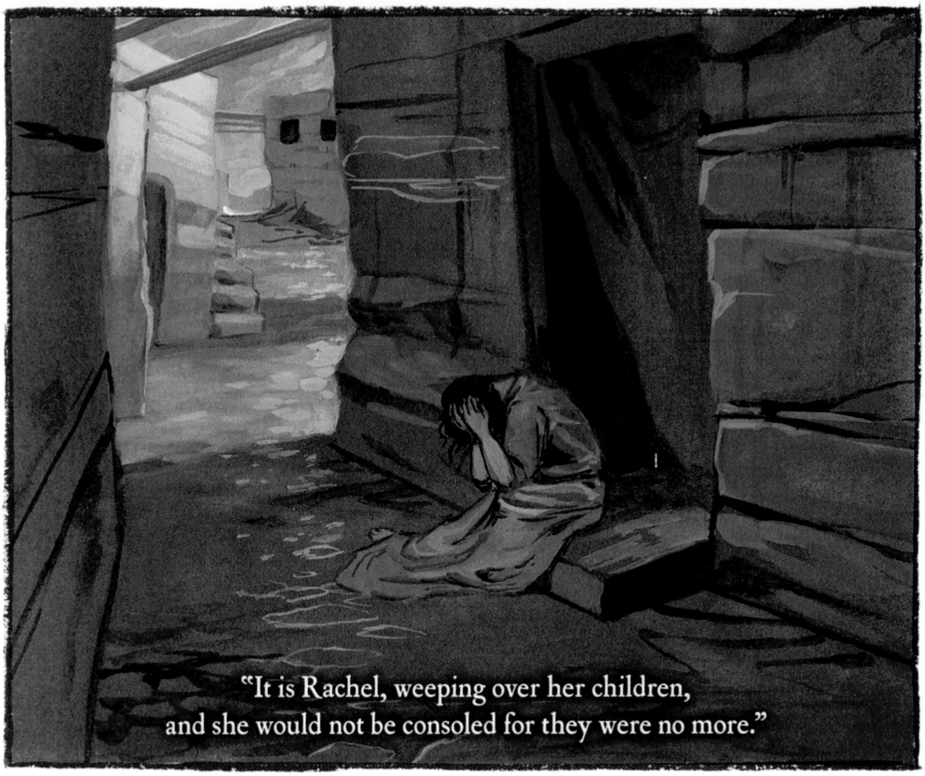
"It is Rachel, weeping over her children,
and she would not be consoled for they were no more."

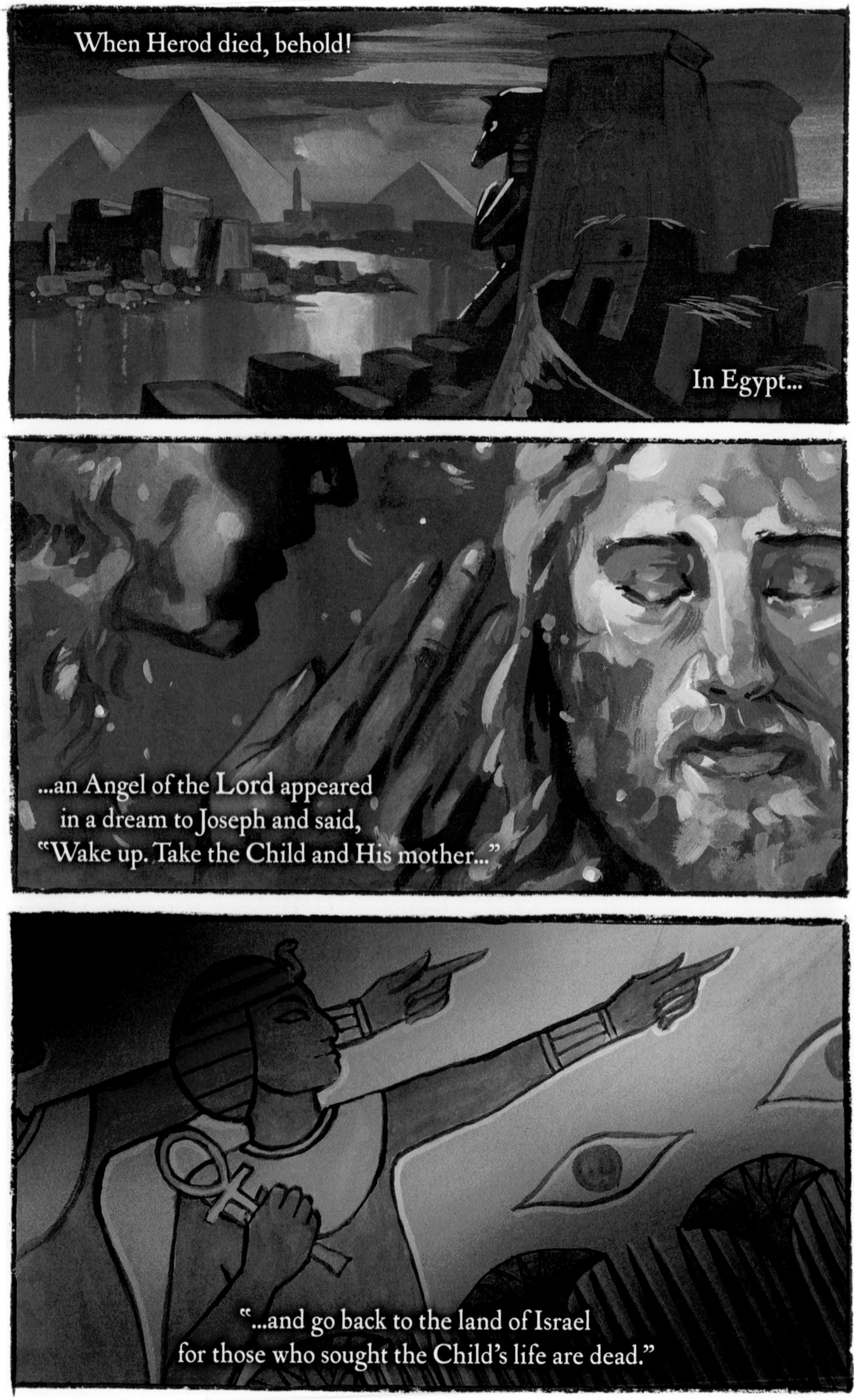
When Herod died, behold!
In Egypt...
...an Angel of the Lord appeared in a dream to Joseph and said, "Wake up. Take the Child and His mother..."
"...and go back to the land of Israel for those who sought the Child's life are dead."

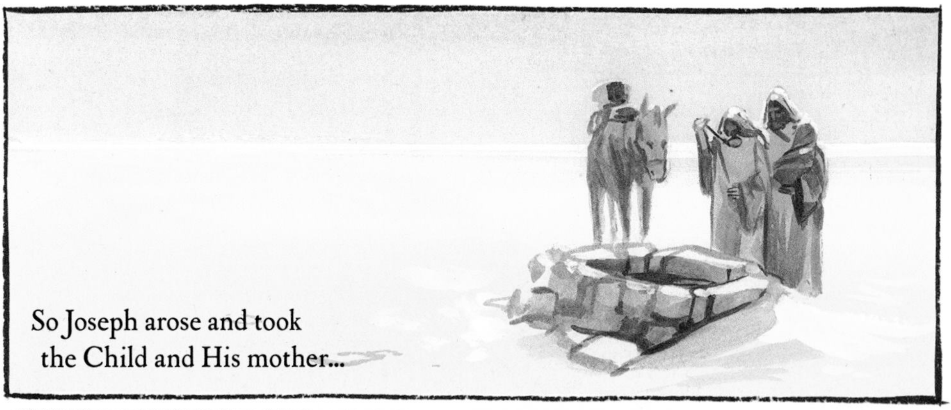
So Joseph arose and took the Child and His mother...

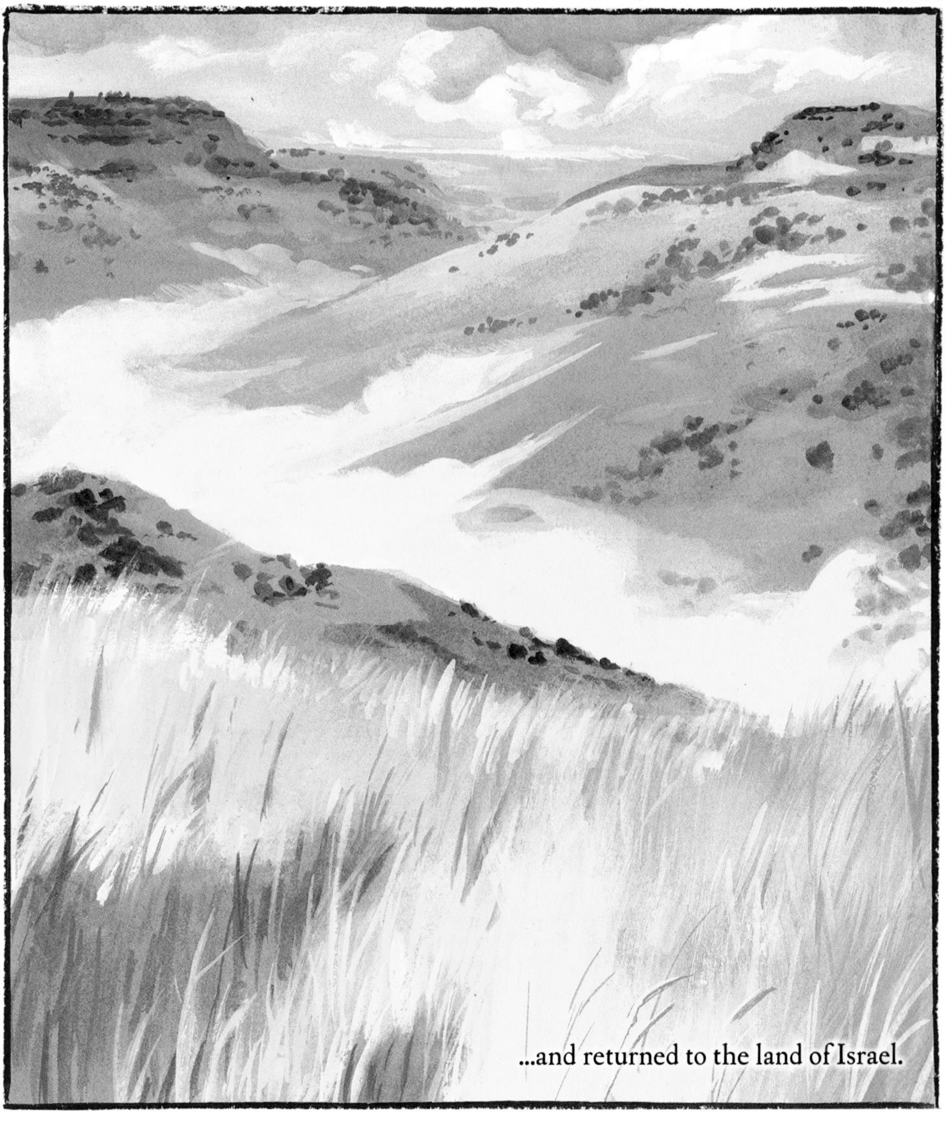
...and returned to the land of Israel.

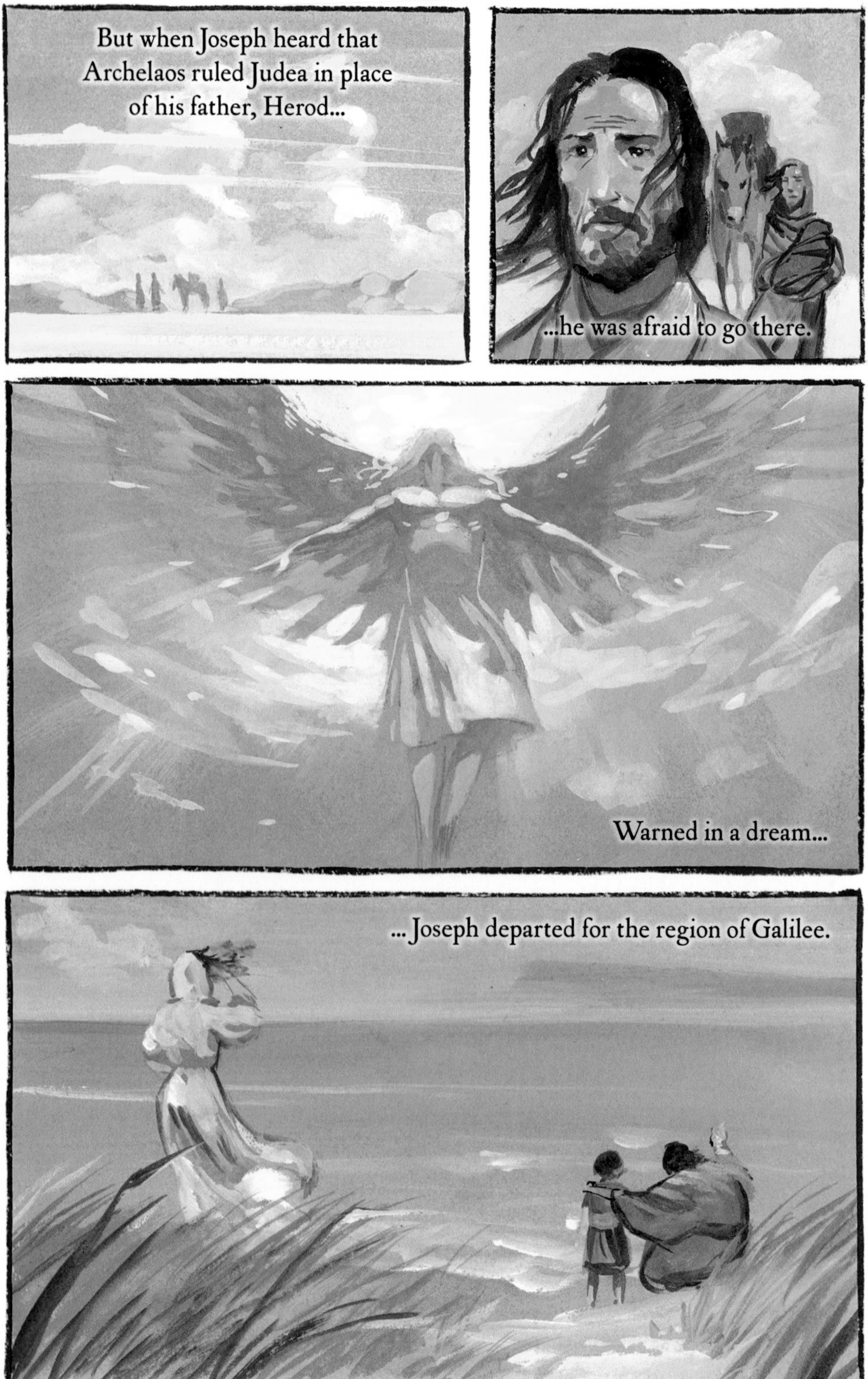
But when Joseph heard that Archelaos ruled Judea in place of his father, Herod...
...he was afraid to go there.
Warned in a dream...
...Joseph departed for the region of Galilee.

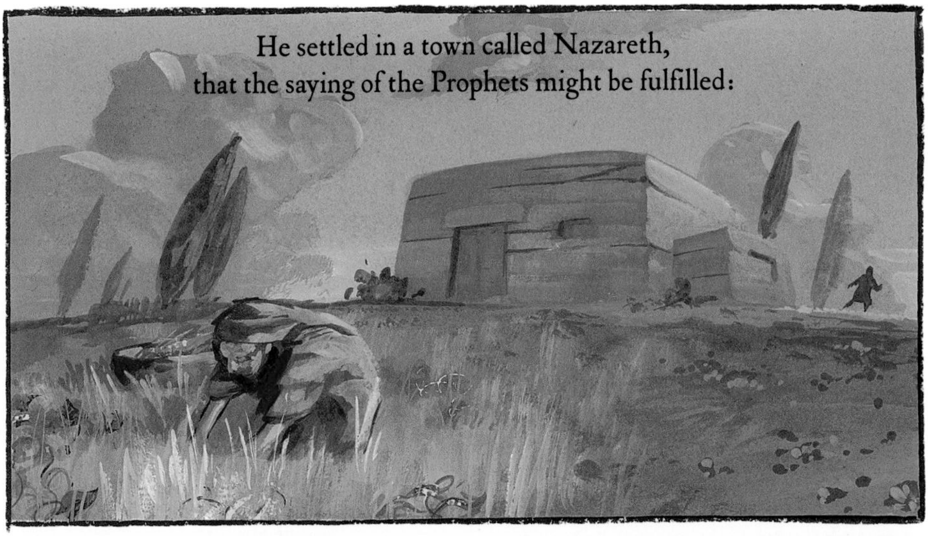
He settled in a town called Nazareth,
that the saying of the Prophets might be fulfilled:

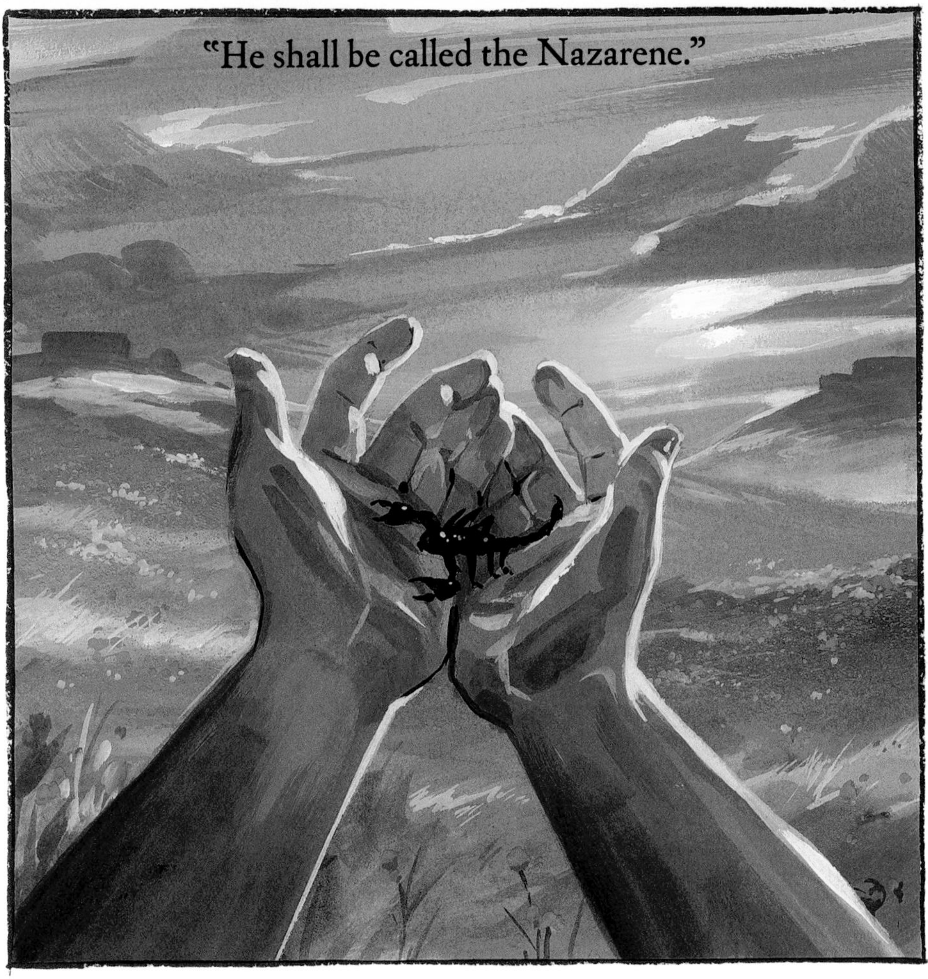
"He shall be called the Nazarene."

Boy Jesus

LUKE 2:41–52

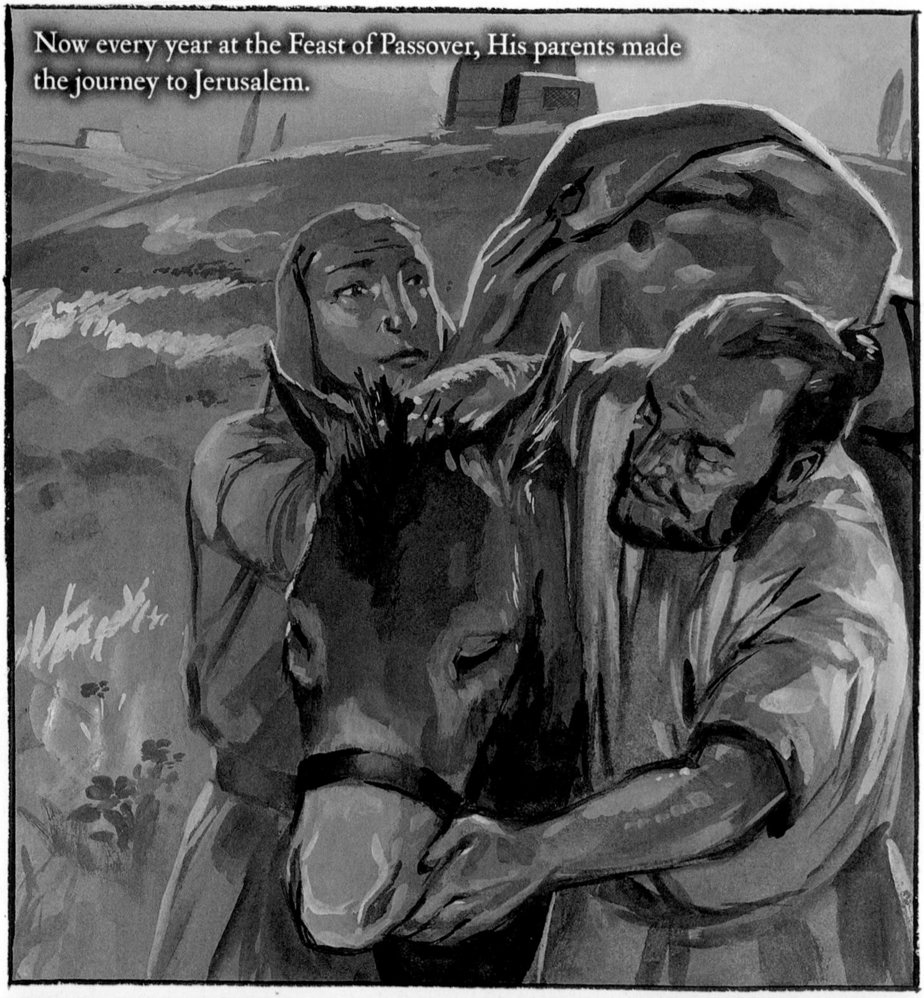
Now every year at the Feast of Passover, His parents made the journey to Jerusalem.

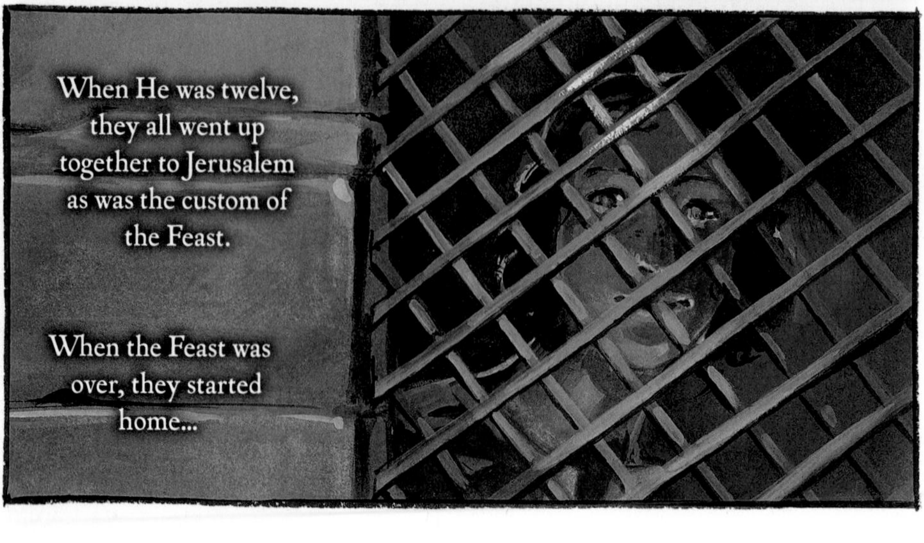
When He was twelve, they all went up together to Jerusalem as was the custom of the Feast.
When the Feast was over, they started home...

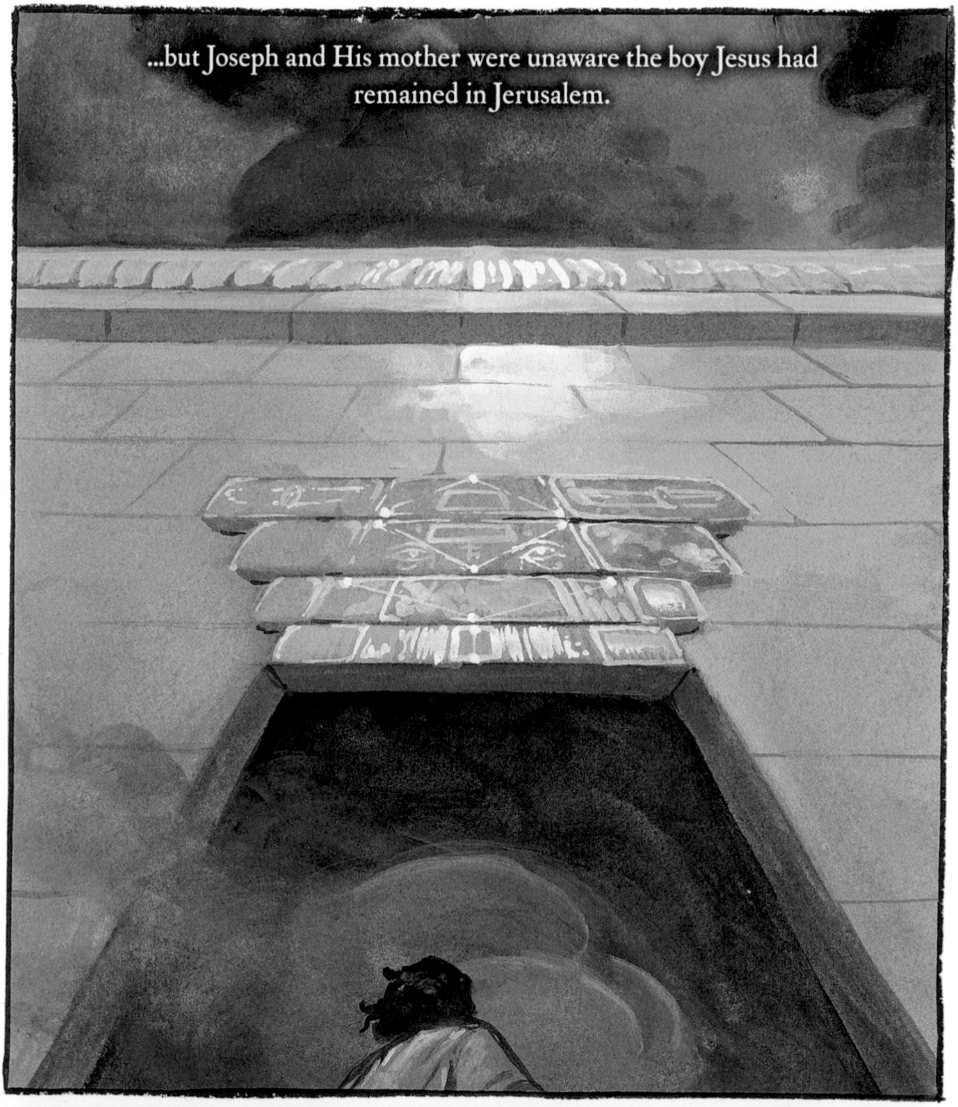
...but Joseph and His mother were unaware the boy Jesus had remained in Jerusalem.

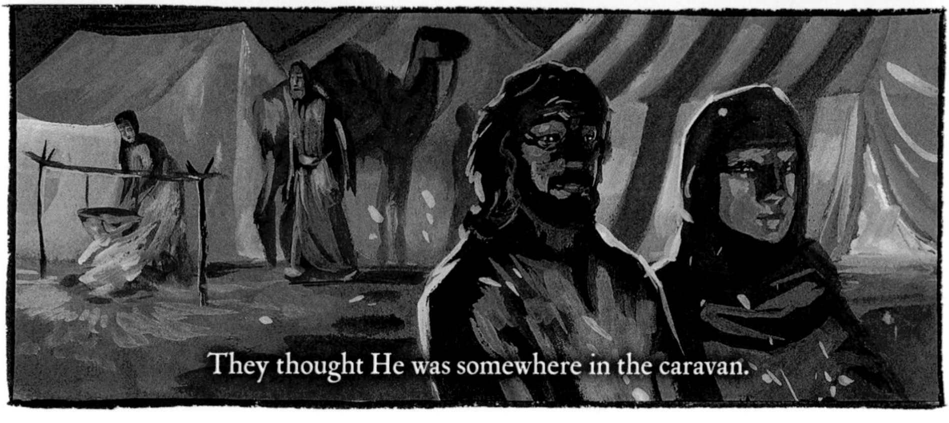
They thought He was somewhere in the caravan.

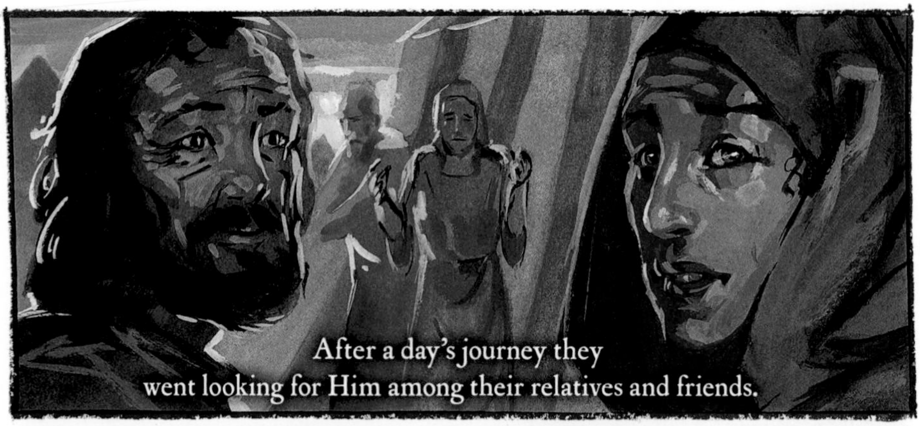
After a day's journey they
went looking for Him among their relatives and friends.

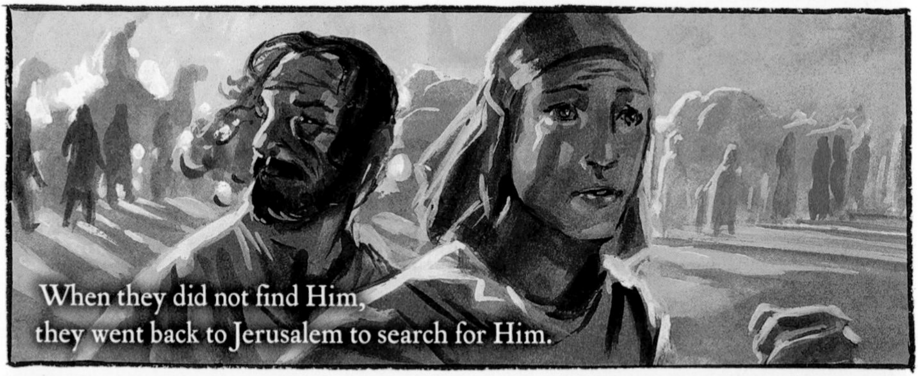
When they did not find Him,
they went back to Jerusalem to search for Him.

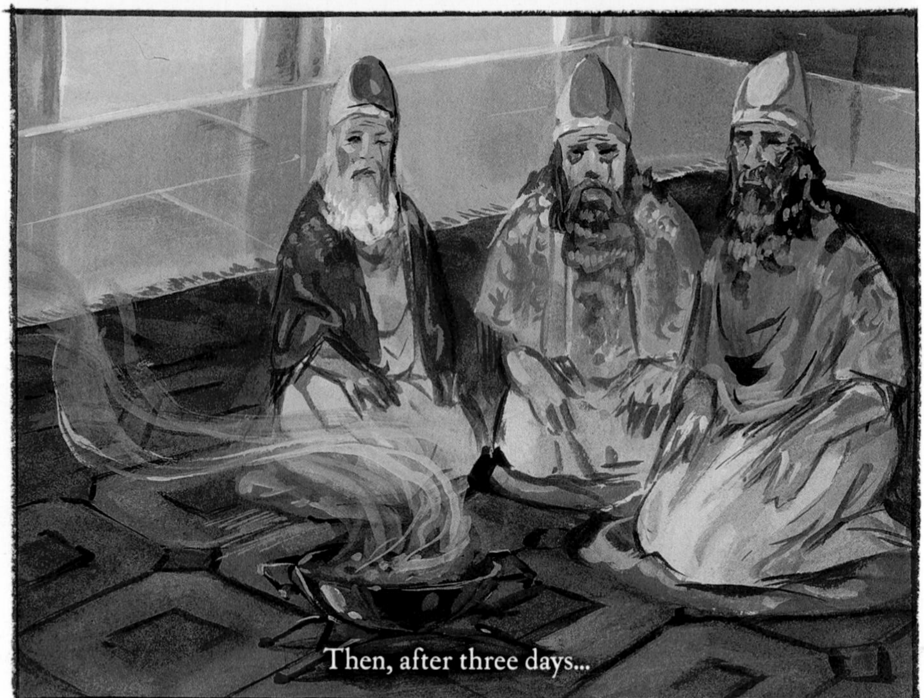
Then, after three days...

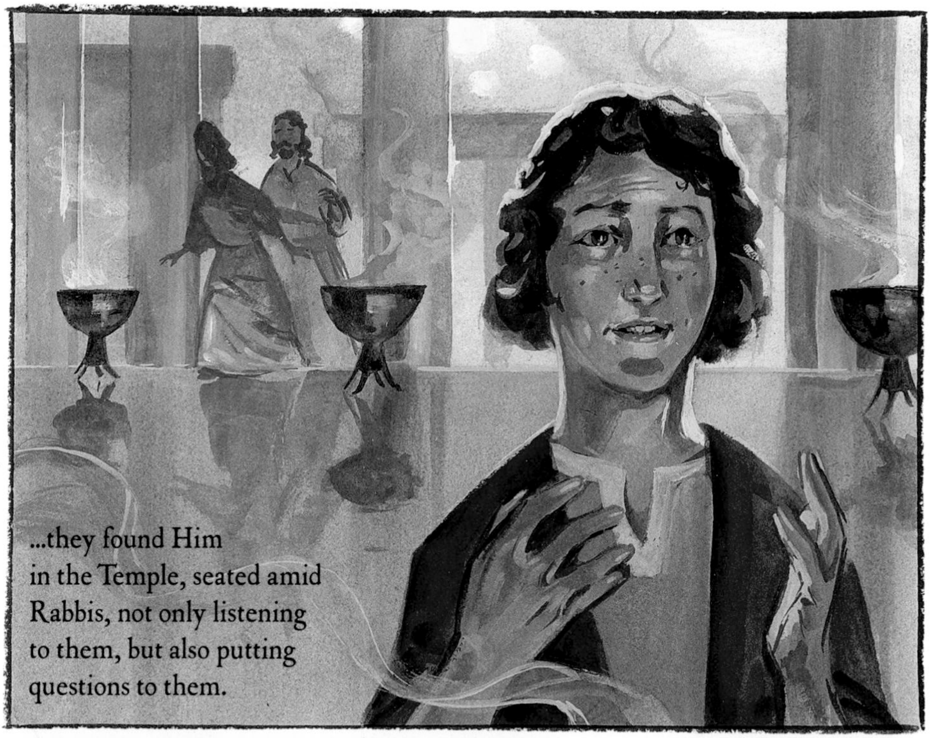
...they found Him in the Temple, seated amid Rabbis, not only listening to them, but also putting questions to them.

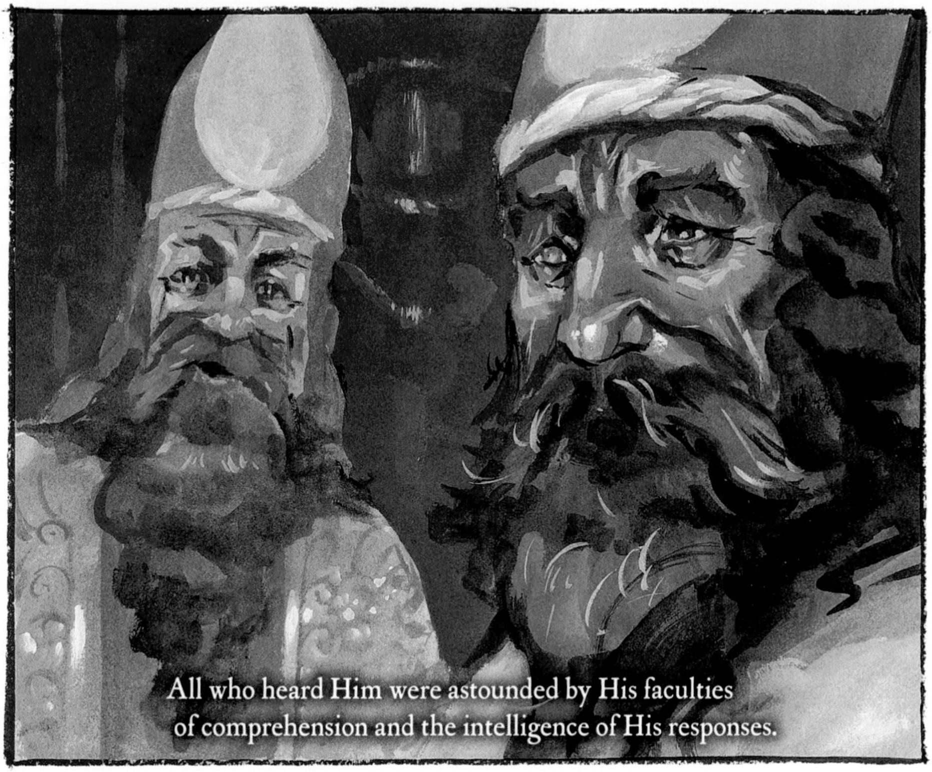
All who heard Him were astounded by His faculties of comprehension and the intelligence of His responses.

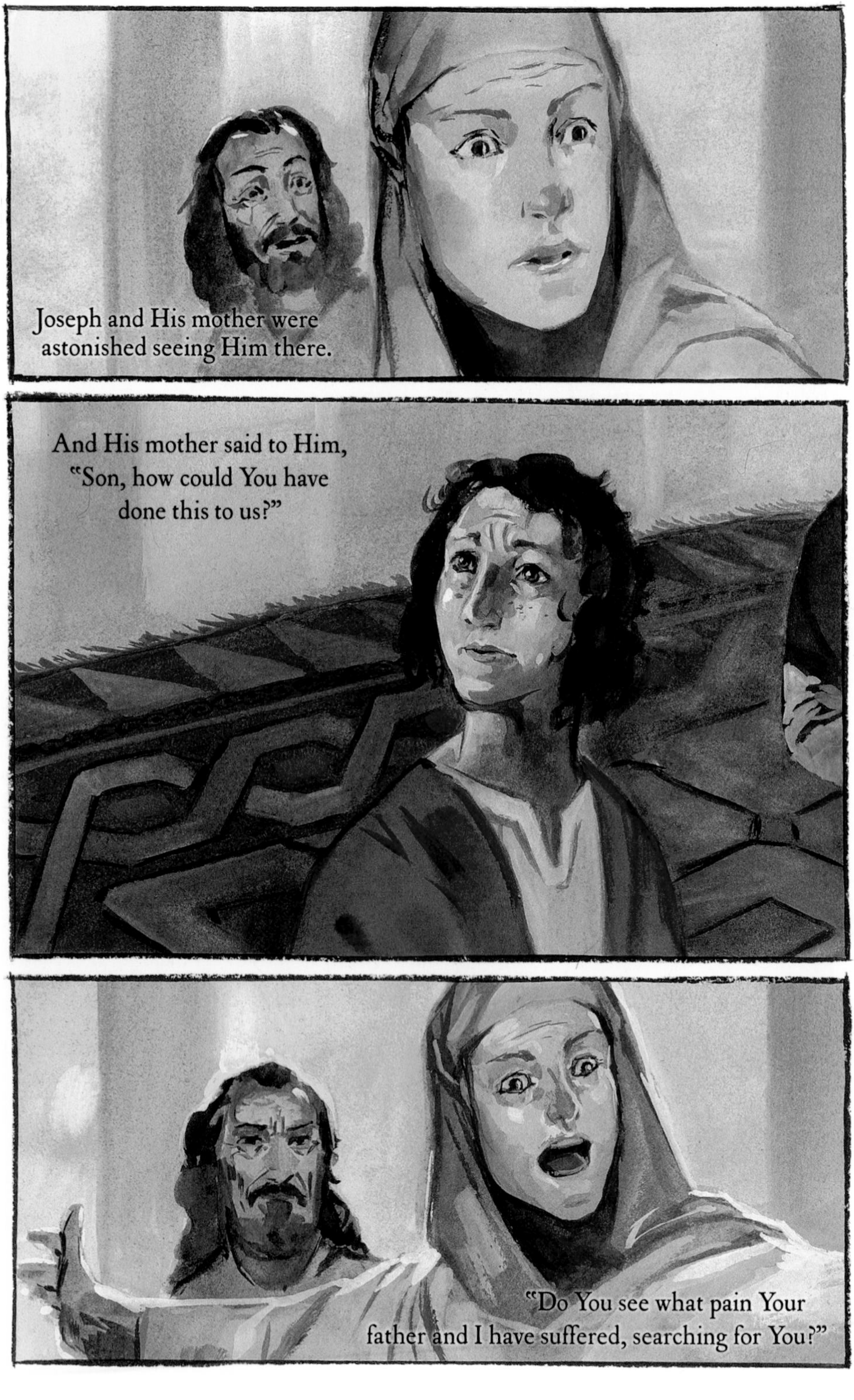
Joseph and His mother were astonished seeing Him there.
And His mother said to Him, "Son, how could You have done this to us?"
"Do You see what pain Your father and I have suffered, searching for You?"

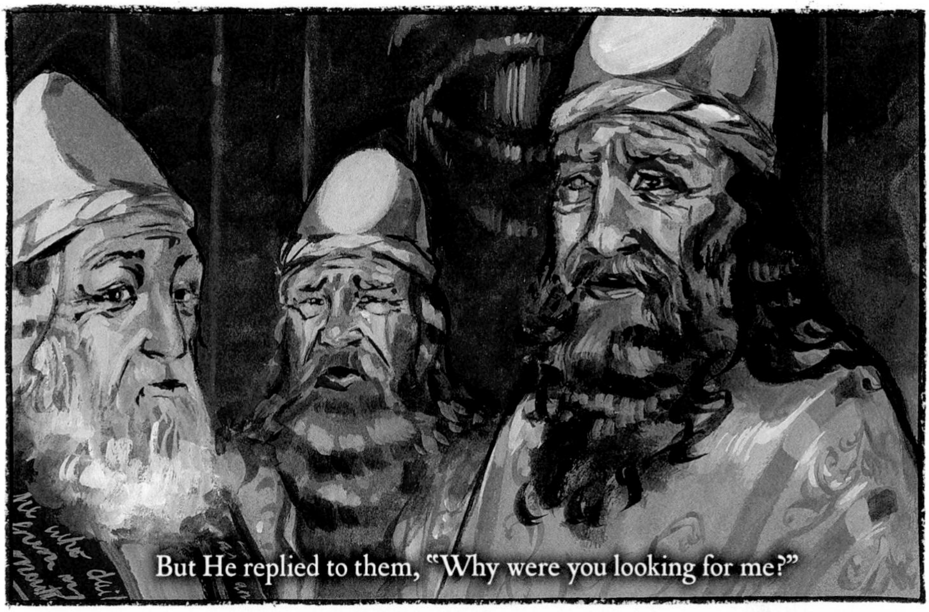
But He replied to them, "Why were you looking for me?"

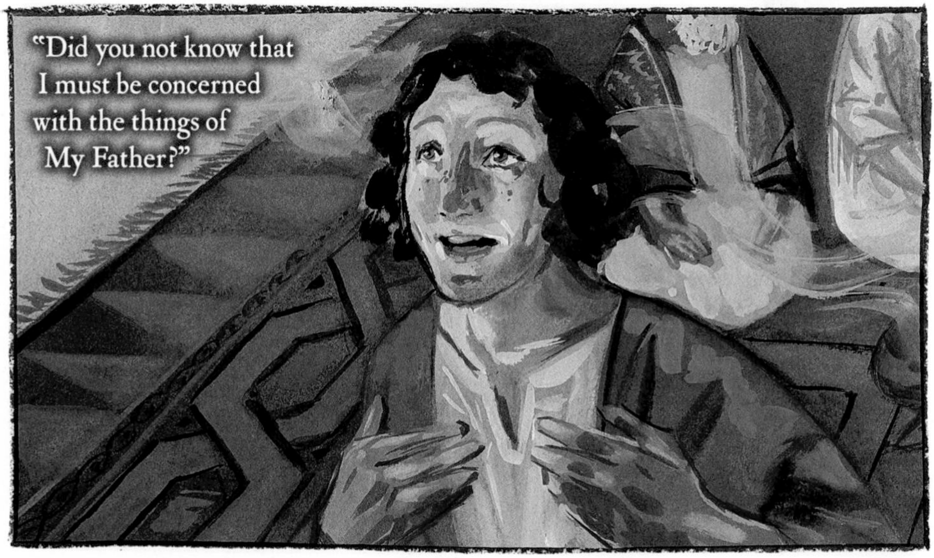
"Did you not know that I must be concerned with the things of My Father?"

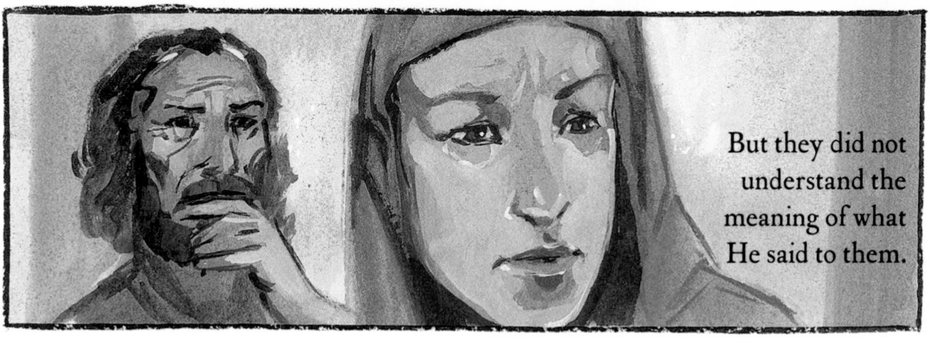
But they did not understand the meaning of what He said to them.

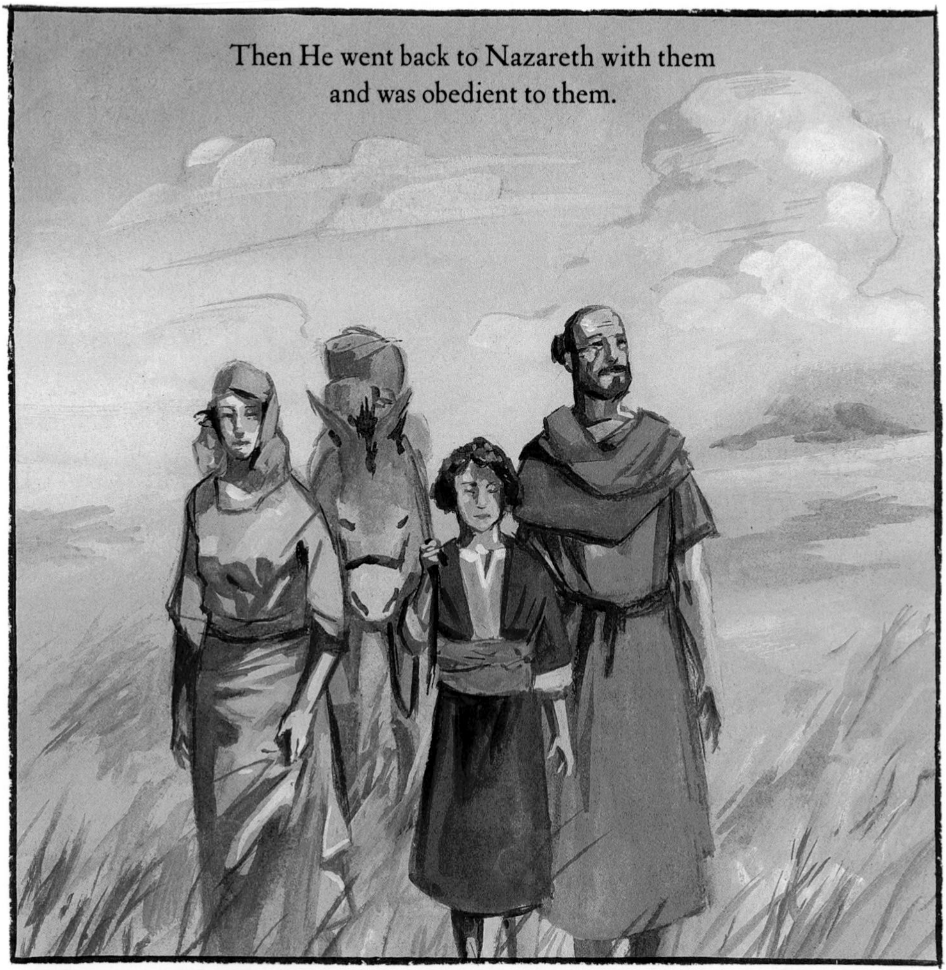
Then He went back to Nazareth with them
and was obedient to them.

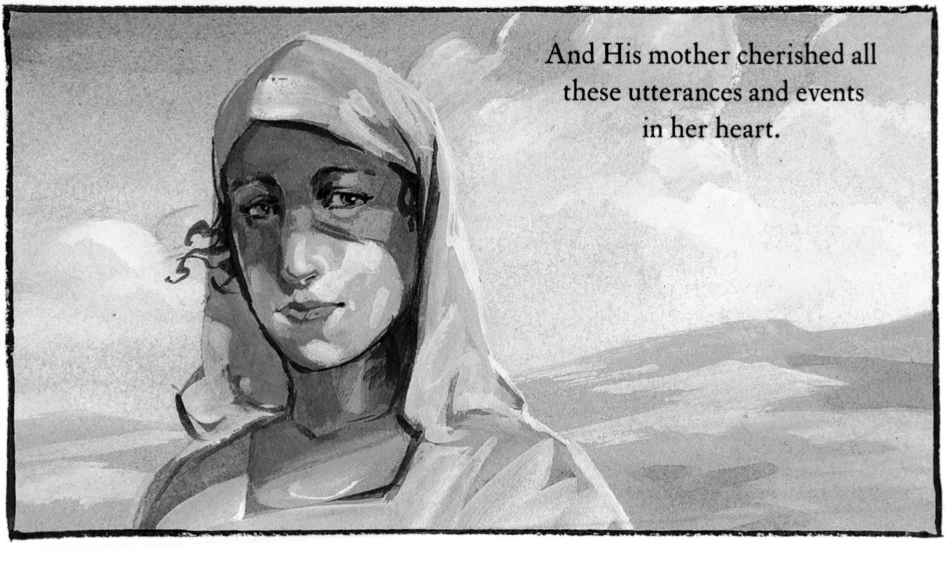
And His mother cherished all
these utterances and events
in her heart.

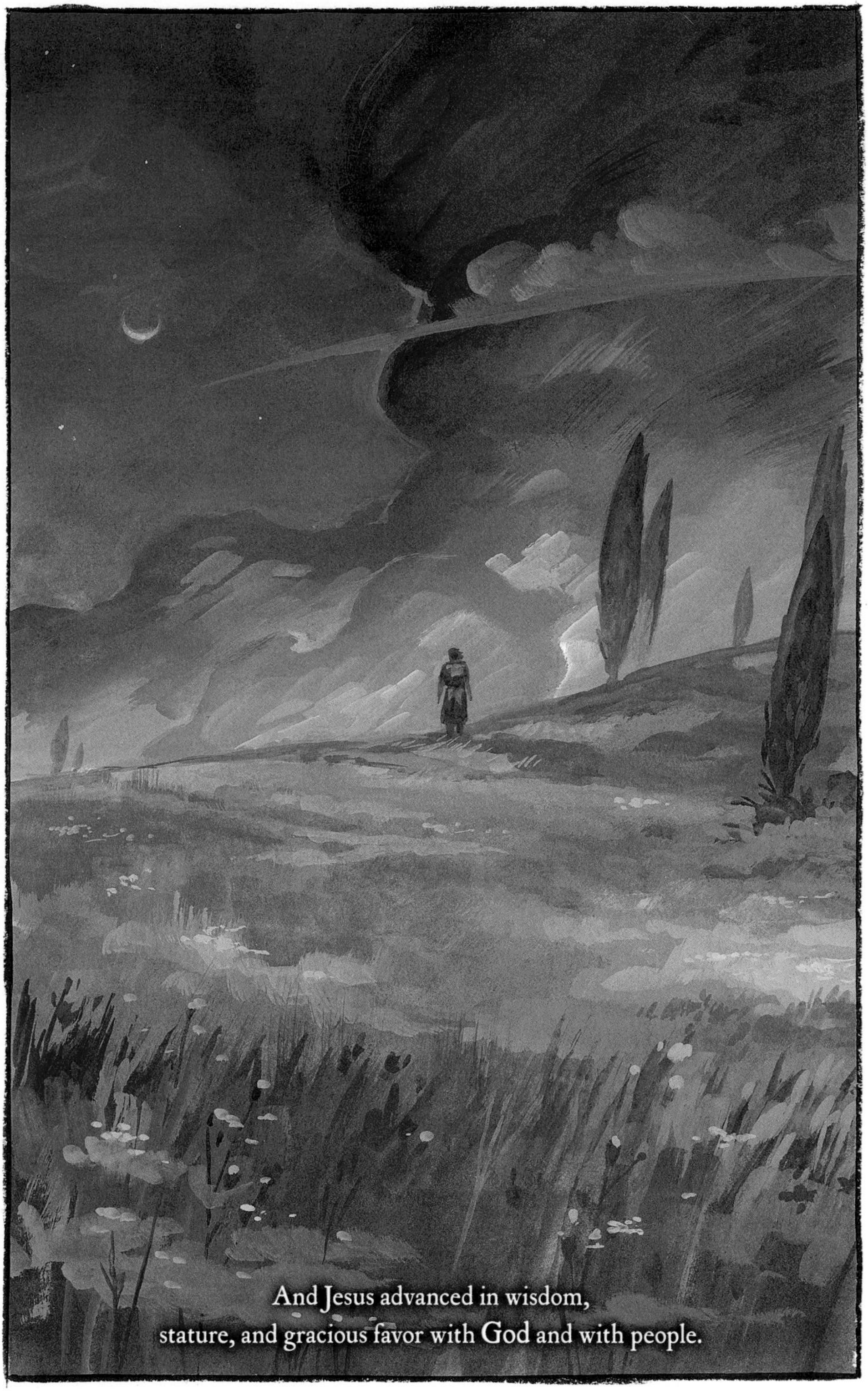
And Jesus advanced in wisdom,
stature, and gracious favor with God and with people.

Voice in the Desert

LUKE 3:1–3; JOHN 1:19–23; MARK 1:2,3; LUKE 3:5,6

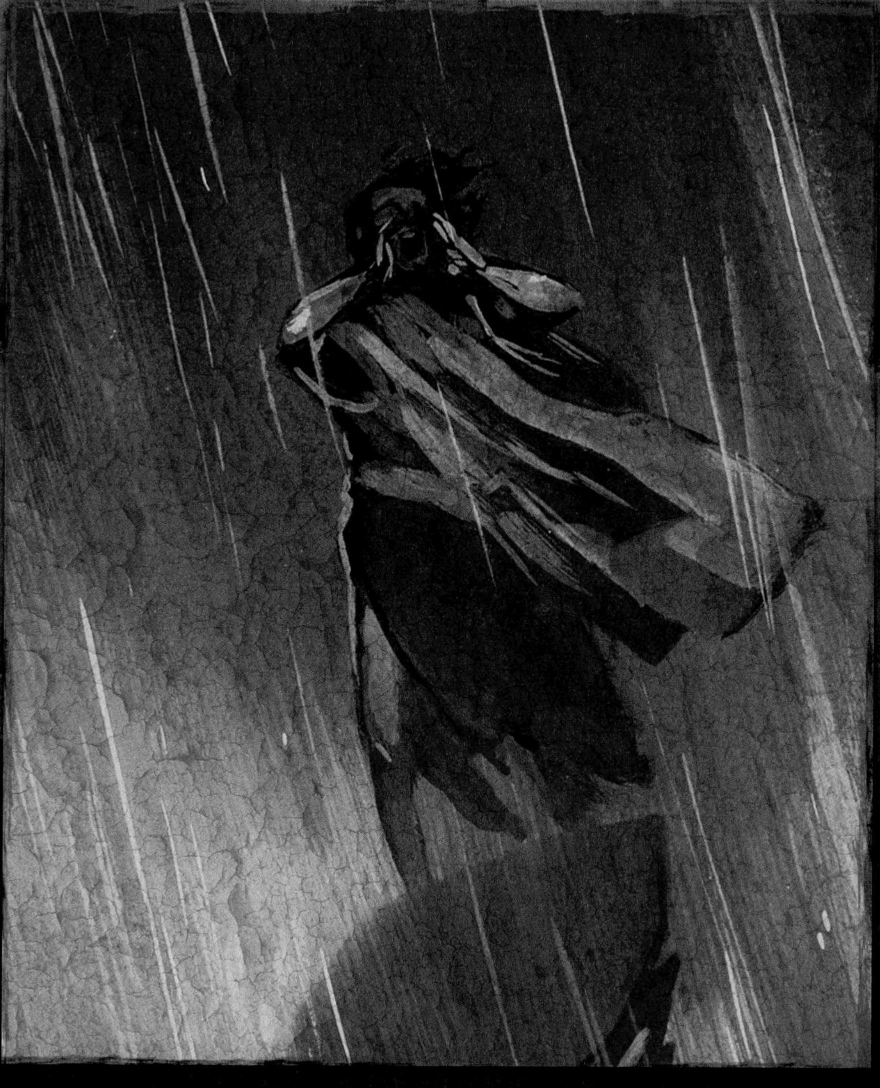

Now in the fifteenth year of the rule of Tiberius Caesar,
when Pontius Pilate was the provincial governor of Judea...

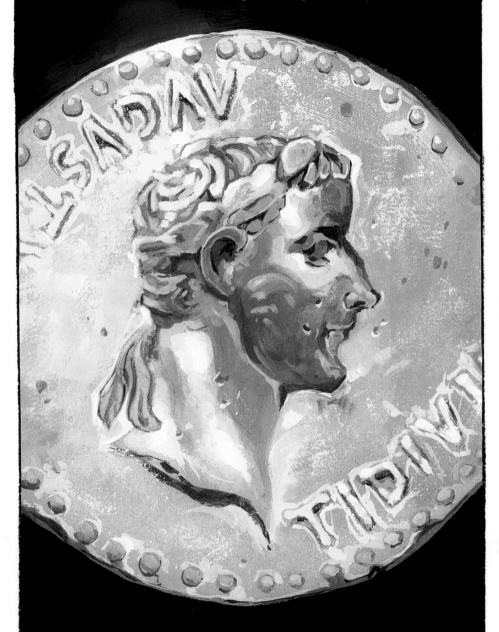

...Herod the Tetrarch of Galilee,
his brother Philip the Tetrarch of Itouraia and the region of
Trachonitis, and Lysanios the Tetrarch of Abilene...

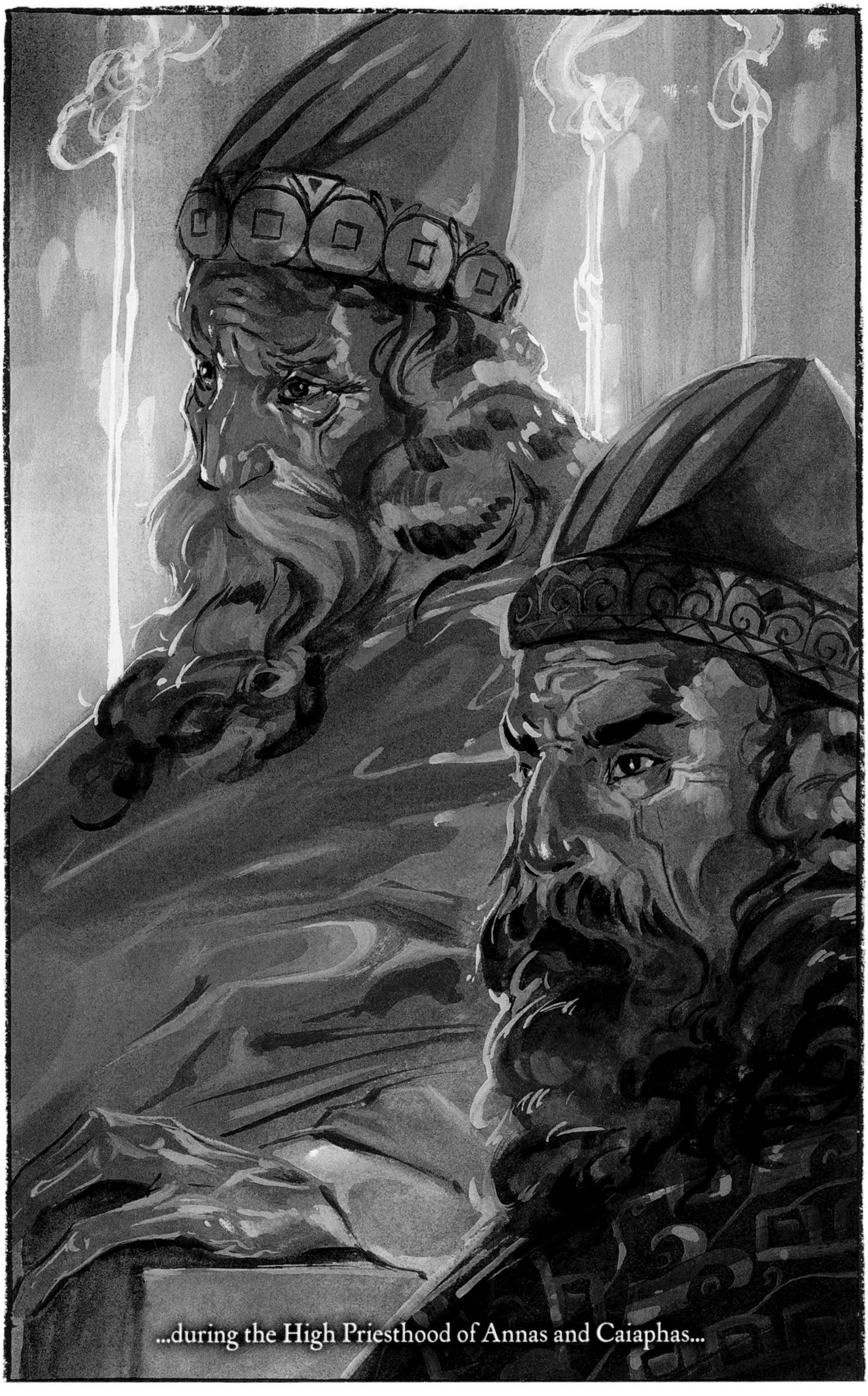
...during the High Priesthood of Annas and Caiaphas...

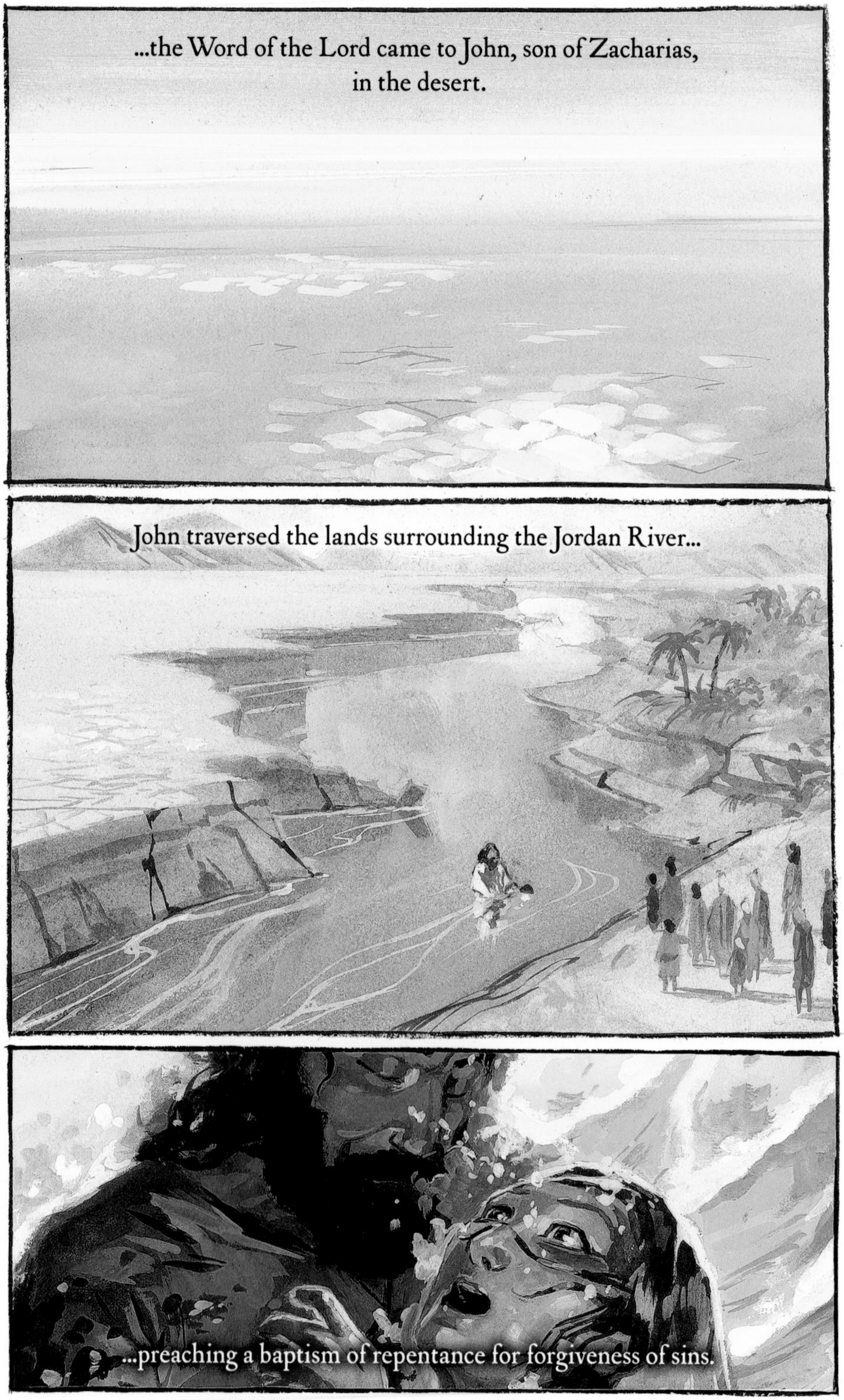
...the Word of the Lord came to John, son of Zacharias, in the desert.
John traversed the lands surrounding the Jordan River...
...preaching a baptism of repentance for forgiveness of sins.

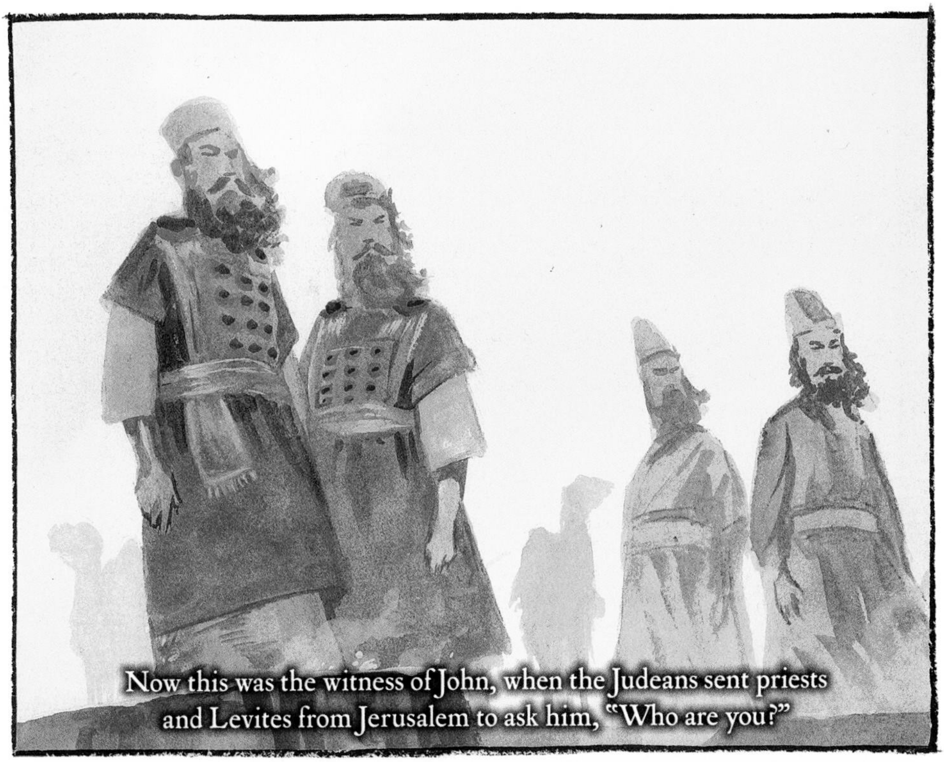
Now this was the witness of John, when the Judeans sent priests and Levites from Jerusalem to ask him, "Who are you?"

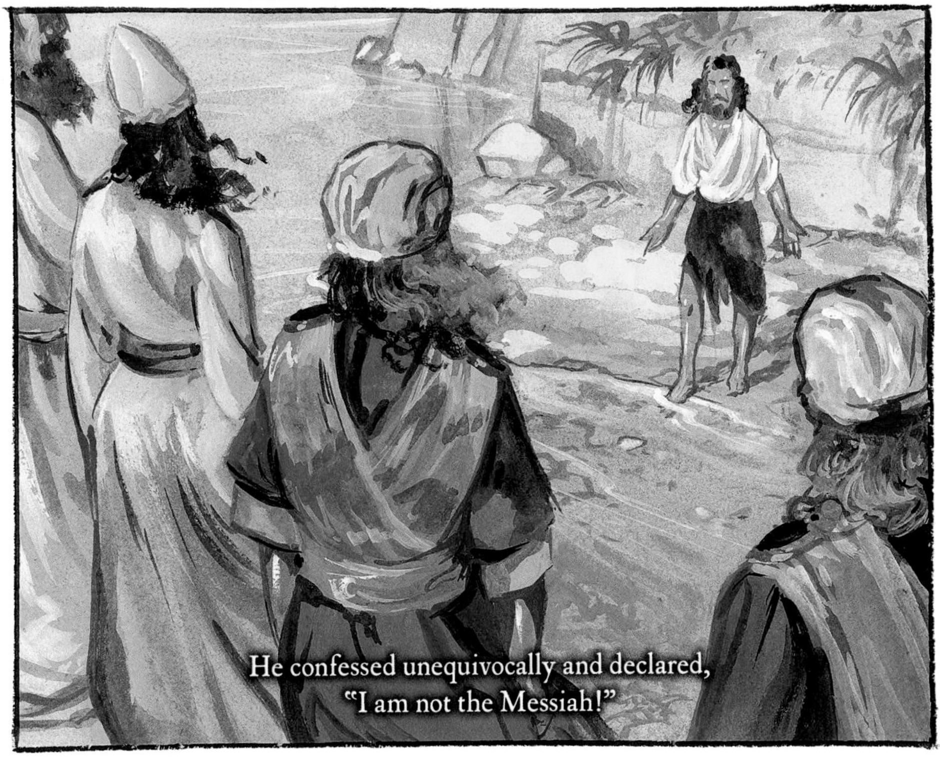
He confessed unequivocally and declared, "I am not the Messiah!"

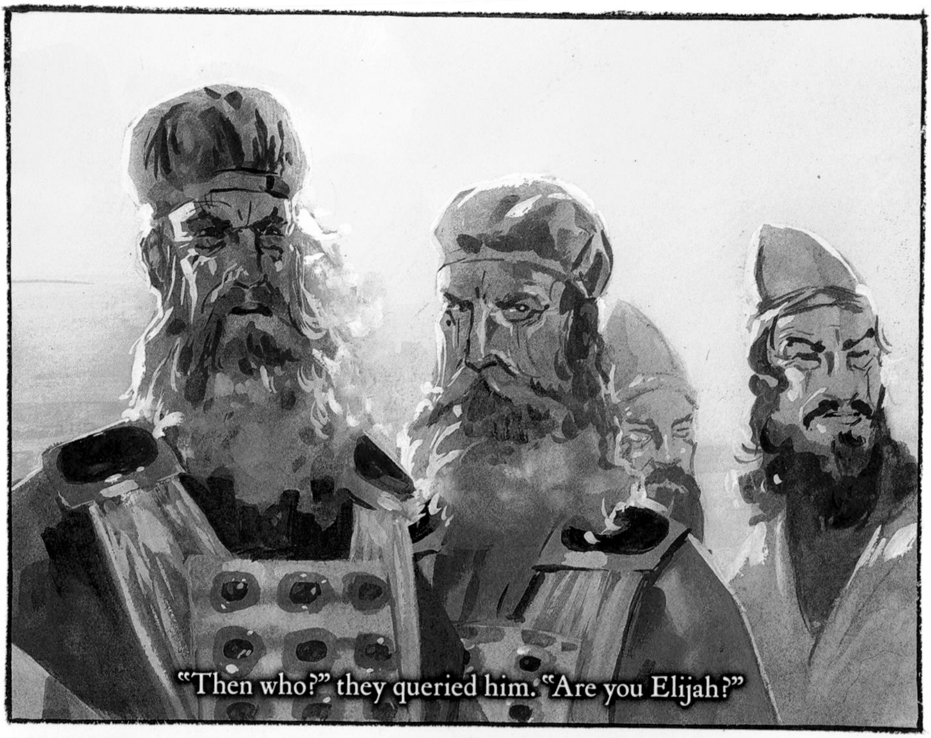
"Then who?" they queried him. "Are you Elijah?"

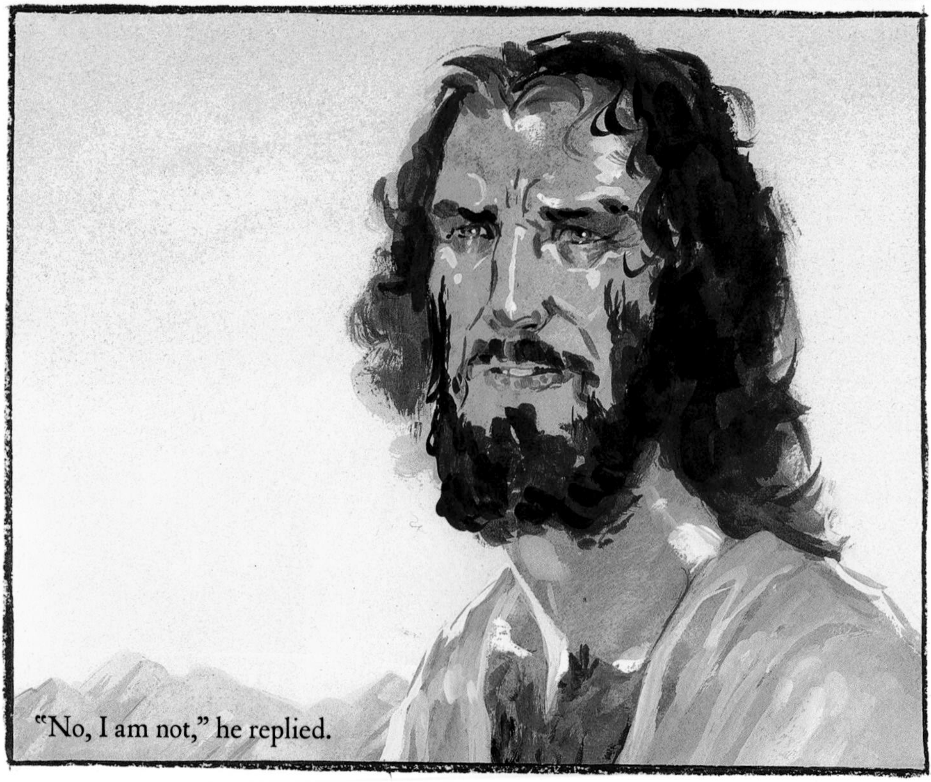
"No, I am not," he replied.

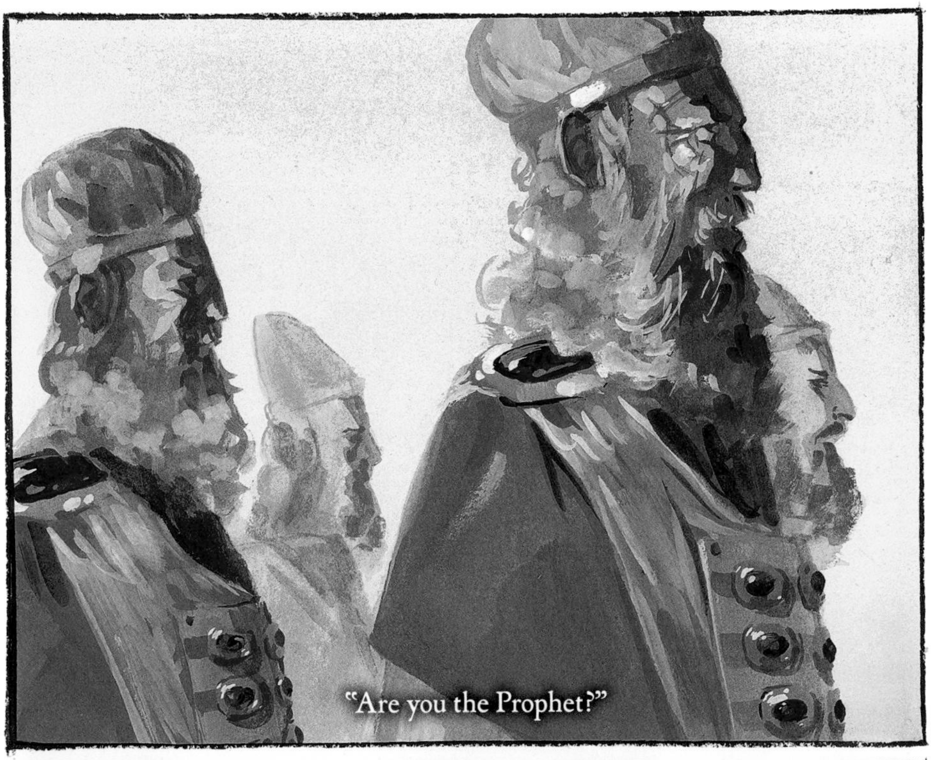
"Are you the Prophet?"

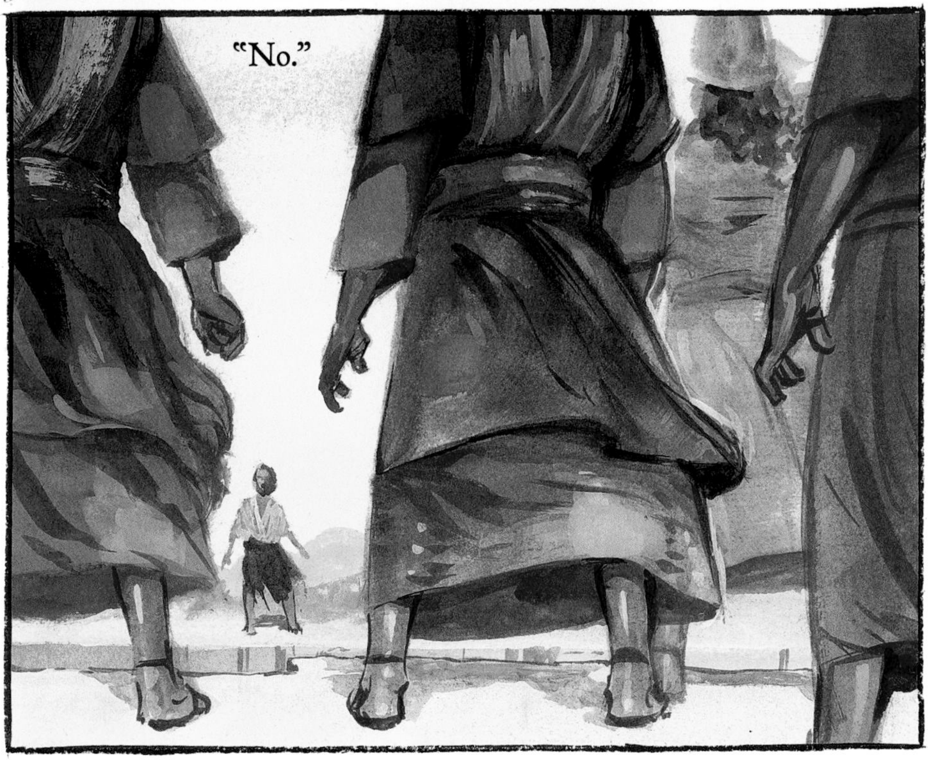
"No."

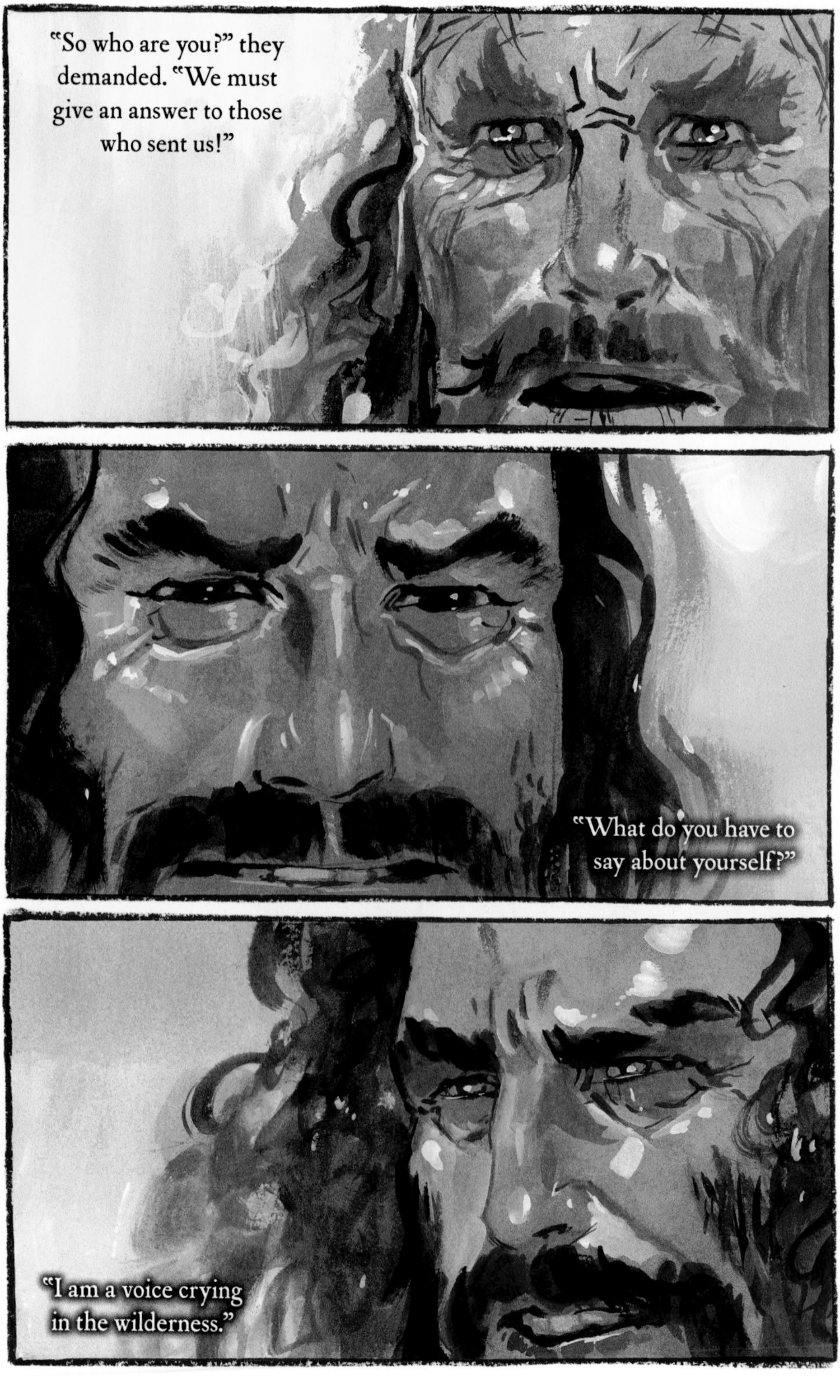
"So who are you?" they demanded. "We must give an answer to those who sent us!"
"What do you have to say about yourself?"
"I am a voice crying in the wilderness."

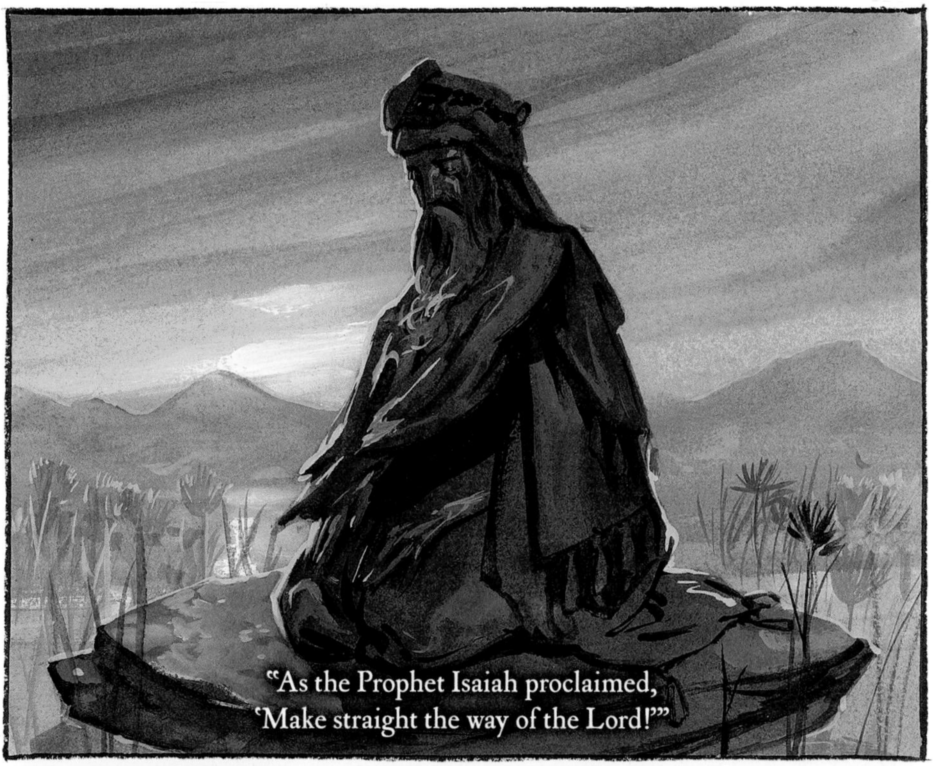
"As the Prophet Isaiah proclaimed, 'Make straight the way of the Lord!'"

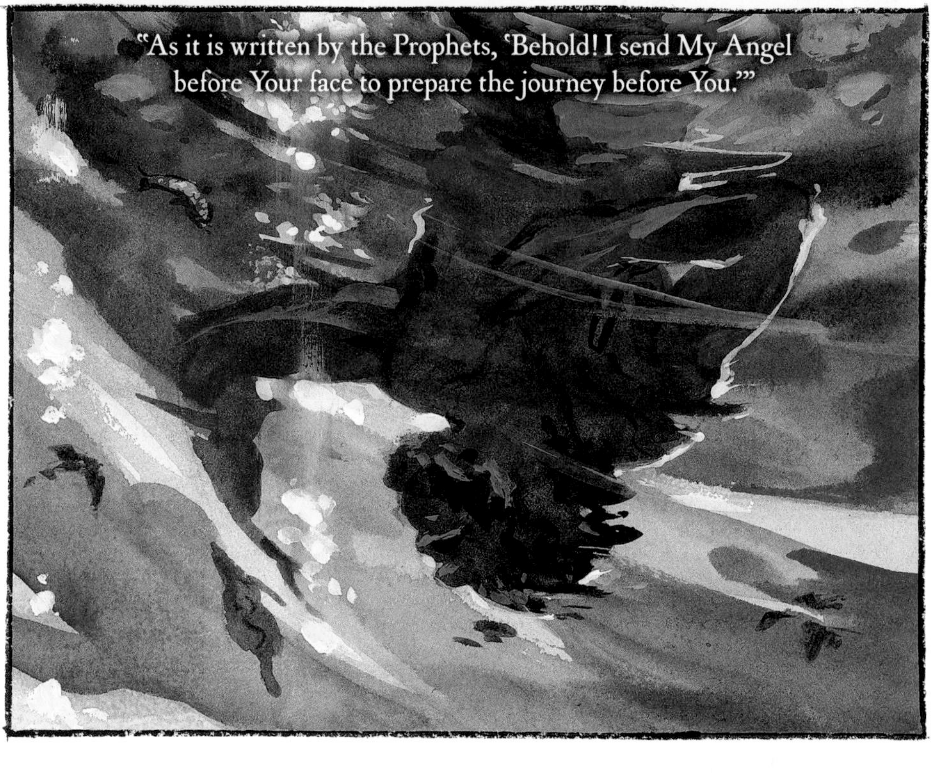
"As it is written by the Prophets, 'Behold! I send My Angel before Your face to prepare the journey before You.'"

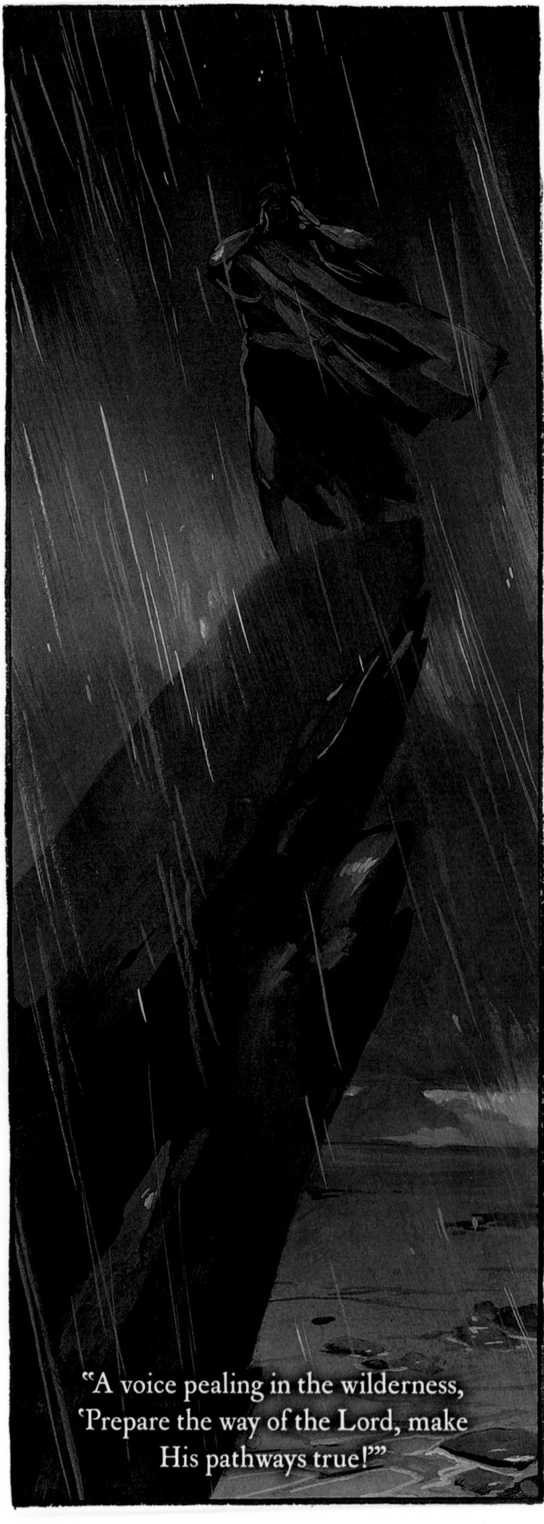
"A voice pealing in the wilderness, 'Prepare the way of the Lord, make His pathways true!'"

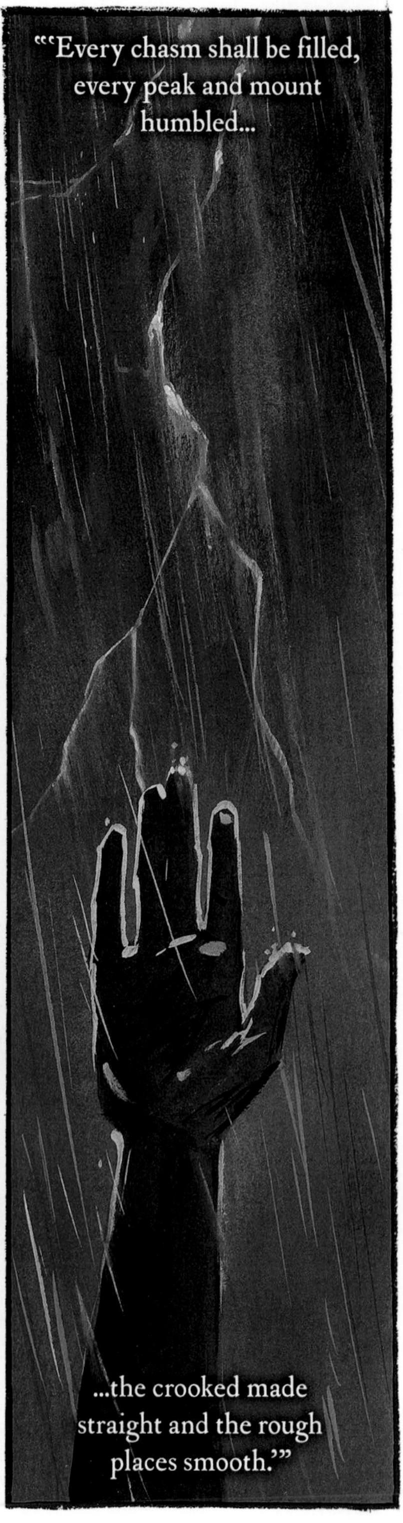
"'Every chasm shall be filled, every peak and mount humbled...
...the crooked made straight and the rough places smooth.'"

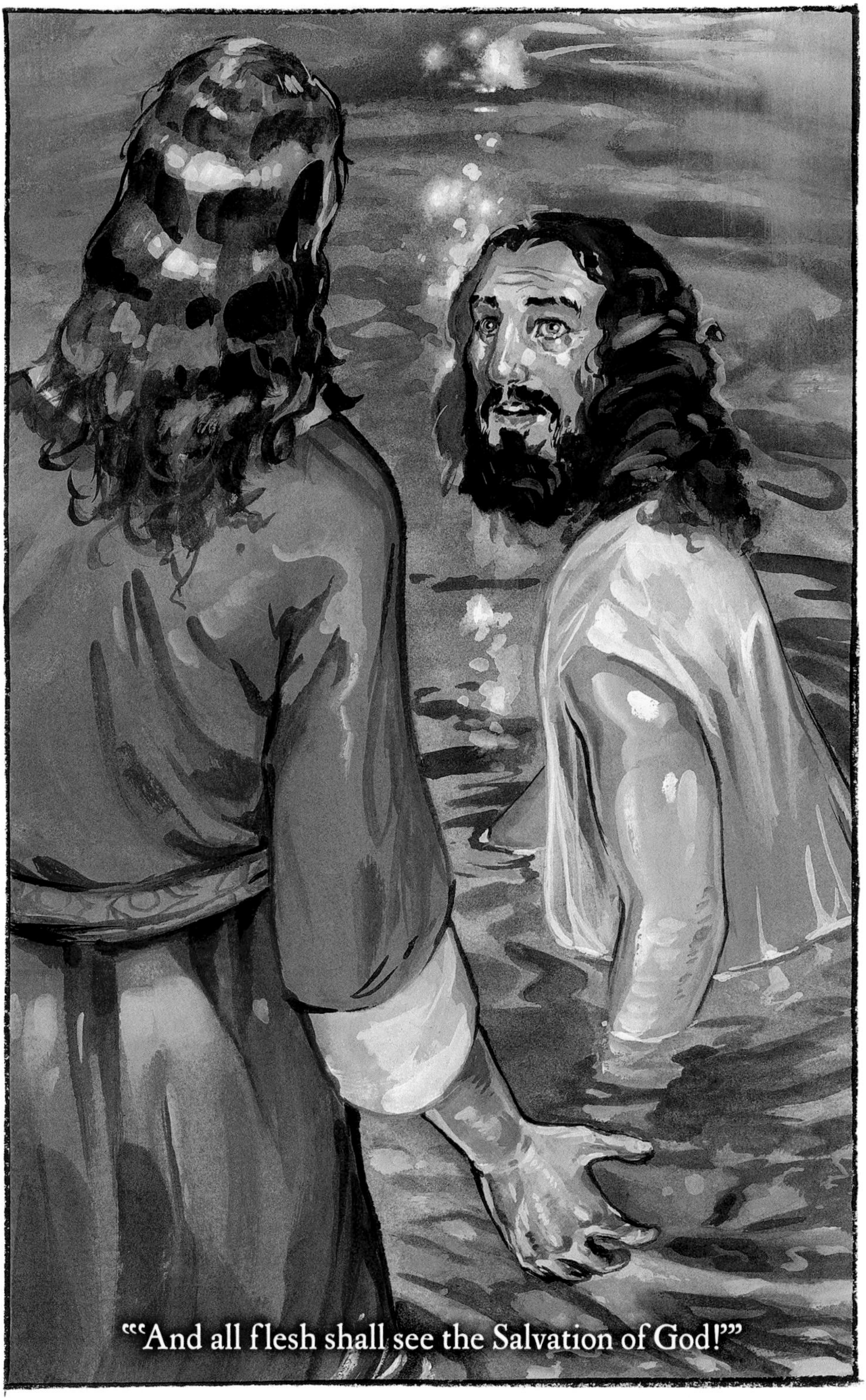
"'And all flesh shall see the Salvation of God!'"

Genealogy According to Matthew

MATTHEW 1:2–17

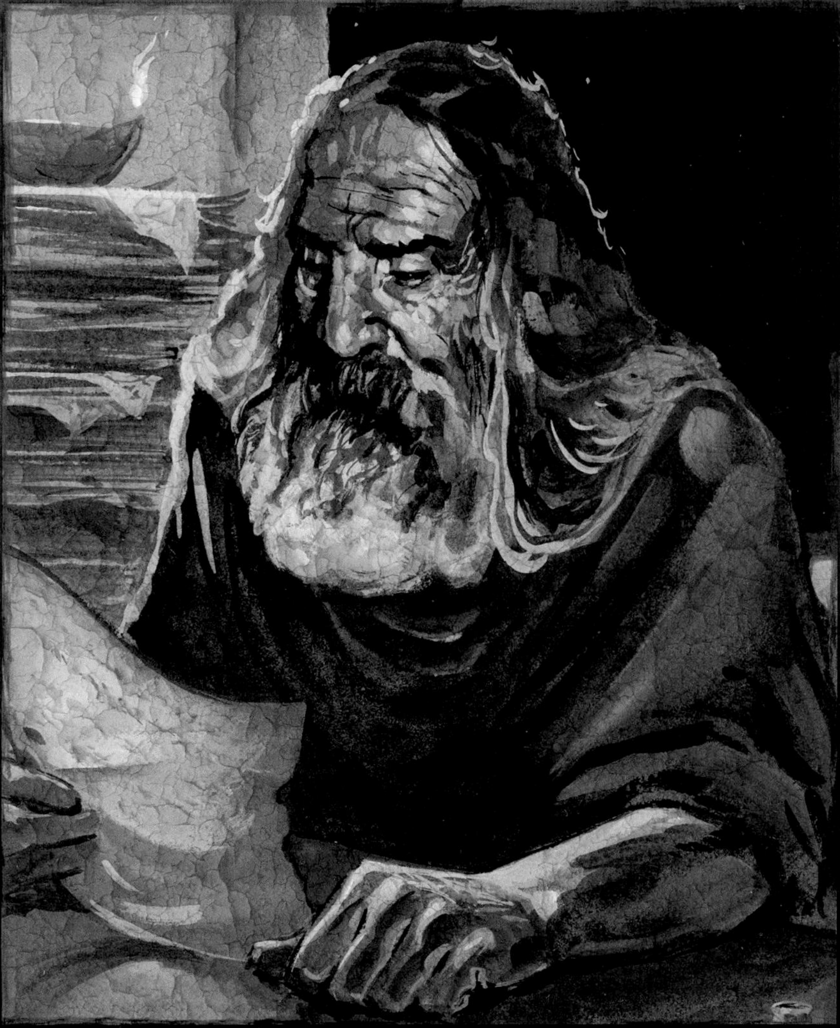

1:2) Abraham fathered Isaac. Isaac fathered Jacob. Jacob fathered Judah and his brothers.

1:3) Judah fathered Phares and Zara by Thamar. Phares fathered Esrom. Esrom fathered Aram.

1:4) Aram fathered Aminadab. Aminadab fathered Naason. Naason fathered Salmon.

1:5) Salmon fathered Booz by Rahab. Booz fathered Obed by Ruth. Obed fathered Jesse.

1:6) Jesse fathered King David. King David fathered Solomon by the wife of Ouriah.

1:7) Solomon fathered Roboam. Roboam fathered Abia. Abia fathered Asa.

1:8) Asa fathered Iosaphat. Iosaphat fathered Ioram. Ioram fathered Ozias.

1:9) Ozias fathered Ioatham. Ioatham fathered Achaz. Achaz fathered Ezekias.

1:10) Ezekias fathered Manasses. Manasses fathered Amon. Amon fathered Josias.

1:11) Josias fathered Jechonias and his brothers, at the time of the Babylonian Exile.

1:12) After the exile to Babylon, Jechonias fathered Salathiel. Salathiel fathered Zorobabel.

1:13) Zorobabel fathered Abioud. Abioud fathered Eliakeim. Eliakeim fathered Azor.

1:14) Azor fathered Sadok. Sadok fathered Acheim. Acheim fathered Elioud.

1:15) Elioud fathered Eleazar. Eleazar fathered Matthan. Matthan fathered Jacob.

1:16) Jacob fathered Joseph, the man betrothed to Mary. From her, Mary, Jesus was born, the One Who is called the Christ—the Anointed One.

1:17) So then, all the generations from Abraham to David were fourteen generations, and from David to the Babylonian Exile were fourteen generations, and from the Babylonian Exile to the Christ were fourteen generations.

Genealogy According to Luke

LUKE 3:23–38

3:23b) Jesus was (so it was thought) the son of Joseph, who was the son of Eli,

3:24) the son of Matthan, the son of Levi, the son of Melchi, the son of Ioann, the son of Joseph,

3:25) the son of Matthew, the son of Amos, the son of Naoum, the son of Eslim, the son of Naggai,

3:26) the son of Maath, the son of Matthew, the son of Semeü, the son of Iosech, the son of Ioda,

3:27) the son of Ioann, the son of Rhesa, the son of Zorobabel, the son of Salathiel, the son of Neri,

3:28) the son of Melchi, the son of Addi, the son of Kosam, the son of Elmodam, the son of Er,

3:29) the son of Joses, the son of Eliezer, the son of Ioreim, the son of Mathat, the son of Levi,

3:30) the son of Symeon, the son of Judah, the son of Joseph, the son of Jonas, the son of Eliakeim,

3:31) the son of Melea, the son of Maïnan, the son of Mattathas, the son of Nathan, the son of David,

3:32) the son of Jesse, the son of Obed, the son of Booz, the son of Salmon, the son of Naason,

3:33) the son of Aminadab, the son of Aram, the son of Ioram, the son of Esrom, the son of Phares, the son of Judah,

3:34) the son of Jacob, the son of Isaac, the son of Abraham, the son of Thara, the son of Nachor,

3:35) the son of Serouch, the son of Ragav, the son of Phalek, the son of Eber, the son of Sala,

3:36) the son of Caïnan, the son of Arphaxad, the son of Sem, the son of Noah, the son of Lamech,

3:37) the son of Mathousala, the son of Enoch, the son of Jared, the son of Maleleil, the son of Caïnan,

3:38) the son of Enos, the son of Seth, the son of Adam, the son of God.

Index of Scriptural Verses

Index of Scriptural Verses

Index of Scriptural Verses

ACKNOWLEDGMENTS

All visual art relies to some extent on the traditions of visual art that came before it. The art in these pages has been inspired and influenced by several master art makers from earlier eras, many of whom worked in the Biblical genre. We would like to recognize the painters and film directors who stimulated us to a higher level of visual storytelling. We drew inspiration from graphic artists such as Gustave Dore, James Tissot, Michelangelo, Rembrandt, Delacroix, Luc-Olivier Merson; from cinematic artists such as Cecil B. DeMille, John Ford, David Lean, Sergio Leone and Akira Kurosawa. This list is by no means complete. Our storytelling choices were informed by a nearly inexhaustible fountain of visual culture related (directly and indirectly) to the Bible that comes to us down through the ages.

Also, we thank Chris Diamantopoulos and Suzanne Dunn for their wise counsel and unflagging support throughout all the stages of this process.

Carlton Riffel played an essential role in lettering and design. I personally feel deeply grateful for his resourcefulness and reassuring Huck Finn smile.

And we would specially like to thank Mark Arey and the late Philemon Sevastiades for their translation and Mark in particular for his selection and arrangement of the Gospel verses that provide the foundation for the sequential art on these pages.

Matt Dorff
Adapter & Editor

THE CLIMACTIC BATTLE BETWEEN
GOOD AND EVIL

The final book of the Bible has challenged, inspired, and astonished readers for nearly 2000 years. The book of Revelation may be the most analyzed text in all of Scripture. And yet it remains the most mysterious.

Now comes an illustrated graphic novel version with all 404 verses of this amazing book. Stand in the Apostle John's sandals and watch the New Testament's climactic war between good and evil unfold in dramatic and dazzling imagery. See the Lamb, the Seven-Headed Dragon, and the Beast as never before. Take a thrilling ride through ancient prophecy. Discover anew the story of the ultimate fulfillment of John's faith as the final battle is fought between God and Satan.

Including a translation from the ancient Greek by Fr. Mark Arey and Fr. Philemon Sevastiades, an adaptation by Matt Dorff, and illustrations by renowned artist Chris Koelle, *The Book of Revelation* is an emotionally stirring and thought-provoking way to experience this timeless narrative.

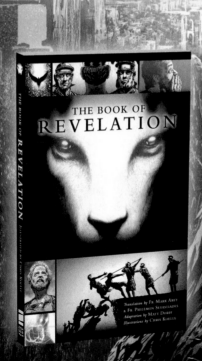

Available NOW at your favorite bookseller